YORK MEDIEVAL TEXTS

General Editors
ELIZABETH SALTER & DEREK PEARSALL
University of York

The Middle Scots Poets

A. M. KINGHORN

Reader in English, University of the West Indies

 EDWARD ARNOLD

First published 1970 by
Edward Arnold (Publishers) Ltd
41 Maddox Street, London W1

PR
8656
.K5
1970 / 46,274

Cloth edition SBN: 7131 5466 7
Paper edition SBN: 7131 5467 5

Printed in Great Britain by Billing & Sons Limited
Guildford and London

General Preface

The present series of *York Medieval Texts* is designed for undergraduates and, where the text is appropriate, for upper forms of schools. Its aim is to provide editions of major pieces of Middle English writing in a form which will make them accessible without loss of historical authenticity. Texts are chosen because of their importance and artistic merit, and individual volumes may contain a single work, coherent extracts from a longer work, or representative examples of a genre. The principle governing the presentation of the text is to preserve the character of the English while eliminating unnecessary encumbrances such as obsolete letters and manuscript errors. Glossary and explanatory notes operate together to clarify the text; special attention is paid to the interpretation of passages which are syntactically rather than lexically difficult. The Introduction to each volume, like the rest of the apparatus, is designed to set the work in its proper literary context, and to provide the critical guidance most helpful to present-day readers. The intention of the series is exclusively literary: the Editors hope to attract a wider audience not only for works within the accepted literary canon, but also for those which have until now been regarded as 'specialist' in appeal, or which have been presented as if they were.

The choice of poems included in this volume has been governed by the editor's wish to illustrate both range and variety in the works of the Scots makars and, in so doing, to provide a useful group of texts suitable for undergraduate study.

Of the twelve selections, nine furnish complete texts of the poems, and one, from Henryson's *Orpheus and Eurydice*, omits only the concluding *moralitas*. In addition, a number of passages are quoted at length in the course of the critical introduction. These are intended not only to illuminate the argument of the introduction itself, but also to enlarge the scope of the volume, for they include examples taken from works not represented in the list of contents. For this reason the glossary is linked to the introduction as well as to the main text.

Acknowledgements

I gratefully acknowledge permission given by the editors and publishers of the *Modern Language Review, Studies in Scottish Literature* and the *University of Texas Studies in Literature and Language* to incorporate material previously published in articles. Reference to these is made in the bibliography.

Particular acknowledgement is due to Dr James Craigie and the Council of the Scottish Text Society for allowing me to print from their collections of manuscripts, and to the editors of Douglas's *Aeneid* (Dr David F. C. Coldwell) and *Hary's Wallace* (Mr M. P. McDiarmid) for permitting the use in the Introduction of passages from their recent Scottish Text Society editions. Mr W. Mackay Mackenzie's edition of *The Kingis Quair* has provided a valuable aid to the preparation of the passage (I) from that work, and I must thank the publishers for allowing me to use it.

Assistance given to me by the Librarian and staff of the University of the West Indies Library, Mona, made it possible for this book to be prepared in Jamaica. I should also like to acknowledge the help of Mr Derek Pearsall and Professor Elizabeth Salter, the General Editors of the series; of Mr Edward Maddrell, for his note on music; of Mr D. D. Murison, editor of the *Scottish National Dictionary*, whose expert knowledge has elucidated many difficulties in the glossary; and of Mrs M. Turpin, who typed the Introduction. Finally, I should like to add a special note of appreciation to my wife, whose aid throughout has been invaluable.

A.M.K.

Contents

Introduction

THE poets or 'makars' whose works form the subject of this volume lived in Scotland (with one possible exception) during the fifteenth and sixteenth centuries. Personal information concerning medieval writers is in the majority of cases scanty, frequently extending to little more than their names. Anonymity is the general rule and biography based on internal evidence in the works themselves is to be viewed with suspicion because of its subjective character. What seems to be a revelation by the poet about himself may really be 'an element in the design of the works, a part of the poets' technique',[1] or at most a self-dramatization. James I's personal account, even if it be in truth of his own authorship, is a convention of the dream-vision tradition and, as such, valueless as autobiography. Dunbar's grumbles about his elusive pension and Henryson's interests in medical matters do not isolate them as individuals. More is known about the facts of Douglas's life, but his later prominence in the unsavoury intrigues of post-Flodden times sheds no light on his literary achievements. The political lessons of the *Aeneid* may be seen to mirror Renaissance concerns with statecraft, but the translator himself remains, in company with his fellow-poets, a shadowy figure. The makars are to be evaluated not as unique artists living separate 'lives' but by what they did with what they shared—firstly, a common bond with Chaucer, whom they respected, even revered, as a master-craftsman, and secondly, a complicated inheritance of literary practice, both European and regional, going back far beyond Chaucer.

Historical Background

The shining personality of their time was James IV of Scotland (1472–1513), whom his near-contemporary George Buchanan described as being possessed of a sound mind in a sound body but not bookish.[2] James seems to have been an extrovert compelled by mainly physical interests. He enjoyed field sports, open-air revels, music and dancing, cards and dice-games, and travelled a great deal about his kingdom to meet the poor peasants with whose welfare he tried to be concerned. No impassable gulf separated James and his travelling court from the impoverished folk who gave him their allegiance, for the country was poor and the knight's castle modest. The ordinary man had lived for centuries in a hovel, shared with his single cow, holding a strip of land on a

[1] G. Kane, 'The Autobiographical Fallacy in Chaucer and Langland Studies': Chambers Memorial Lecture, University College, London, 2 March 1965 (London, 1965), p. 6.

[2] 'Ingenio quidem acri, sed vitio temporis ab literis inculto' (*Rerum Scoti-carum Historia*, 1582, p. xiii). See R. L. Mackie, *King James IV of Scotland* (Edinburgh and London, 1958), p. 118.

A*

five-year lease with hardly any encouragement to improve his portion. The Scots clergy was an ignorant body, its members equipped by the 'sang scule'[3] with a rudimentary knowledge of church music and in some instances drilled in Latin in the grammar school, a feature of almost every 'burgh' or trading-community in the land. Practically the sole reliable item of biographical information concerning Henryson states that he once held the position of school-master in the grammar school of Dunfermline, appointed by the Abbot to instruct boys in Latin language and literature.

The Scots population was about one-fifth that of England,[4] distributed mostly in the south, but in spite of this relatively small number there were by 1500 three university foundations—St. Andrews (1411) Glasgow (1451) and Aberdeen (1495). St Andrews was considered superior to Glasgow in endowment and scholarship, and when James IV came to the throne had over a hundred undergraduates. Both St Andrews and Glasgow attracted arts students, but theologians usually travelled to Paris or Orleans where they might profit from the instruction of the most learned Catholic teachers in Europe. William Dunbar and Gawain Douglas were probably both students at St Andrews, and it is likely that Douglas proceeded to Paris for theological training. By contemporary standards he was the most learned Scotsman of his time, an early example of the Northern 'Renaissance man'.

Printing was introduced into Scotland in 1507 by Walter Chepman and Androw Myllar, who brought a press from France and were given a royal licence. Although the chief purpose of the press was to print official documents, its output did include eleven works of literature, in whole or in part. Henryson's *Orpheus and Eurydice*, Dunbar's *Flyting*, *Lament*, *Goldyn Targe* and *Twa Mariit Wemen and the Wedo*, and Blyn Hary's *Wallace* were published by Chepman and Myllar, whose leanings towards contemporary poets may be taken as a demonstration of nationalist feeling. Such sentiments, deeply rooted in a semi-legendary past, had been particularly evident since the last quarter of the fifteenth century. In 1482 Edward IV invaded Scotland, laid waste the Borders and occupied Edinburgh, establishing the Duke of Albany as governor in place of James III, whose hold on the country was growing weaker. He had tried to

[3] Song schools were connected with the cathedrals and trained boys for the choir, providing them at the same time with a rudimentary education. By 1450 they were established not only in the seats of great abbeys but in all the leading burghs. They survived as separate institutions until the eighteenth century.

[4] I.e. probably about 300,000. Edinburgh, Dundee, Aberdeen, Perth, Glasgow, St Andrews, Stirling and Ayr were the leading burghs, with populations of 2000 or more. Accurate statistics are not available. *Cf.* T. M. (Baron) Cooper, 'The Population of Medieval Scotland' (*Scottish Historical Review*, XXVI, 1947), pp. 2–9.

promote matrimonial alliances with the English nobility in the face of a hatred of the English dating back to the Wars of Independence, and had thus aroused the enmity of his barons, who charged him with 'inbringing of Englishmen' and held him in personal contempt for his lack of martial qualities. Scotland's traditional ally against England was France, an alliance strongly supported both by the barons and the ecclesiastics, in whom political power mainly resided. Little goodwill existed towards England, and James's quarrelsome character and obvious lack of administrative talent played into the hands of his many enemies who numbered, among others close to him, his own brothers.[5]

James III did, however, pave the way for conditions favourable to the arts, particularly in architecture, and Edinburgh came to assume something of its subsequent importance as a centre of trade, the principal burgh and capital of the kingdom. Increasing wealth in the hands of a minority of important burghers was frequently invested in secular building, an art in which James III took a strong personal interest. Improvement of his own residences at Stirling and Linlithgow reflects this enthusiasm. The burgh communities developed in spite of old feudal ties and indicated how the face of society was changing; the burghers sought mutual protection, guarded their newly-acquired privileges zealously and distrusted outsiders. In this respect they may be compared with members of European guilds, which demonstrated similar tendencies towards isolation.

Nevertheless, much of the old Scots feudal system remained, though it should be noted that this structure was not the hierarchical feudalism of England but instead more of a social relationship influenced by clan solidarity. In effect, this meant that there was no built-in rivalry separating nobles from clergy, since bishops were drawn from the ranks of the nobility and, in accordance with clan loyalties, blood links and family ties tended to overweigh social distinctions. The importance of kinship distinguished Scotland's internal politics from those of England or France, since Scottish legislation was not necessarily biased in favour of the upper classes—rather the contrary in fact—and the 'bond of manrent', that is, hereditary service pledged in return for protection, was always a strong feature of clan solidarity. This is the background of Blyn Hary's *Wallace*, composed in about 1475 as a manifesto of the common people's loyalty and, by the same token, as a criticism of the low estate of the existing Scots court which, when faced by the English enemy, tried to placate him. *Wallace* recalled the heroic behaviour of the common people nearly two centuries before, just as Barbour had celebrated the campaign of the Scots nobles under Bruce; but in the nation ruled by James III, such a spirit does not seem to have been prominent amongst the landowning fraternity.

[5] See G. Donaldson, *Scottish Kings* (London, 1967) and R. L. Mackie, *op. cit.*, for succinct accounts of James III's relations with his nobles.

The reign of James IV was more favourable to poetry, since the king, in contrast to his predecessor, liked to present himself both as a patron of the arts and as a just governor. Pedro de Ayala's flattering account of Scotland, and Piccolomini's more austere picture, together with internal evidence provided in certain contemporary poems—the latter probably nearer to the actual facts—help one to imagine what conditions were like.[6] The king's vices included a strong desire for military fame, and his posturing in this respect led in the end to the disaster of Flodden; Dunbar's comments on corruptions, both moral and financial, which prevailed at court, and Henryson's reflections on the low state of public morality, encouraged by slow process of law, suggest that their world was full of disappointments for them. Some knowledge of the life and times of James IV is indispensable to any study of the content and variety of their works, for the activities of his court inspired and encouraged Dunbar to write on many subjects, and the three estates over which James ruled provided Henryson with a rich source of material for satire and complaint cast in the form of fables.

This was the last independent period in Scottish history. James's marriage in 1503 to Henry VII's elder daughter Margaret, celebrated in Dunbar's *Thressil and the Rois*, brought about a short-lived truce with England, but Scotland's alliance with France and Henry VIII's threatening policy towards the French made friendship with the English politically impossible. Henry landed at Calais in 1513, one year after Scotland had renewed her 'auld alliance' with France, and James, feeling himself thereby obliged to rattle his sabre in the name of Scottish 'knychthode', invaded England. The direct result was the utter defeat of the Scots armies at Flodden. James himself and many of his nobles died on the battlefield, and the English defeat by Bruce at Bannockburn was avenged by a slaughter of more than ten thousand Scots, a blow from which the nation never fully recovered.

Throughout the period, colourful as it may have been at the level of the court, the ordinary peasant's lot did not change and the prosperity which was beginning to touch the king, the nobles and the important burghers affected the peasants not at all. Their lives were harsh and unattractive by our standards and were spent from day to day, monotonously, in an unpleasant climate of snow, sleet and heavy rain, broken by short summers which provided rare opportunities for open-air celebration. The poets of the time refer to the weather rather more than do their English contemporaries, and the popular tradition of

[6] See W. C. Dickinson, *Scotland From the Earliest Times to 1603* (London and Edinburgh, 1961; 2nd edn. revised, 1965), pp. 274–5. Ayala, Spanish Ambassador to James IV's Court, said that the king spoke six languages in addition to English and Gaelic and was active as a just administrator. Piccolomini, who became Pope Pius II, visited Scotland in 1435, when James I was on the throne and conditions for the most part were bleak.

poetry-making frequently took as its subject fairs, incidents in public places, and gatherings held in summer, when the people could shed their winter sorrows and abandon themselves to joyful occasions with a wild, unbridled zest. *Cokelbie Sow, Peblis to the Play, The Cursing of Sir John Rowell* and other poems in the Scots comic tradition, which stretched from James I to Burns, all display a boisterous lack of caution, crude cynicism, ribaldry and a taste for violent physical movement that contrasts violently with the contemplative writings of a poet like Henryson or of Dunbar in his pessimistic moods.

The Nature of Middle Scots Poetry

Scots poetry of the fifteenth and sixteenth centuries presents problems both linguistic and literary. The term 'Middle Scots' was first employed by Victorian scholars to describe the language of written communication in the Scottish Lowlands as transmitted by James I, Blyn Hary, Henryson, Dunbar, Douglas and Lyndsay in verse, and John Gau, Sir Gilbert Haye, John of Ireland, John Bellenden, James VI and the anonymous compiler of *The Complaynt of Scotland* in prose. A hard-dying academic tradition claims 'Middle Scots' to have been a written language only, never actually spoken; but modern studies have indicated that the vocabulary of medieval Scots writers, while rich in literary embellishment and 'aureation', had as much of living speech in it as that of Burns. Dunbar's *Tretis of the Twa Mariit Wemen and the Wedo* combines ornament, educated speech and colloquial idiom in the one poem. *The Goldyn Targe* is gem-encrusted, an important example of lofty poeticism, self-supported by Latinized or 'aureate' diction, while *The Flyting of Dunbar and Kennedie*, an incidental parody of the style of popular denunciatory preaching, is linguistically almost a negation of the aureate. *The Petition of the Gray Horse, Auld Dunbar* is conversational in tone, and the procession of deceased and moribund poets in *Lament for the Makars* is prosaically described in catalogue fashion, as though by a muttering priest bereft of personal concern.

Dunbar and his contemporaries wrote for an educated audience in and around the court of James IV and drew upon the verbal resources of the sophisticated, grammar-school-educated man familiar with classical Latin. Reinforced by direct borrowings from modern French and from colloquial Latin, such a medium was certainly not remote from the popular speech. Douglas complained that his 'Scottis' was inadequate for the highest flights and that its oral range was limited, thus justifying his borrowings from Latin, French and English for the purpose of translating Virgil. Henryson, especially in the *Morall Fabillis*, depends a good deal less upon artifice than do either Dunbar or Douglas, and his animals speak in the manner of Dunfermline officials, lawyers or schoolmasters like himself whose diction was precise and to the point. Orpheus, Eurydice and Cresseid, all Scots in classical garb, are inherited poetic creations, but Robyne and Makyne's rustic love-idyll is conducted in a plausible imitation of the intimate accents of real life. *The Thre Deid Pollis* mingles the aureate with the unadorned colloquy of a contemporary moral lesson as it might have been delivered from the burgh pulpit.

The same variations in usage are to be noted in Blyn Hary's *Wallace* and, a century earlier, in Barbour's *Bruce*, both of which survive in a late fifteenth-century manuscript. Since neither *Bruce* nor *Wallace* are represented in this volume, a few examples of literary and colloquial diction taken from each of these long works may not come amiss at this stage. From *Bruce*, a passage describing the reconnaissance by Scottish scouts of the English army lying before Bannockburn:

> And soon the great host have they seen
> Where shieldis shin and war so sheen,
> And basnetis weill burnisht brycht,
> That gave agane the sun great licht.
> They saw so feill browdyn baneris
> Standards, pennownys upon spearis,
> And so feill knychtis upon steedis
> All flawamand into their weedis ... (XI, 460–7)

and another, in which Bruce is consulting his men before committing himself and them, to the battle. It is almost *vers libre*:

> 'I trow that gude ending
> Sall follow till our beginning.
> The whether I say nocht this you till
> For that ye suld follow my will
> To fecht, for in you sall all be;
> For gif ye think speedful that we
> Fecht, we sall fecht; and, gif ye will,
> We leave, your liking to fulfil ... (XII, 189–96)

Wallace is a century richer in such contrasts. From the highly stylized:

> The mery day sprang fra the oryent,
> With bemys brycht enlumynyt the occident.
> Eftir Titan, Phebus, up rysyt fayr,
> Heich in the sper the signes maid declayr.
> Zepherus began his morrow cours.
> The swete vapour thus fra the ground resours.
> The humyll breyth doun fra the hewyn awaill
> In every meide, baythe fyrth, forrest and daill.
> The cler rede amang the rochis rang

> Throuch greyn branchis, quhar burdis blythly sang
> With ioyus voice in hevynly armony. (VIII, 1183–13)

the poet moves quickly to a conversation between Wallace and Edward I's
queen, Eleanor, engaged on her suppliant mission:

> Wallace askyt quhat hyr cummyng mycht meyn.
> 'For pes,' scho said, 'at we haiff to yow socht.
> This byrnand wer in baill has mony brocht.
> Ye grant us pees for him that deit on tre.'
> Wallace ansuerd, 'Madeym, that may nocht be.
> Ingland has doyne as gret harmys till us
> We may nocht pas and lychtly leiff it thus.'
> 'Yeis,' said the queyne, 'for crystyn folk we ar,
> For goddis saik, sen we desyr no mar,
> We awcht haiff pes.' 'Madeym, that I deny.
> The perfyt caus I sal yow schaw, for quhy
> Ye seke na pes bot for your awn availl...' (VIII, 1284–95)

and at the end of the work there is a lament for the martyred hero cast in the
accents of Germanic rhetoric, where one is reminded of the Anglo-Saxon
Wanderer and of the 'ubi sunt' formulas of early Christian homilies:

> Allace, Scotland, to quhom sall thow compleyn!
> Allace, fra payn quha sall the now restreyn!
> Allace, thi help is fastlie brocht to ground,
> Thi best chyftane in braith bandis is bound
> Allace, thow has now lost thi gyd off lycht!
> Allace, quha sall defend the in thi rycht!
> Allace, thi payn approchis wondyr ner!
> With sorow sone thow mon bene set in feyr
> Thi gracious gyd, thi grettast gouernour,
>
> Allace, our neir is cumyn his fatell hour!
> Allace, quha sall the beit now off thi baill!
> Allace, quhen sall off harmys thow be haill!
> Quha sall the defend? quha sall the now mak fre!
> Allace, in wer quha sall thi helper be!
> Quha sall the help? quha sall the now radem!
> Allace, quha sall the Saxons fra the flem! (XI, 1109–24)

This stems from a Germanic tradition at least six hundred years older than
Chaucer; both Barbour and Blyn Hary were writing in securely-established
northern traditions quite distinct from those imported into England and seized

by Chaucer for his own purposes. Any unqualified application of the term 'Scottish Chaucerians' to the poets represented in this volume has therefore to be rejected. Chaucer himself assimilated from France the modes of dream-allegory and *fabliau* or short humorous satirical tale, and from Italy the narrative modes of Boccaccio, yet it is far from the truth to say that Chaucer 'imitated' the foreign styles which he modified, enhanced and adapted to suit existing English traditions. To call him merely 'the great translator' is to do him little justice.

The Scots and Chaucer

The Scots were undoubtedly inspired by Chaucer, and by the Chaucerian strain in Lydgate; in various ways, some obvious (subject-matter), some harder to define (style, language-formulas and literary reference), they absorbed his example. But no two Scots were influenced by Chaucer in exactly the same way, and there is much in their poetry which is not to be found in Chaucer. 'Chaucerianism' is an 'academic' label: apart from some obvious linguistic stylistic and conventional similarities, found mainly in James I's *Kingis Quair*, Chaucer's influence is mostly indirect and in some cases very weak.

A related objection may be found to 'Scottish', which refers to the Lowland part of the country as distinct from Highland or Gaelic. It has been suggested by several modern critics that the influence of Gaelic or Celtic on Middle Scots writing was strong.[7] Although none of the writers could have known the Gaelic language,[8] its residual impact—what linguists call the 'deep structures' of speech—touched the poetic hearts of Henryson, Dunbar and Douglas even when they were trying hard to affect literary conventions borrowed from foreign sources. The Lowland Scots language is usually said to be a development from northern Middle English and it is easy to show that there is little or no difference between the written language as used by Barbour and by his English near-contemporary Minot. In fact, the poets of James IV's reign actually referred to their tongue as 'Inglis' (thereby distinguishing it from Gaelic), and though Henryson's writing shows that a division between English and Scots had appeared, it was not until 1513 that Douglas actually called his native medium 'Scottis'.[9] However, this should not be taken as evidence that 'Scottis' was considered to be a provincial extension of 'Inglis'. Not only was it not provincial, but the Scots literary tradition, linked closely with French,

[7] See K. Wittig, *The Scottish Tradition in Literature* (Edinburgh and London, 1958), p. 61. One of the charges levelled at Dunbar by Kennedie was that he rejected 'Irische' or Gaelic (*Flyting*, 345–8).

[8] James IV's knowledge of Gaelic (see *n.* 6, p. 4) may not have been very great, in spite of what Ayala claimed.

[9] *Aeneid*, Prologue to Book I, 118.

Italian[10] and Dutch cultures, was 'European' in a sense that English never was.

What is implied by 'Scottis', therefore, is far more than a difference of language; in fact, it had to do not only with language, but also with racial inheritance and national character, topography and climate. Shaped by such conditions and influences, the poetry of later medieval Scotland is rich and individual. Remarkable for its technical sophistication and control, it is also remarkable for its sensuous and pictorial strength. On the one hand there is Dunbar, whose poetry reached a technical standard quite unknown in England— a virtuoso quality comparable to that of southern French troubadour verse, or to that of Villon. Dunbar's compositions in elaborate 'aureate' modes—his courtly marriage-poem, *The Thressil and the Rois*, for instance—draw on the most varied resources of language and style for their ceremonial purposes. In Henryson, by contrast, one is aware of the poet's eye resting steadily on the realities of winter-season and winter-landscape. The settings are not those of lush Italian or French landscapes nor any imported Mediterranean scene;[11] when he writes about Orpheus's descent to the underworld, he does not take the terrain of hell on trust from Virgil or Dante. Douglas, too, in his *Aeneid*-Prologues, reveals a keen sense of the changing aspects of the Scottish country-side. There is nothing second-hand about his reaction to the northern winter— 'the tyme and sesson bittir, cald and paill'—and if some of the images for the fine-weather descriptions are borrowed, his original perception still makes itself felt. Here a summer day ends:

> Amyd the hawchis, and every lusty vaill,
> The recent dew begynnys doun to scaill,
> To meys the byrnyng quhar the son had schyne,
> Quhilk tho was to the neddir warld declyne:
> At every pilis poynt and cornys croppis
> The techrys stude, as lemand beryall droppis,
> And on the hailsum herbis, cleyn but wedis,
> Lyke cristal knoppis or smal silver bedis.
> The lyght begouth to quynchyng owt and faill,
> The day to dyrkyn, declyne and devaill;
> The gummys rysis, doun fallis the donk rym,
> Baith heir and thar scuggis and schaddois dym.

[10] The Italian influence, through Chaucer, was indirect until the middle of the sixteenth century, though Douglas refers briefly to Boccaccio in *The Palice of Honour* (line 915); Lyndsay's *Dreme* is reminiscent of Dante's *Commedia* but his source was probably a fifteenth-century French redaction. The medium of Scots cultural relations continued to be Latin, the quality of which was especially high in Scotland.

[11] A point first made by Allan Ramsay in *Preface to Ever Green* (1724).

Upgois the bak with hir pelit ledderyn flycht,
The lark discendis from the skyis hycht,
Syngand hir complyng sang, efter hir gys,
To tak hir rest, at matyn hour to rys.
Owt our the swyre swymmys the soppis of myst,
The nycht furthspred hir cloke with sabill lyst,
That all the bewte of the fructuus feld
Was with the erthis umbrage cleyn ourheld;
Baith man and beste, fyrth, flude and woddis wild
Involvyt in tha schaddois warryn syld.
Still war the fowlis fleis in the air,
All stoit and catall seysit in thar lair,
And every thing, quharso thame lykis best,
Bownys to tak the hailsum nychtis rest
Eftir the days laubour and the heyt.   (Prol. XIII, 21-47)

There is nothing quite like this in English poetry until the eighteenth century. Chaucer gives no hint of any desire or capacity to evoke such a scene; only one of Chaucer's contemporaries, the anonymous author of the alliterative romance, *Sir Gawain and the Green Knight*, shows a similar interest in recording what he observed of seasonal landscapes.

The Scots developed their own literary language partly as a rival to Latin, adequate for the kind of lofty sententiousness with which they were by this time familiar from reading the works of Virgil, Ovid and Horace. The patriotic desire to purify Latin, to investigate the uses of ordinary nouns, to explore the resources of the Latin language and to achieve a Ciceronian accuracy in prose composition which characterized the Italian Renaissance was extended to vernacular languages, and is best seen in the many translations from classical authors not only into Italian, but into French and English. Douglas represents this movement in Scotland where, as in other European countries, it was felt that since language was not a fixed entity but instead a product of human effort, it was every writer's patriotic duty to add to the glories of his own national tradition. Douglas's 'Scottis' translation of *Aeneid* was the earliest translation of that work into any tributary of 'Inglis'.[12] It was also a major literary work in its own right.

From Dunbar's *Lament for the Makaris* one may learn the names of over a score of Scots poets, of whom fewer than half are known by their works. It

---

[12] Caxton's *Eneydos* (1490) was a translation of the prose *Livre des Eneydes*. In spite of Douglas's attack on it (*Aeneid*, Prol. to Book I, 138ff.), Caxton's adaptation caught more of the spirit of Virgil's original than any previous vernacular redactions. See L. B. Hall, 'Caxton's "Eneydos" and the Redactions of Virgil (*Mediaeval Studies*, XXII (1960), 136-47).

seems that, in the century following Chaucer, Scotland was just as active in the writing of verse as England (or any European country) and, judging by the works which remain, stood, together with Italy and France, at the summit of contemporary poetic achievement. Scottish literature is not to be judged in terms of English literature. It is rooted in different soil, depends on different conventions and feelings, and although it makes use of many familiar literary devices, handles them in a way alien to that of the English. Dunbar called his fellow-poets 'makars'; this is a more appropriate term than 'Chaucerians', for it suggests both nationality and the presence of the spirit of technical invention in a new language distinct, in this case, from 'Inglis'.

The poetry of the makars, with notable exceptions, does not treat of the sumptuous or of the excessively decorative—not surprising in a land economically poor and cursed by bleak weather. Barbour and his shadowy successor Blyn Hary wrote epics of valour in the spirit of noble romances and, as spokesmen for a well-established patriotism, showed how it had burst forth at a time of need. Dunbar was an intensely individualistic poet whose ascendant *persona* was that of a confessor; in contrast, Henryson's powerful moral detachment affected all his writings. Douglas was first and foremost a learned experimenter of the Renaissance, seeking to establish by translation that an amalgam of two languages might serve to interpret Virgil.

The Kingis Quair

Closest of all to Chaucer's early style is *The Kingis Quair*, usually credited to James I (1394–1437), who is supposed to have written it during his imprisonment in England. There are, though, too many echoes in it of late fifteenth-century English verse patterns to make the attractive hypothesis of his authorship entirely acceptable. James was taken into custody by English pirates, who intercepted him on the way to France and, a boy not quite twelve years of age, he became by this stroke of fortune a captive of Henry IV and, later, of Henry V, whom he accompanied to France. His mature years were thus spent under the eye of the English, nominally a prisoner of his country's long-standing enemies. After Henry V's death in 1422, England was governed by a regency dominated by Henry Beaufort, Bishop of Winchester, and his brother the Duke of Exeter, which fact suggested to the Scots diplomats negotiating for James's release the possibility of a matrimonial alliance between their king and an English noblewoman. The Duke of Exeter's niece, Jane Beaufort, seems to have been a strong candidate for James's hand, and, though the Scots king's wishes in the matter are not recorded, it is likely that he did not object. At all events, the pair were married in February, 1424.

This is the historical background to *The Kingis Quair*,[13] a poem written in a

[13] See G. Donaldson, *op. cit.*, pp. 63ff.

mixture of Scots and English forms of different periods in Chaucerian allegorical mould, dependent upon *The Romance of the Rose* framework and, according to the manuscript, the creation of the king himself. The author affects to be describing his own love-affair, viewed in retrospect with continued satisfaction, and the sense of his character and personality is strong throughout the poem. C. S. Lewis and others have considered that its originality lies in the use of the dream-allegory and other literary devices of French origin to celebrate a real courtship leading to marriage and not, as was usual at the time, a fanciful, idealized and impersonal one. More recent study of the poem has been inclined to disregard autobiographical content in favour of the philosophical.[14] Personal experience becomes a basis for a record of how the poet tried to reconcile his own problems with the pervasive presence of Fortune; as in the case of Boethius, the poet is seeking an escape from the impersonal wheel. The author of the *Quair* finds his deliverance in a dream which resolves his youthful difficulties and in which he is liberated by Love and Philosophy. His personal experiences and the dream-vision cannot be separated.

According to this argument, authorship becomes less significant. Of all Scots late medieval poems the *Quair* bears the closest resemblance to Chaucer's style in invention, but the lyrical impact is much more intense and concentrated than that of Chaucer. The music and colours of nature, the descriptions of fishes, beasts and trees, and the intimate personal tone of the writer recall the English secular songs of the fourteenth century, while the splendid spectacle, rhythm and rich adornments anticipate Spenser, though in the more consciously-disciplined manner which, as we have already noted, is characteristic of all the 'makars'. The writer's claim to truth of experience gives the poem a vital force which the more languid works of Chaucer's English imitators do not possess, and the narrative culminates in a celebration of marriage, for which the poet thanks the gods, the wheel of fortune, the well-disposed nightingale, the gilly-flower, the enclosing castle wall, the saints, the month of March (the month of the king's capture in 1406) and all the natural and divine powers to which he owed his earthly bliss. This is the antithesis of the misery of Boethius, whose life began so happily, and whose book had sent the poet off into meditations on the unpredictable ways of Fortune, thus providing the conventional framework for the narrative.

Other English poems such as *The Flower and the Leaf*, *The Assembly of Ladies* and *The Court of Love* are comparable in the extent of their direct debt to Chaucer, while Scottish compositions like *The Quare of Jelousy* and *Lancelot of the Laik* are written in the same amalgam of English and Scots forms. Lydgate's *Temple of Glas*, composed during James's lifetime, almost certainly

[14] Lewis in *The Allegory of Love* (Oxford, 1936), p. 235; and see articles by Preston, Rohrberger, MacQueen and von Hendy listed in select bibliography, section 5.

influenced *The Kingis Quair* for there are many close resemblances, and Lydgate's name occurs in a final stanza which recommends the *Quair* to disciples of the poet's acknowledged masters, Gower and Chaucer. There is no traceable connexion with Gower, though his name is mentioned first. If James I did indeed write the poem from his own heart, less than a quarter of a century after Chaucer's death, he must be credited with the infusion of a new spirit into this established mode, for in the medieval convention of *amour courtois*, a husband's love for his own wife was considered to be almost a discreditable emotion.

If James was not the author, the development away from Chaucerian example becomes less startling: if, for instance, the author was a late fifteenth-century poet assuming the *persona* of James sixty years after his death. The poem then takes a minor place, along with other anonymous works, as a late Chaucerian allegory composed by a nameless Scotsman writing with considerable originality in an old-fashioned style. For the critic, it is tempting to accept James as the original author, the language as southern English of the early fifteenth century and the dominating Scottish forms as the work of two scribes of the late fifteenth century, thus dealing with the complex problem of reconciling the main contradictions which a study of the *Quair* involves.[15] But on existing textual evidence, questions of authorship and date must remain unsettled and it is not beyond the bounds of possibility that it may not be a Scottish poem at all.

The 'Christ's Kirk' Tradition

In strange contrast to *The Kingis Quair* are two burlesque poems, *Christ's Kirk on the Green* and *Peblis to the Play*, both attributed by early commentators to the same royal author. With them and others such as *Cokelbie Sow* and *The Wife of Auchtermuchty* begins a Scots comic tradition of 'making' which culminated in Fergusson's *Leith Races* and Burns's *Holy Fair*. It continues, though in a debased form, to this day. In fact, it is this tradition which really links the medieval with the modern phase of Scottish poetry, since the 'Chaucerian'

[15] See Sir W. A. Craigie, 'The Language of *The Kingis Quair*', *Essays and Studies*, XXV (1939), 22–38. However, the heading to the poem in the unique MS 'Heirefter follows the quair Maid be King James of Scotland the first callit the Kingis Quair and Maid quhen his Ma. wes in England' may be a sixteenth-century addition deriving from the unconfirmed and confused statement in John Major's Latin *History of Britain* (1521). Referring to the King's literary gifts, Major observed that 'he composed a skilful book about the queen while he was a prisoner, before he married her' (artificiosum libellum de regina dum captivus erat composuit, antequam eam in conjugem duceret: *Historia Majoris Britanniae*, lib. I, cap. xiv). The language is less 'English' than Craigie alleged.

impetus died with Montgomerie's *Cherry and the Slae*, composed about 1580. The vitality of Dunbar and the easy flexibility of Henryson were each *sui generis*, and Douglas's achievement in translation could not be built upon by others because of the rapid linguistic changes which followed the disaster of Flodden. When eighteenth-century collectors and popularizers like Watson and Ramsay sought a living force in native verse it was in this old comic tradition, carried on in such poems as *Habbie Simson, the Piper of Kilbarchan* and similar mock-elegies composed in seventeenth-century Scotland, that they found it. Ramsay's own original work, which gave the example to Fergusson and Burns, was heavily indebted to this burlesque tradition, and in the *Elegies* (on Maggy Johnston, John Cowper and Lucky Wood) and in *Lucky Spence's Last Advice*, it may be seen how he himself carried it on.[16]

The makars themselves were stimulated by *Christ's Kirk*, both in manner and matter. By means of a combination of technical devices, such as rapid transitions from one scene to the next, vividly etched detail and a stereotyped metrical pattern, consisting of two quatrains of alternating four- and three-stress lines ending in a bob and wheel of one or two lines, sometimes varied in individual poems, the poet, posing as detached spectator, manages to impart a raciness sufficient to carry forward an otherwise slender subject and to give solidity to a train of diverse images by making them appear to move, rather like Langland's device of 'crowded plurals'. Dunbar's *Dance in the Quenis Chalmir, Dance of the Sevin Deidly Sinnis, The Sowtar and Tailyouris War* and *The Fenyeit Friar of Tungland* all fall into this category, and Henryson's *Robyne and Makyne* employs a stanza form identical with that of *Christ's Kirk*, but leaving out the bob and wheel.

Later makars like Lyndsay and Alexander Scott, as well as Dunbar, wrote poems using the mock-tournament device as a basis for satire, and there are many anonymous pieces which draw upon the model of *Christ's Kirk*—*The Cursing of Sir John Rowell* and *Rauf Coilyear* being two of the best known. These racy narratives represent the gems of the northern alliterative tradition, which the makars adopted in combination with regular rhythm as the best medium for the communication of their energetic and often extravagant verses. *Rauf Coilyear* is an excellent example of the union of two patterns:

> Gowlis glitterand full gay, glemand in grene;
> Flowris with flourdelycis formest in feir
> With mony flamand ferly, ma than fyftene;
> The rufe reulit about in reuall of reid,
> Rois reulit ryally,
> Columbyn and lely,
> Thair was ane hailsum harbery,
> Into riche steid. (669–76)

[16] *Poems* (1721).

The 'wheel' which closes the stanza emphasizes the dancing rhythm and is a device of which all the makars make expert use. Dunbar is especially fond of dancing scenes, where the speed of the verse requires accentuation and the tendency of the lines encourages chanting. Both *Christ's Kirk* and *Peblis to the Play* are cast in the same rollicking metre, which suits the wild, outspoken and vituperative character of Scots popular poetry, studded with proverbial usage and catalogues of insulting terms, as in Skelton, Rabelais and, in the present century, James Joyce.

Flyting

This brings us to an important feature of Scots 'making'—the tendency to indulge in 'flyting', or 'quarrelling' verse, cast in terms of extravagant formality and representing a duel with rhetorical weapons. Flyting implies debate, for reply is always invited from a foeman worthy of the server's verbal fusillade who can at will return fire with comparable accuracy and devastation. Dunbar's *Flyting with Kennedie* exploits every extravagance of language conceivable for the purpose of nailing the opponent to the wall, but the whole effect is one of mockery, not only of the poets concerned but also of the rhetorical devices which are deliberately exaggerated for the sake of an intellectual game. It is hard to judge the extent of animosity which lies behind such lines as these of Dunbar's, but it was probably very slight since his reference to Kennedie's death in the *Lament* is tender:

> Mauch muttoun, byt buttoun, peilit gluttoun, air to Hilhous;
> Rank beggar, ostir dregar, foule fleggar in the flet;
> Chittirlilling, ruch rilling, lik schilling in the milhous;
> Baird rehator, theif of natour, fals tratour, feyindis gett;
> Filling of tauch, rak sauch, cry crauch, thow art oursett;
> Muttoun dryver, girnall ryver, yadswyvar, fowll fell the:
> Herretyk, lunatyk, purspyk, carlingis pet,
> Rottin crok, dirtin dok, cry cok, or I sall quell the.

followed by Kennedie's reply:

> Dathane devillis sone, and dragon dispitous,
> Abironis birth, and bred with Beliall;
> Wod werwoif, worme, and scorpion vennemous,
> Lucifers laid, fowll feyindis face infernall;
> Sodomyt, syphareit fra sanctis celestiall,
> Put I nocht sylence to the, schiphird knaif,
> And thow of new begynis to ryme and raif,
> Thow salbe maid blait, bleir eit, bestiall.

Translation destroys the effect, which depends largely upon incessant alliteration.

Other Scots flytings, such as those between James V and Sir David Lyndsay or between Montgomerie and Polwart later in the century, were not, apparently, taken as evidence of genuine antagonism. James VI's treatise on literary criticism, *Reuelis and Cautelis*,[17] refers to flyting as an accepted exercise and it can certainly be paralleled in other literatures, usually in a much milder form. Scots lent itself to the violent kind of expression on which flyting depends, and there is nothing quite like it either in English or in other European literatures such as Provençal, where poetical skill was often displayed in debate form. Two-sided scurrility, maintained for as long a period as the participants can manage, is essentially comic in result and it is unlikely that personal hurt was the object. The effect is inclined to be one of an academic parade of technical skill and knowledge by a pair of lively minds duelling with the arms of their profession. Flyting persists in Scottish literature to this day and the tendency to break out into a catalogue of abusive epithets is apparent in verse composed well before Dunbar's time. *Cokelbie Sow* and *The Cursing of Sir John Rowell*, both known to Dunbar, are the earliest examples left to posterity of this dominant tendency of the makars. Fergusson, Burns, R. L. Stevenson and Hugh McDiarmid are in this way descendants of Dunbar. In fact, when McDiarmid, writing in 1927, issued his manifesto for the revival of Scots language for poetry,[18] it was to Dunbar that he looked for example, for in linguistic and thematic variety Dunbar is the richest of all Scots poets.

William Dunbar

Dunbar affords the clearest indication of what is really meant by 'Chaucerian'. When Chaucer translated *Le Roman de la Rose* he invented a poetic diction, and of this Dunbar is fully conscious. When he called Chaucer 'rose of rethoris all' Dunbar was hinting at the nature of his own debt to the English poet. The 'aureate style' and Douglas's 'sugurit sang' are the result of experimentation with European rhetorical conventions and with Chaucerian modifications of these. In his freedom of expression Dunbar are not anchored to traditions, however, and his characteristics are distinct. His ability to turn his hand to almost any kind of verse on almost any subject calls to mind the earlier (Latin) verse of the continental *vagantes*. A list of his works shows him jumping from one topic to another, writing comic lyrics like *On his Heid-ake*, parodies like *The Sowtar and Tailyouris War*, scurrilous commentaries like *To the Quene*,

[17] In *Essayes of a Prentise in the Divine Art of Poesie* (1584): 'Rules and Cautions to be observed and avoided in Scots poetry', published in Arber reprint series.
[18] C. M. Grieve ('Hugh MacDiarmid'), *Albyn: or Scotland and the Future* (London, 1927), p. 35.

serious lyrics on the transience of life, devotional lyrics, formal allegories and obsequies, poems praising women and others condemning their mercenary conduct, sardonic petitions for his own overdue preferment, pieces which owe their inspiration to personages at court like James Dog and Thomas Norny, macaronic compositions in two or three languages like *The Testament of Mr Andro Kennedy*, vignettes of Edinburgh life, debates, religious and moral verses and even one or two apparently malevolent attacks, such as the *Epitaph for Donald Owre*. The *Flyting* with Kennedie is, as noted before, in ultimate intention good-natured.

His poems tend to be short. The *Flyting* takes up five hundred and fifty lines, *The Twa Mariit Wemen and the Wedo*, his most ambitious work, five hundred and thirty lines. It is a burlesque on the confession convention involving the innocent fair maidens of romance, and its metrical ancestors are to be found, not in the Chaucerian tradition, but in northern English unrhymed alliterative verse romances.[19] It is, in fact, Dunbar's only extended essay in alliterative writing. The qualities of dignity and magnificence which suited spacious heroic themes also made the alliterative measure a fit medium for satire and burlesque, as we have pointed out, and in the hands of a skilled makar like Dunbar it was remarkably effective.

The Twa Mariit Wemen and the Wedo marks the contrast between outer show and inner truth in the case of the three females, probably drawn from the life with actual court ladies as models. Formally, the work is a debate among a trio of expensively-attired women celebrating Midsummer's Eve in a lush garden. The poet overhears them *en cachette* behind a hedge. The garden is the familiar earthly paradise of the *Rose* and the ladies, lavishly described, show their familiarity with the diction of *amour courtois* and the religion of Eros, along with the adulterer's virtues of secrecy and 'pity' so dear to medieval writers on love between the sexes. The reader soon discovers, however, that despite their superficial courtliness, the trio regard marriage as no more than licensed harlotry. Their attitude has to be considered against the economic background of medieval society, where the giving of dowries played an important role in the arrangement of marriages and the wife often found herself the sole executrix of her deceased husband's estate. Even poor girls sought to acquire a suitable dowry by receiving alms and imitating the practices of the better-endowed classes. For this reason, the impact of Dunbar's anti-feminist satire today is probably more savage and less comic in its effect than it was when he wrote it. Although for the modern reader the rose-garden maidens are gold-diggers (of a type presumably common in James's materialistic court), the coarseness of their sentiments and the lewdness of their conversation must be considered against its appropriate social setting and not judged in accordance with Renais-

[19] See the article by Edwin G. Morgan listed in select bibliography, section 5.

sance poetic idealization of the married state. The poet's attitude is akin to that of medieval clerics in the tradition of St Jerome, who condemned women for their supposedly insatiable sensuality.

There is, moreover, a strong 'literary' ring about the poem, which burlesques the romances by making the women spiritual heirs to the Wife of Bath, in her own turn one of a long line of predatory females whose ultimate source is Ovid.[20] The lines contain many echoes from ballad, proverbial and romance sources as well as the deliberate taking-off of rhetorical formulas from the aureate vocabulary of the makars themselves.

> Quhat throw the sugarat sound of hir sang glaid,
> And throw the savour sanative of the sueit flouris,
> I drew in derne to the dyk to dirkin efter mirthis;
> The dew donkit the daill and dynnit the feulis. (7–10)

—a verbal scene which is set in violent contrast to the robust descriptions of the sexual habits of the various husbands, who differ only in degree of contemptibility. One is forced to conclude that the pairs are well matched, and the bawdy language essential to the subject matter.

The Goldyn Targe and *The Twa Mariit Wemen* may usefully be compared. Both were inspired by the allegorical tradition of Chaucer and his French predecessors, but whereas the latter poem distorted the tradition for purposes of burlesque, the former translated it into current poetic diction. The *Targe* opens conventionally, in the rose garden, and the battle between Reason and the Flesh, described in terms of contemporary military tactics, is in itself presented according to accepted pattern and the allegorical personages are familiar enough. But the dream is obviously not a pleasant one in its closing moments and the poet's abrupt return to reality conveys a sense of emotional shock: he awakens 'wyth spirit affrayde' to the joyful choir of birds which had helped to lull him to sleep. The pictures of nature, whether richly artificial or simple, are always visually exciting; Dunbar has an unerring sense of the value of colour in composition:

> I saw approch, agayn the orient sky,
> A saill, als quhite as blossum upon spray,
> Wyth merse of gold, brycht as the stern of day.... (50–2)

The mythological figures whom he introduces did parade in popular pageants, and to those living at the time were not simply literary abstractions. It is

---

[20] E.g. Anus in the twelfth-century Latin play *Pamphilus, de Amore*; la Vieille in *Le Roman de la Rose*; Ghismonda in Boccaccio's *Decamerone* (1st story, 4th day); the six old women in *Les Evangiles des Quenouilles* (c. 1450); la Belle Hĕaulmiére in Villon's *Testament*; Celestina in de Rojas' Spanish tragedy.

possible that the allegory has a political significance, and refers to Franco-Scottish alliances, but there is no internal allusion to support such a theory, as there is in *The Thressil and the Rois*.

The influence of the pulpit is also evident in the vocabulary of those makars who were in holy orders or who took a keen interest in ecclesiastical affairs during the years of polemic preceding the Reformation. Flyting is strongly influenced by the Goliardic Latin poems which, under the name *sermones*, and using the same techniques, castigated the more blatant corruptions of the times.

The tendency to borrow from the language of preachers emerges not only in flyting but also in a certain love of morbidity and obsession with the ugly and repellent. Henryson's *Thre Deid Pollis* and Dunbar's *Of Manis Mortalitie*, with its sinister refrain:

> Quod tu in cinerem reverteris

both harp on the common late medieval theme of life as but a brief pathway to the grave. Dunbar and Villon share this obsession with death and dying which the 'Ubi sunt?' tradition reflects both as a reality and as a symbol. As a reality death appears in various forms—as a corpse in Dunbar's *Of Manis Mortalitie*, and in Villon's *Epitaphe*, where six gallows-birds dangle, exposed to the wind, rain, sun and flying scavengers. Sometimes it stimulated the poet to elegy, such as that on Bernard Stewart, Lord of Aubigny, a famous soldier and ambassador to Louis XIII, who died suddenly whilst on an official visit to Edinburgh. Dunbar regrets the sudden uprooting of this 'flour of chevalrie' and bursts into lament:

> O duilfull death! O dragon dolorous!
>   Quhy hes thow done so dulfullie devoir
> The prince of knychtheid, nobill and chevilrous ... !   (17–19)

Dunbar ends his *Meditatioun in Wyntir* by solacing himself with anticipation of the vivid enjoyments and ephemeral delights of the warm season:

> Cum, lustie symmer! with thi flowris
> That I may leif in sum disport.   (49–50)

Meditatioun in Wyntir captures the poet's nocturnal apprehensions in the style of a confession; his will to write 'sangis, ballatis, and ... playis' has been sapped by the 'dirk and drublie dayis' of the Scottish winter. He is not certain whether or not worldly affairs should hold but a passing attraction for him and he is 'assayit on everie side' by allegorical figures who offer advice. Despair, Patience and Prudence are followed by Age, who reminds him that he will be called to account for the use he made of his time on earth. Finally Death is depicted as throwing his gates wide open, after the style of contemporary murals, and speaks as he does in the contemporary play of *Everyman*:

> Syne Deid castis upe his yettis wyd,
> Saying, 'Thir oppin sall the abyd;
>   Albeid that thow were never sa stout,
>   Undir this lyntall sall thow lowt:
> Thair is nane uther way besyde.' (36–40)

The stanza is anti-climactic in that Death's appearance is no surprise and does not heighten the tension as it might have done had Age succeeded instead of preceded:

> And than sayis Age, 'My friend, cum neir,
> And be not strange, I the requeir:
>   Cum, brodir, by the hand me tak
>   Remember thow hes compt to mak
> Off all thi tyme thow spendit heir.' (31–5)

Dunbar's anticipation of summer does little to convince us that he is really going to enjoy the pleasures of life, for though Age is a much less abstract figure than Death in this short procession and is depicted as a friendly ally against the grim and impersonal Reaper, the poem as a whole has the quality of a daydream and the personifications lack shape and substance. For all his weightiness, Dunbar is writing first and foremost in a poetic convention and striking an attitude in accordance with the fashion of the pulpit without thinking of other individuals.

More seemingly personal is *Lament for the Makaris, quhen he wes seik*, but this poem was probably written in about 1506, a number of years before Dunbar's death, so that its urgency was not as great as the procession-convention makes it appear. The simulated tone is that of a man who realizes that his time in a deceptive and fleeting world is almost over; his advice to the living to prepare for death so that 'Eftir our deid that lif may we' was a stereotype of the contemporary sermon. The refrain with which each stanza concludes recalls other poets' names in terms of his own predicament, but his attention to his fellows is a poetic device to relate the theme of change to himself, identified as one bringing up the rear in the line of dead and dying makers. In *None May Assure in This Warld*, the poet says that his only hope is for a seat in Heaven; earthly prizes go to sycophants, but he himself has missed his chance, and in spite of his long service has been given no reward. He consoles himself by remembering that riches will not help anyone to evade judgment and the accompanying torments of hell, and holds fast to a prayer for heavenly consolation. The rhetorical line 'Quhat is this lyfe bot ane straucht way to deid?' reveals a pervasive aspect of Dunbar's poetic character. His inclination to make hay while the sun shines is invariably tempered by a sad musing over life's disappointments and the clerkly image of 'Timor Mortis'.

Dunbar's poems yield no solid autobiographical information. Whether he entered the priesthood or not, the scope of his travels abroad, the nature of his frustrations at court and the results of his efforts to secure a benefice—none of these questions is answered in the poems. The dominant impression, however, is that Dunbar was a solitary person whose relations with others were prickly and who rarely betrayed fondness for specific individuals of either sex. His is not a convivial figure and he frequently mentions his lack of company. In *Of Deming* he is

> Musing allone this hinder nicht

and in *The Twa Mariit Wemen and the Wedo* we are told that

> I muvit furth allane, neir as midnicht wes past.

Several poems start conventionally by telling us of his sleeplessness. *The Birth of Antichrist* introduces the poet waiting for dawn, musing on his plight and on the sorry state of the world, while *Meditatioun in Wyntir*, as we have noted, is of the same kind, painting a picture of unsettled gloom, not much relieved at the end by the glimpse of summer. The motifs derived from French with which Dunbar introduces many of his poems are given a personal character and the writer speaks as a man on his own who trusts in no one, as in *None May Assure In This Warld*, one of his most despondent utterances:

> Quhom to sall I compleine my wo,
> And kythe my cairis ane or mo?
> I knaw not amang riche or pure
> Quha is my freind, quha is my fo. (1–4)

and complains about unfair distribution of rewards. Many pieces concern his supplications for a pension which, as a court poet entertaining patrons, he felt to be his entitlement. One such effusion informs the King:

> Off sic hie feistis of sanctis in glorie,
> Baithe of commoun and propir storie,
>   Quhair lairdis war patronis, oft I sang thame
> *Charitas pro Dei amore;*
>   And yit I gat na thing amang thame.
>
> ('To The King', 11–15)

and there are several other complaints of a similar nature. Of these *The Petition of the Gray Horse, Auld Dunbar* is the most personal and appealing: it is less serious than most of the others and concerns the king's failure to supply him with a gift of clothing:

> I am ane auld hors, as ye knaw,
> That ever in duill dois drug and draw;
> Gryt court hors puttis me fra the staw,
> To fang the fog be firthe and fald.
>   Schir, lat it never in toun be tald,
>   That I suld be ane Yuillis yald!   (31–36)

His religious poems, often glossed over by commentators in favour of his comic verses, rise above the themes of Court life and his personal difficulties. *Of the Nativitie of Christ* is a masterpiece of incisive language, with a Latin phrase from Isaiah, 'Et nobis puer natus est' concluding each stanza and anticipating the symmetry of *Epithalamion*. *On the Resurrection of Christ*, a hymn for the morning of Easter Sunday, etches an allegory in swift strokes, looking forward to Bunyan's description of Christian's combat with Apollyon; a chanted refrain concludes each stanza:

> Done is a battell on the dragon blak,
> Our campioun Chryst confountet hes his force:
> The yettis of hell ar brokin with a crak,
> The signe triumphall rasit is of the croce,
> The divillis trymmillis with hiddouss voce,
> The saulis ar borrowit and to the bliss can go,
> Chryst with his blud our ransonis dois indoce:
> *Surrexit Dominus de sepulchro.*

> Dungin is the deidly dragon Lucifer,
> The crewall serpent with the mortall stang;
> The auld kene tegir with his teith on char,
> Quhilk in a wait hes lyne for us so lang,
> Thinking to grip us in his clowss strang;
> The merciful Lord wald nocht that it wer so,
> He maid him for to felye of that fang:
> *Surrexit etc.*   (1–16)

Ane Ballat of our Lady is a complicated structure of coinages and borrowings from literary sources and Latin hymns on the Virgin, modified to suit the rhyme, through which Dunbar expresses religious fervour:

> Hodiern, modern, sempitern,
>   Angelicall regyne!
> Our tern infern for to dispern
>   Helpe, rialest rosyne!

> *Ave Maria, gracia plena!*
> Haile, fresche floure femynyne!
> Yerne us, guberne, virgin matern,
>   Of reuth baith rute and ryne. (5–12)

From an exercise like this it may be judged that the outstanding feature of Dunbar's work, to which he owes his influential place in Scottish literary history, is his meticulous verbal craftsmanship developed at a time before the makars' vocabulary had become impoverished and when it could still be used as a vehicle even for classical epic. As a virtuoso of poetic language he had no equal among his contemporaries, and his polished technique has been cited as evidence that his appeal is intellectual rather than deeply emotional. In contrast, Henryson's poems are sometimes said to be written 'to the heart' without display of verbal wizardry. Although this is a superficial conclusion, there is no doubt that the most obvious characteristic of Dunbar's methods is the degree to which he explored and organized the resources of this short-lived literary language and adapted it for the writing of poetry in a number of medieval stylistic conventions and complex metrical patterns, allegorically, descriptively, lyrically, satirically, in dialogue, in testament, burlesque, *pastourelle* and flyting. Though other poets, for example, Skelton in English and George Buchanan in Latin, cultivated similar habits, Dunbar is without equal in Scottis.

Robert Henryson

Chronologically, Henryson precedes Dunbar, since the latter mentions him in *Lament for the Makaris* as having already died in Dunfermline. Henryson was not unduly influenced by Chaucerian rhetorical practice.[21] Much of his work is shot through with a genial but retiring quality and, though he did not leave very much, in emotional intensity and in relation of quality to quantity, he far surpassed the other makars. His masterpiece is *The Testament of Cresseid*, in which his direct debts to Chaucer are limited to the names of the main characters in the traditional tale and to the use of the English poet as a model for diction. In fact, there is little to distinguish Henryson's verse-technique in this poem from Chaucer's except the Scotsman's stronger taste for alliteration, but whereas Chaucer translated and developed Boccaccio's *Il Filostrato* for his *Troilus and Criseyde*, Henryson took up the old story at the point where Chaucer

---

[21] A. C. Spearing's essay, 'Conciseness and the Testament of Cresseid' (*Criticism and Mediaeval Poetry*, London, 1964, 118–44), finds that the paramount quality of the poem is brevity, well established throughout the Middle Ages as an ideal of style in certain types of writing, such as the chronicle or the literature of instruction, but not, especially, in poetry. As an ideal of poetic utterance, brevity was given a new lease of life as the oral tradition declined and printed books began to replace it (Spearing, *op. cit.*, 126–31).

left off and applied his fine talents to the creation of an original imaginative work.

Viewed in relation to *Troilus and Criseyde*, Henryson's *Testament* seems to require little interpretation. Taking up the thread of Chaucer's narrative, Henryson pays Cresseid back for her infidelity in harsh terms and makes a superficial appeal to a self-righteous male morality by reducing 'the flour and *A per se*' to a 'late lipper', whose testament bequeaths her body to the worms, her material goods to the Church, and her soul to Heaven. Neo-classical critics seeking to re-establish criteria of literary art based on symmetry find in the *Testament* an emotional satisfaction lacking in *Troilus and Criseyde*, but at the same time they admit that the English poem is, with all its faults, closer to real life. The *Testament* has in fact been blurred by this continued insistence that it be evaluated in terms of Chaucer's earlier achievement. Independent reading shows it to be an allegorical work written with distinct motives and under different social conditions from those which governed *Troilus and Criseyde*. The 'doolie sessoun' and the Trojan setting are at odds[22] and the 'typically Chaucerian elements' which some critics claim to find in Henryson do not blend easily with the 'typically Scots morality' by which human beings are expected to reap what they sow. There is not much to connect the two poems except a common interest in the old legend of the lovers, Henryson's reference to his predecessor's work and the unexplained fate of Cresseid after her desertion by the lustful Diomede. The *Testament* is a fresh moral allegory having general human application. Cresseid, punished for her 'brukkilnes', is both a universal figure of womanhood and a symbol of sinful and suffering humanity. Unlike Dunbar, Henryson does not write like a disappointed cynic; unlike Lyndsay, he was not a clamorous social propagandist, but he shared with both a keen sense of moral indignation. Nearly all his writings show this and *The Testament* is no exception.

Cresseid, a breaker of moral and theological laws, is punished by the physical affliction of leprosy, thought at that time to be a form of venereal disease[23] and described in the poem with apparent accuracy. After much physical scourging, through her eventual repentance and her testament relinquishing earthly things, she is permitted to die in the purified state of an aspirant to the conventual life, her carnal sin forgiven. Whereas at the end of his poem Chaucer affects to see the real values of life as transcendental and makes his Troilus reject earthly love as blind and wasteful, Henryson at the last promotes sympathy for Cresseid's miserable lot on this earth. But his stern morality is always in control. In

[22] See J. MacQueen, *Robert Henryson, a Study of the Major Narrative Poems* (Oxford 1967), pp. 50–1.

[23] See D. Fox, ed., *The Testament of Cresseid* (London and Edinburgh, 1968), introduction, pp. 23–30, and *n*. 30 (below, p. 30).

principle Henryson displays little sympathy for the shortcomings of fallen humanity, writing his poems as a practical lesson with a constructive solution. His strong and unyielding sense of justice runs through the entire *Testament* and in the central section, cast in the form of a dream-vision, Cresseid is formally accused, denounces Venus and Cupid and is judged guilty and sentenced by an assembly of planetary gods, who speak according to their traditional literary characters. Her *Complaint*, revealing her in all her misery, is followed by a brief meeting with Troilus, which impresses upon her, and on the reader, the full impact of what she has earned by her infidelity. There is no 'feminine psychology' in the poem and the static figure of Cresseid is simply a support for the workings of ideal justice and repentance. Henryson's poem is a sermon—not an attack on womankind or on any specific woman, but an exhortation to Christian justice, to make men awaken to the miserable facts of contemporary life.

The *Morall Fabillis*, written probably before 1480, are all closely connected with church and state corruptions,[24] though they are written in a lighter vein. Henryson has recast certain of Aesop's *Fables* and added others, like *The Fox, the Wolf and the Cadger* which may be of his original composition. The heavily moralistic Aesop is transformed in his hands and the old stories, without loss of narrative attraction, now become the vehicles for political and social commentary. *The Taill of the Uponlandis Mous and the Burges Mous* illustrates his capacity to make insignificant creatures speak and act like human beings whilst at the same time preserving their traditional animal traits. *The Taill of the Fox and the Wolf* is a criticism of mendicant friars and their irresponsible exercise of the mendicant's office, that is, of receiving confession without genuine contrition. The *Taill of the Wolf and the Lamb* upholds a thinly-disguised political allegory and points out that real justice is to be found only in heaven, since on earth, notwithstanding the civil law, might is right. *The Taill of the Scheip and the Doig* draws a realistic picture of the effects of tyranny on the powerless. In such pieces Henryson anticipated the intense feeling which inspired in Lyndsay's *Ane Satyre of the Thre Estaits* its author's virulent hatred of social injustice and petty tyranny. Each 'Taill' is followed by an explanatory *moralitas* and although the creatures whose actions have been described are thus shown to be symbolic, there is no diminishing of human interest in the narrative itself.

The *Taill of Schir Chantecleir and the Foxe* is a good example of how Henryson's treatment of a theme differs from Chaucer's. There is no similarity between this 'Fabill' and *The Nonnes Preestes Tale* apart from their dependence on Aesop's story. Chaucer allowed his audience to take or leave the moral lesson, but Henryson spells it out in detail and warns man to flee from the twin sins of

---

[24] See M. W. Stearns, *Robert Henryson* (New York, 1949), a treatment of the effects of contemporary social conditions on Henryson's art.

flattery and vainglory which the fox and the cock respectively represent. Instead of Chaucerian digressions on dreams and a development of the husband-wife, cock-hen relationship as a human document merging with a parody of the romance style, one is presented with an uncomplicated narrative of the tempter fox and the conceited cock who falls for a simple confidence trick. The hen–mistresses of Chaucer's version are introduced by name only after the fox has taken Chantecleir by the throat. Each offers her opinion of their unfortunate paramour. The trio, Partlot, Sprutok and Coppok represent various attitudes to love, courtly, realistic and cynical. Coppok, who speaks last, denounces the cock-lover and says that his sins have found him out and that his fate is God's justice. At this point the widow-woman of the fable sends her dogs to rescue Chantecleir, who persuades the fox to release him and, in spite of the latter's further blandishments, flies back to safety. There is no suggestion, as in Chaucer, of any cosmic allegory nor that any direct biblical reference is implied: the *moralitas* explains the whole in terms of two stock deadly sins. Henryson's version emphasizes character and action rather than setting, giving only slender hints of the northern landscape, and his straightforward narrative and colloquial dialogue is less 'literary' than Chaucer's. It is more obviously rooted in the spoken language—perhaps because he was not himself of the Court circle and wrote deliberately for the literate citizen whose dissatisfaction with social conditions he reflected. Though he may lack the versatility and glitter of Dunbar, Henryson reveals in these adaptations of Aesop a more profound poetic character who speaks more directly than Dunbar to a socially-conscious age like our own. He claims that

> In hamelie language and in termes rude
> Me neidis wryte, for quhy of Eloquence
> Nor Rethorike, I never Understude   (*Prol.* 36–8)

and, compared with his fellow-makers, he seems to have been little affected by Chaucer; though such a view fails to take into account more subtle influences of tone, verse formation and the art of reflecting his own personality without seeming to do so, itself a strong characteristic of Chaucer.

The specifically 'medieval' side of Henryson is more clearly seen in his minor works. Modern critics have in the main restricted their attention to *The Testament of Cresseid* with some incursions into the *Fabillis*. Fourteen other poems attributed to him are each worthy of more detailed attention than they have hitherto been given. As in the *Testament* and the *Fabillis*, the most prominent feature of these minor pieces is the quality of the poet's learning and the technique through which he incorporates it into his verse. His classical interests and bookish inclinations, far more pronounced than Dunbar's, are evident in nearly every poem and the generally slow tempo of his writing gives an impression of weightiness absent from Dunbar. Henryson displays the learning of a conservative scholar of his time and country; not a mercurial soul like Dunbar, he is less given to emotional fluctuations of mood and spirit, and his addresses often adopt the tone of deliberate preaching. His vocabulary is less mannered than Dunbar's and appears closer to what we believe to have been popular speech. The atmosphere he creates is pastoral and of the countryside rather than courtly and of the burgh, and he contemplates the vicissitudes of the world from the point of view of his 'rurall mous' whose 'sempill lyfe withoutin dreid' is the ideal to be sought and cherished. If there is something of Catullus in Dunbar, Henryson may be said to look at life through Horatian spectacles.

Robene and Makyne is perhaps the best illustration of the way in which Henryson can marshal his talents as a lyrical poet in the service of a conventional form. The subject is love between rustics, its form is that of the *débat* and it is written, though only superficially, in the style of the Old French *pastourelles*.[25] The conversational dialogue between the Scots lover and his lass conveys a simple moral of the 'gather ye rosebuds' kind and each stanza is subtly different from its predecessor in mood or in the picture it creates. Robene is keeping his sheep when Makyne reveals her long-standing love for him and tells him that unless he returns it she will surely die. Robene protests his ignorance of love, whereupon Makyne immediately reveals an unexpected sophistication and shows her familiarity with the language and practices of *amour courtois*. But Robene is half-hearted and wants to postpone the proferred sexual association until a vague tomorrow; in spite of her entreaties, he leaves her desolate. Later, he has second thoughts, but by this time so has she, and echoes the sentiments of a familiar proverb:

> The man that will nocht quhen he may
> Sall haif nocht quhen he wald.   (91–2)

Unwilling in his turn to accept rejection, Robene counters this with an enticing picture of dalliance to which the maiden remains indifferent. Thus the tables are turned; it is Robene who is finally left to mourn and Makyne to laugh and we leave him where we found him, looking after his sheep, stricken with remorse. The poem has strong dramatic qualities, for the stanzas are in themselves little scenes and the Scots dialogue is colourful and dramatic. Although the inevitable moral purpose is plain and the conventionally-named characters may well mask a significant contemporary allegory, as they do in the *Fabillis*, this is Henryson's lightest poem, essentially a song, with alternating moods of hope and despair conveyed in established traditions of ballad, proverb and native irony.

[25] See A. K. Moore, 'Robene and Makyne' (*Modern Language Review* XLIII, 1948, 400–3), who rejects the argument that Henryson was indebted to French sources.

It is tempting to cite *Orpheus and Eurydice* as early work, though there is no real evidence for this. The longest of the minor poems, it is based on Nicholas Trivet's interpretation of the Orpheus legend as told by Boethius and has little in common with the Middle English *Sir Orfeo*. There is little human interest, for Orpheus is a symbol, allegorically justified in the *moralitas* as the union of Phoebus (wisdom) and Calliope (eloquence) and described as the intellectual part of man's soul. Eurydice represents desire led by temptation and the narrative is an allegory of the early Christian *Psychomachia*, the battle within man's soul between the rational and sensual sides of man's nature. Orpheus's inability to resist a backward glance at Eurydice stands for the triumph of worldly lust and vain prosperity over reason. This is the standard Thomist and Aristotelian interpretation of the legend, and Henryson adds nothing to it except details.[26]

Familiar too are the devices by means of which he gives the poem extra weight—the musical references (taken from Boethius), the procession of nine muses, the elongated classical allusions and the *mappa mundi*. The freshness of the work emerges in its scenic descriptions. Henryson's glance at Orpheus's path towards Hell is an act of memory—the dreary moor, with its thick thorn bushes and the slippery track through the field have about them a humorous authenticity unmatched in contemporary English poetry. Hell is a 'dully place', 'a grundless deip dungeoun' with all its attendant material horrors, fire and stink and poison and torment, where dwell the undead 'ay deand, and nevirmoir sall de'. There we encounter the familiar grouping of medieval sinners, starting with classical and Hebrew tyrants and evildoers and including contemporary prelates convicted of abuses—popes, cardinals, bishops, abbots and other men of religion who had misused their offices, all tormented in the flames. References of this nature are the stock-in-trade of the late medieval satirist, but the domestication of the topography of hell and the importation of mythological personages, Cerberus, the Eumenides, Ixion, Tantalus and Titius, together with the unmistakeably Lowland accents of Pluto, Proserpyne and Orpheus himself place this work squarely on the Scots side of the Border.

The narrative is sketchy and follows the classical versions;[27] Orpheus only rarely comes alive, but in the three opening stanzas of the *Complaint* he cries inconsolably and poignantly for his vanished wife:

> Quhair art thow gone, my luve Ewridicess?

and takes leave of his old haunts. The work shows Henryson to be an accomplished technician but its heavy dependence on stock material and a comparison with his *Testament* reveal a certain rawness that may be associated with apprentice immaturity of conception not obvious in his other long poems.

[26] See MacQueen, *op. cit.*, pp. 30–1, and below, p. 100.

[27] Ovid, *Metamorphoses* VII; Virgil, *Georgics* II; Boethius, *De Consolatione Philosophiae* III, Metrum 12.

The Thre Deid Pollis treats of a familiar medieval subject, death, and may be compared with Dunbar's *Of Manis Mortalitie* or with Villon's *Epitaphe*. Henryson's poem dwells closely on death's repulsive physical aspects which will be visited on all men. The poem is stronger in pictorial qualities than Dunbar's, though not as vivid as Villon's. The audience is asked to imagine the skulls in a row, real ones or effigies on a tomb, under the gloomy poet's contemplative eye. They stand out starkly, with cavernous eye-sockets leering from hairless domes and behind them, in a mocking double-vision, the 'lusty gallandis gay' who will some day be as they are now, 'holkit and how' and 'wallowit as the weid', and the 'ladies quyht', their physical charms enhanced by precious stones and jewellery, who shall inevitably lie 'with peilit pollis' and empty brain cavities.

Having issued this grim reminder, the poet hammers home a stereotyped moral, warning his audience against pride, asking them to be humble and to seek mercy since earthly vanities and ceremonial pomp, mortal achievement and human learning are in the end best symbolized by an empty death's head. He makes a special appeal to the aged, shortly to die, exhorting them to fall upon their knees and to ask forgiveness and concludes with a general injunction, aimed at all mankind, to pray for salvation to the Redeemer. The piece is a sermon in miniature, depending for its effect on the pervasive presence of the trio of grinning skulls and the terror of physical change with which the medieval mind was affected.

In many of his short poems Henryson talks like a calm monk who knows that all is vanity and offers consolation from the point of view of a man matured by experience. It is this tone which separates his from Dunbar's religious lyrics: Henryson is far surer of his place in the scheme of things and he talks without animus as one enabled by his faith to reject the ultimately worthless and to hold fast to what he thinks really valuable. He seems to have little enthusiasm for the attractions of urban life or for the court preferment which cost Dunbar so many sleepless nights. Pieces like *The Ressoning betwix Age and Youth* and *The Prais of Age* convey a personal message not often present in medieval verses treating the well-known theme of instability. *The Want of Wyse Men* and *Aganis Haisty Credence of Titlaris* are both closer to Dunbar, and even to Lyndsay, in spirit; they illuminate the crude political atmosphere of the 'estates', where fools were loose-tongued, and numerous irresponsible tale-bearers were hearkened to in high places. But, unlike Dunbar, Henryson is speaking as a poor outsider whose sufferings from the unwisdom of governors are indirect; in the second poem, he warns a governor against listening to unsolicited or lying reports without weighing the evidence. The final stanza paints a grotesque portrait of the 'bakbyttar', reminiscent of Langland and the morality plays:[28]

[28] Contemporary Scots drama, with which Henryson must have been

> Within ane hude he hes ane dowbill face,
> Ane bludy tung, undir a fair pretence. (53–4)

Ane Prayer for the Pest has much in common with the sentiment of the *Morall Fabillis*, particularly that of *The Scheip and the Doig*, a plea for the poor written as if by one of their number. In sending up this supplication asking for preservation 'fra this perreuls pestilens' Henryson poses as a spokesman for the ordinary man, later summed up by Lyndsay in the figure of John the Commonweal, whose burdens were unfair, whose treatment by the powerful was unjust and who lacked all protection but the power of prayer. If Henryson is in any sense a court poet, he comes out of a very different stable from 'the auld gray horse Dunbar', who is no champion of the oppressed and harps mainly on himself and his own insecurity at the hands of the kings and nobles. Henryson's greater impersonality is not a sign of remoteness but of selflessness; this social concern is more durable than any fascinations of language and for this reason he speaks to our time far more directly than any of his contemporaries.

Sum Practysis of Medecyne stands out from all the other poems because it is Henryson's single exercise in burlesque, a parody of the prescriptions of contemporary apothecaries directed at an audience which knows of their ever-complicated character (a legacy of Arabian compilers and the medical schools of Salerno and Montpellier which followed the example set by their treatises). Henryson achieved his satirical object by listing, in popular alliterative measure, items in a compound which are far-fetched, non-existent or irrelevant as a cure for the ailment they claimed to master. One is reminded of Villon's *ballade* suggesting a remedy for stewing envious tongues;[29] but whereas Villon is twisted by contempt, Henryson is impelled by a good-natured leg-pulling spirit to burlesque the practices of a profession for which he had a high regard. Henryson is expert at describing the external symptoms of a disease and commentators occasionally recall that his account of Cresseid's leprosy was cited by Sir James Young Simpson[30] as dating the incidence of Greek elephantiasis in

---

familiar, does not seem to have been as widespread in performance as the English Miracles and Moralities, and we lack first-hand evidence concerning actual productions. Lyndsay's *Satyre* (*q.v.*) was clearly written about 1530 for a popular audience accustomed to witnessing conventional serious drama as well as farce, and though it is the only surviving complete text of a medieval Scots play was surely not an isolated example. Many burgh records mention dramatic performances of all kinds from the mid-fifteenth century onwards. (See A. J. Mill, *Mediaeval Plays in Scotland*, Edinburgh and London, 1927.)

[29] *Le Testament*, 1425–54.

[30] In *Edinburgh Medical and Surgical Journal* (1841). The Greeks called true leprosy 'elephantiasis' and Simpson (also largely responsible for the story that Robert Bruce was a leper) was over-confident about identifying the disease

Northern Europe. Henryson may have enjoyed the dual role of schoolmaster and chaplain of a leper hospital,[31] not an unknown combination in the Scotland of that time, but, whatever the sources of his information may have been, *Sum Practysis* supplies additional evidence of his keen interest in healing.

All Henryson's poems are obviously the work of a skilled makar who tells us little about himself, though he seems to have moved in the world as an active teacher and helper of men. His mainly serious character and steadiness of purpose is mirrored in his handling of late medieval subjects—rustic love, religious faith, prayer, moral dialogue, incidents of classical legend, complaint against current abuses and death, both as a symbol of spiritlessness and as a stark reality. He is not much given to broad humour and this single burlesque is mild and kindly meant—he is temperamentally too sympathetic and fastidious for 'flyting'. No single line of his carries a dart to wound specific individuals and, compared with Dunbar, whose moods can vary from scorn to anguish within the same poem, Henryson is consistent and predictable throughout the entire

---

from written records. The old medical term 'lepra' was generic and included various skin diseases as well as, for example, bubonic plague, smallpox, syphilis in a post-primary stage of rashes, and lesions. Psoriasis, scabies, eruptions of boils or sores such as were said to have afflicted Job and Lazarus (whose name became a synonym for the disease itself or for its carrier, as in *TC* 343, 531) and even species of horse- or plant-mange were referred to as 'leprosy'. Biblical usage strongly influenced the medieval conception of the disease: 'leprosy' could mean simply a state of misery and poverty such as a beggar endured, and 'Lazarus' often signified a beggar, afflicted by loneliness and the rejection of his fellows, such as true leprosy brought with it. The metaphor of a loathsome disease conveys the impression of isolation. Simpson's researches notwithstanding, leprosy as described or referred to in early documents does not necessarily imply the infection of Hansen's bacillus. See W. MacArthur, 'Mediaeval Leprosy in the British Isles', *Leprosy Review*, XXIV (Jan., 1953), 8–19.

[31] Perhaps because of a long-established though dubious interpretation of *Isaiah* 53,4 by the early rabbis and by St Jerome in his translation of the Vulgate, the word 'stricken' was taken to mean the servant was a leper. Wycliffe continued the tradition, and thus the teachings of the Church encouraged particular kindness to lepers. By Henryson's time there were in Europe several thousand lazar- or leper-houses, some dating from the Conquest. Most of these were almshouses, founded to support the sick and poor, and seem to have had little to do with sufferers from 'elephantiasis Graecorum'. They were certainly not designed to segregate lepers from the rest of the population and it is not the case that some form of quarantine saved the countryside from widespread contagion. The disease is not especially contagious and quarantine was not known until the fifteenth century. See Wilfred Bonser, *The Medical Background of Anglo-Saxon England* (London, 1963), 371–4 and MacArthur, *op. cit.*

canon of his works. The pace of his poetry is leisured but rarely laboured, in spite of the strong moralizing character of most of it. He never experiments with a daring vocabulary in order to justify an otherwise slender offering and his verse is less colourful, less dashing, less varied metrically and generally more sober than Dunbar's. He has not served as a model for later poets, as Dunbar has done, and his firm intellectual rooting in the traditional learning of the Middle Ages, combined with an ascetic conservatism of temperament, has made him an occasionally admired but largely neglected makar. Only within recent years have there been strong indications of a movement to place Henryson first among Middle Scots poets.

Gavin Douglas

Scotland also has her 'great translator',[32] for Gavin Douglas's reputation[33] rests on his rendering of Virgil's *Aeneid* into Scots, completed in 1513, after eighteen months' work, shortly before Flodden and the virtual extinction of the flower of Scotland. Because it was produced quickly in a period of political and linguistic transition it has suffered by being regarded as a literary curiosity, praised for its exuberant richness and Spenserian pictorial qualities and passed over without careful examination.

Douglas wrote it under the spell of a righteous patriotism at a time when the military and political threat from England was rapidly increasing. His immediate object was to stabilize and to enrich his native language which, as has been noted, he called 'Scottis', and to endow it with eminence as a European literary medium fitted, like Latin, for heroic utterance. Earlier Scots epics, *Bruce* and *Wallace*, had been written in 'Inglis' and lacked resources uniquely national. Even in his day the language was, on Douglas's own admission, inadequate for the highest flights; its range was limited and a hundred years later *Aeneid* could not have been attempted in 'Scottis':

> Yit stude he nevir weill in our tung endyte
> Less than it be by me now at this tyme   (*Prol.* I, 494–5)

These are prophetic lines, for religious and political pressures peculiar to Scotland soon afterwards combined to bring about the disintegration of 'Scottis' as a vehicle for literature of the first order.

[32] 'Grant translateur noble geffroy chaucier' (from a *ballade* by Eustache Deschamps, *c.* 1386). See above, p. 8.

[33] In addition to the *Aeneid*, Douglas is credited with having written three poems: 'The Palice of Honour', 'Conscience' and King Hart', but of these only the first is indisputably of his authorship. See P. J. Bawcutt, ed., *The Shorter Poems of Gavin Douglas* (Scottish Text Society: Edinburgh and London, 1967), introduction.

When he said that he lacked the 'fowth' or abundance of language,[34] Douglas was not simply expressing a conventional humility in the august company of 'maist reverend Virgill, of Latyn poetis prynce': the clash of arms at Flodden became the symbol of the end of the old Scotland and of the destruction of the young seed of her Renaissance. Political trends towards Union implied a movement in favour of anglicization and a London-centred culture; ironically it was *a patria sua exsul*, under Wolsey's protection, that Douglas himself died in 1522, proscribed in his native land as rebel and traitor. He left behind him a great translation of *Aeneid*[35] in a language soon to become tragically unread and unreadable, and cast in medieval styles which even in his own time were considered old-fashioned outside Scotland. Douglas was at heart a schoolman and although his 'nature' poetry anticipated Thomson's *Seasons*, his Scottis was built up on the electic principle, taking its own where it could be found from Latin, French, the literary Scottis of his predecessors and even 'Inglis':

> Nor yit as cleyn all sudron I refuss,
> Bot sum word I pronounce as nyghtbouris doys:
> Lyke as in Latin beyn Grew termys sum,
> So me behufyt quhilum or than be dum
> Sum bastard Latyn, French or Inglys oys,
> Quhar scant war Scottis—I had nane other choys.   (*Prol.* I, 113–8)

The key to the poem, both as translation and as original work, is the author's periodically whimsical statement in the *Prologue* to Book I on the difficulties of translation. Referring to 'our tongis penuritie' in comparison with the rich resources of Latin, he says that he will not translate word for word but will instead take the advice of Horace and St Gregory and give a free rendering.[36] In the spirit of the Renaissance, Douglas regards the classics as humane letters rather than mystically inspired productions of genius akin to divinity. He is the only makar to venture into the realms of literary criticism and shows himself well informed about the classical peak of culture and language to which his own civilization might aspire. Temperamentally, as a poet, he is a patriot and works

[34] *Aeneid*, Prologue to Book I, 120.
[35] He particularly abhors Caxton's prose redaction (se *n.* 12, p. 10), which he claims has no more to do with the Virgilian original than has the devil with St Augustine and forestalls possible criticism of his own offering by warning his readers:

> 'Beis not ourstudyus to spy a moyt in myne e,
> That in your awyn a ferry boyt can nocht se,
> And do to me as yhe wald be done to.'

(op. cit., Prol. I, 499–501)

[36] See 'The Nature of the Translation' in D. F. C. Coldwell's STS edition, I, introduction, 39ff.

in the European tradition of linguistic experimentation. Such a combination of qualities, allied to a powerful intellect learned in the liberal arts, made Douglas a translator poetically as well as academically original. The *Prologues*, in fact, show less 'originality' than the translation itself, which is a genuine recreation of its model, in spirit and content. There is an effortlessness about Douglas's handling of classical themes which Henryson, among the makars his closest relation, cannot approach without self-consciousness. Orpheus's descent into the underworld is a studied performance compared with Aeneas's descent as translated by Douglas from Book VI:

> Bot lo, a litill befor the son rysyng,
> The grond begouth to rummys, croyn and ryng,
> Undir thar feyt, and woddy toppys hie
> Of thir hillys begyn to move thai se;
> Amang the schaddowys and the skuggis mark
> The hell hundys hard thai yowl and bark,
> At cummyng of the goddes Proserpyne. (Bk VI, iv, 39–45)

Douglas's method of translation depended on the couplet as unit rather than upon the hexameter of the original, and thus he greatly increased the number of lines. He remained nevertheless steadfastly faithful to his resolution

> . . . to mak it braid and plane,
> Kepand na sudron bot our awyn language   (*Prol.* I, 110–1)

and ignored the colder decorum of Renaissance scholarship in favour of rough-hewn equivalence in 'Scottis', so far as the limitations of that medium permitted. The force of his rendering may be felt directly by comparing it with Dryden's English version of the same passage:

> nor ended till the next returning sun,
> Then earth began to bellow, trees to dance,
> And howling dogs in glimmering light advance,
> Ere Hecate came.[37]

which has grace and subtlety but less strength and virility. The trend of English poetry towards 'the grand style' compelled poets to approach their task of creation in a mood of solemnity. By contrast, Douglas made the fullest possible use of the unadorned expressive power of Scottis as it then was and disregarded

[37] ecce autem primi sub lumina solis et ortus
    sub pedibus mugire solum et iuga coepta moveri
    silvarum, visaeque canes ululare per umbram
    adventante dea. (VI, 255–8).

heroic affectation. Within two centuries it was to become a *patois* and associated
with rusticity: for this reason a great gulf now separates it from Virgil and
modern attempts to repeat Douglas's experiments, mostly on a small scale,
have repelled critics who do not understand sufficiently clearly that in the year
of Flodden Douglas's language did not bear the stamp of the provincial. The
briskness and realism of a passage like

> The cartaris smate thar horssis fast in teyn,
> With renyeys slakkyt, and swete drepand bedeyn;
> For, throu the gild and rerd of men so yeld,
> The egyrness of thar frendis thame beheld,
> Schowtand 'Row fast', all the woddis resoundis.
> Endlang the costis the vocis and the sowndis
> Rollys inclusyt, quhill the mekyll hyllys
> Bemys agane, hyt with the brute so schil is[38]   (V, iii, 83–90)

which treats Virgil's characters as though they were contemporaries, may seem
undignified and unheroic to readers conditioned to believe that Virgil represents
the summit of the grand style. C. S. Lewis suggested that many lines 'so pierce
to the very heart of the *Aeneid*'[39] that the effect is one of a freshness lacking in
later English versions like Dryden's. It seems likely indeed that the modern
world has less affinity with the classical world than humanist tradition claims.

The additional *Prologues* to each of the thirteen books[40] contain intimate
vignettes of Scottish life. Their language is generally more directly related to
the aureate diction of Dunbar's allegorical and devotional poetry than to the
language of the actual translation, but as in the case of Dunbar himself, the
sentiments displayed owe little to the study. In *Prologue VII*, Douglas expresses
vividly what he felt about the dismal native winter: 'Bewte was lost, and
barrand schew the landis'—his theme is one of unrelieved ugliness and misery:

[38] nec sic inmissis aurigae undantia lora
concussere iugis, pronique in verbera pendent
tum plausu fremituque virum studiisque faventum
consonat omne nemus, vocemque inclusa volutant
litora, pulsati collis clamore resultant.   (V, 146–50).

[39] *English Literature in the Sixteenth Century* (Oxford, 1954), p. 86.

[40] The extra book, translated from a fifteenth-century continuation by
Mapheus Vegius, which contemporaries linked with the *Aeneid* proper, tells of
Aeneas's marriage to Lavinia and of his death and deification. Douglas affected
to be less than confident about the wisdom of including it and in the Prologue
explains how Mapheus came to him in a vision and persuaded him to do so,
both by argument and by giving the poet-dreamer a score of blows across the
back with a club.

Thik drumly skuggis dyrknyt so the hevyn,
Dym skyis oft furth warpit feirfull levyn,
Flaggis of fire, and mony felloun flaw,
Scharpe soppys of sleit and of the snypand snaw.
The dolly dichis war all donk and wait,
The law valle flodderit all with spait,
The plane stretis and every hie way
Full of floschis, dubbis, myre and clay.
Laggerit leyis wallowit farnys schew,
Browne muris kythit thar wysnyt mossy hew,
Bank, bra and boddum blanchit wolx and bar.
For gurl weddir growit bestis hair.
The wynd maid waif the red wed on the dyke,
Bedowyn in donkis deip was every sike.
Our craggis and the front of rochis seir
Hang gret ische schouchlis lang as ony speir. (47–62)

His description of summer in *Prologue XII* relies somewhat more substantially upon the resources of a literary vocabulary, but the local bird-names bring the portrait close to home:

Dame Naturis menstralis, on that other part,
Thar blysfull bay entonyng every art,
To beyt thir amorus of thar nychtis baill,
The merl, the mavys and the nychtyngale
With mery notis myrthfully furth brest,
Enforcing thame quha mycht do clynk it best:
The cowschet crowdis and pyrkis on the rys,
The styrlyng changis divers stevynnys nys,
The sparrow chyrmys in the wallis clyft,
Goldspynk and lyntquhite fordynnand the lyft;
The gukgo galys, and so quytteris the quaill,
Quhill ryveris rerdit, schawis and every vaill,
And tender twystis trymlyt on the treis
For byrdis sang and bemyng of the beys;
In warblis dulce of hevynly armonyis
The larkis, lowd releschand in the skyis,
Lovys thar lege with tonys curyus,
Baith to Dame Natur and the fresch Venus,
Rendryng hie lawdis in thar observance;
Quhais suguryt throtis maid glaid hartis dans,
And al smail fowlys syngis on the spray: (231–51)

Douglas, who feels the Scottish countryside as a living, moving force, marks its seasonal changes with a sharp attention to details of sound and sight: the reader is persuaded of an authentic 'native' atmosphere. His translation is a source-book of Middle Scots, for no other makar has preserved so completely the *wordhord* available to him.

Sir David Lyndsay

Of those who followed Douglas, the only major figure is that of Sir David Lyndsay, remembered today as the author of a political morality play, *Ane Pleasant Satyre of the Thre Estaits* (*c.* 1530)[41] which has survived as a testament to his dramatic power. Like Dunbar before him, Lyndsay succeeded in imprinting his remarkable vigour on the mind of the audience, but the matter of his art is as Henryson's in the *Fabillis*, and his activities as courtier and diplomat during the years of decision preceding the Reformation are reflected in *The Dreme* (1527) and *The Monarche* (1552).[42] In both of these Lyndsay is distinguished less by his poetry than by a statesmanlike preoccupation with his country's progress: his aim was the reform of Church and State, the purging of the corrupt clergy and nobility, and the improvement of the lot of the Commons. His theme is social justice and, although he employed medieval forms of expression and many stock devices of Chaucerian-French origin, these are but superficial vehicles for the revolutionary content of his works. His verse-satires are reformatory in intention and he has scant respect for poetic ornament as such, so that his poetry suffers from the literary sacrifices which he made to an intense social and evangelical consciousness. It is easy to think of Lyndsay as representing charac-teristic Protestant feeling, although he was in fact a staunch supporter of the old order. In his works the personal complaints of Henryson were replaced by a positive world of combative ideas, summing up popular complaint in his society.

The Dreme contains none of the customary references to poetical predecessors and favourable Muses, and the superficial allegory does little to conceal the apocalyptic visionary character of John the Commonweal,

> Quhose rayment was all raggit, revin, & rent;
> With visage leyne, as he had fastit lent:
> And fordwart fast his wayis he did advance,
> With ane rycht malancolious countynance (921–4)

whom we meet for the second time in *Ane Satyre of the Thre Estaits*. John, like Piers the Plowman for Langland, personifies Lyndsay's human feeling for the

[41] Modernized edn. by M. P. McDiarmid (London, 1967).

[42] D. Hamer, editor, *The Works of Sir David Lyndsay* (Scottish Text Society: Edinburgh and London, 4 vols., 1931–6).

honest toiler who in the ideal Church–State relationship ought to be served by both and not crushed beneath their ponderous weight. John is a sorrowful wanderer, harried and denied justice in the South, in the Highlands and in the Lowlands, and given no place in the social scheme of things; but he promises to return to comfort the Scots when a wise ruler, 'ane gude auld prudent king' succeeds to the throne.

The Thre Estaits is a vision of Lyndsay's ideal government. It is political propaganda in dramatic verse form and its periodic vulgarity is an invitation to violent reformation. A dramatic impulse informs all his verse; his natural bent was the drama and his appeals are direct and factual. He employs *flyting*, not simply for effect, but for obvious illustrative purposes, and uses the confession-convention to show up the real character of figures like pardoners, monks and friars, as well as of traditional morality-play personages like Falset, Dissait, Flatterie, Oppression and Wantoness who in the end meet their just deserts on the scaffold. The human characters, drawn to the life, the Cottar, the Soutar, the Tailor and their respective wives, with the familiar gallery of rogues,

> Fidlers, pypers, and pardoners
> Thir jugglars, jesters, and idill cuitchours,
> Thir carriers and thir quintacensours:
> Thir babil-beirers and thir bairds,
> Thir sweir swyngeours with lords and lairds
> . . . thir great fat freiris
> Augustenes, Carmleits and Cordeleirs
> And all uthers that in cowls bene cled
> Quhilk labours nocht and bene weill fed . . .
>
> (2604–8; 2615–8)

representing the state of the pre-Reformation Church in Lyndsay's Scotland, recall the list of guests at the harlot's 'mangery' in *Cokelbie Sow*. Much of the dialogue is reminiscent of the Wakefield Master,[43] though there is in *Ane Satyre* a stronger element of sheer farce, and the play ends in what one critic has called 'a kind of rough festival of fools,'[44] but with Lyndsay's ideal social

[43] E.g. the Wakefield play of the Judgment, wherein the Demons of Hell recite a list of the categories of people facing damnation:
> Of wraggers and wrears, a bag full of brefes,
> Of carpars and cryars, of mychers and thefes,
> Of lurdans and lyars that no man lefys,
> Of flytars, of flyars and renderers of reffys.

Text from G. England, editor, *The Towneley Plays* (Early English Text Society, Extra Series 71, 1897).

[44] J. Speirs, *The Scots Literary Tradition* (London, 1940), p. 81. Foly's con-

relationship established. It is the only complete example of Scots medieval drama; its closest relative in England is Skelton's *Magnyfycence*, composed in the 1520s, but in technique, language, and exuberant interest *Ane Satyre* is far superior. Although its author made use of many medieval literary devices, including the dream-vision, the walk on a May morning, virtues and vices in the morality tradition and many features of the contemporary satirist's stock-in-trade, the substance of the play is less dated than at first sight appears and both Aristophanes and Shaw would recognize in Lyndsay a kindred spirit.

The Testament and Complaynt of Our Soverane Lordis Papyngo is an unsubtle attack on ecclesiastical abuses, in character essentially dramatic. The dying parrot, overheard by the poet, who is concealed, like the eavesdropper in *The Twa Mariit Wemen and the Wedo*, under a hawthorn, complains of the unreliability of Fortune and regrets her own ambition to rise at court. This is a prelude to her advice to the king and his courtiers on how they should conduct themselves. After this three birds descend, a Pie, a Raven and a Kite, representing a Canon Regular, a Black Monk and a Holy Friar respectively, each claiming to shrive the Papyngo and to be responsible for her earthly goods. The Papyngo distrusts all three and describes the degeneracy of clergy from the time of Constantine. Eventually the Kite confesses her and she draws up a will, leaving parts of her body to various birds. Her heart she bequeaths to the king. However, her executors ignore her last wishes and devour her body. The Kite takes her heart after a wrangle with the others. The testament form was often used as a vehicle for parody and, after Villon, the fashion seems to have spread to Scotland, where, as we have seen, it attracted Dunbar and Henryson before Lyndsay.

Lyndsay's *The Historie of Squyer Meldrum* is another work which includes a poetical testament. Meldrum, a contemporary, was a soldier of fortune whose heroism in war and fortunes in love provided Lyndsay with material for a biographical romance in the tradition of *Bruce* and *Wallace*, celebrating the actual deeds of a flesh-and-blood Scotsman in chivalric terms. Coming as it did at a time when Scottish military fortunes were low, *Squyer Meldrum*, like *Wallace*, was a strongly nationalistic work, whose hero did battle for the honour of Scotland, which he maintained against the English foe with all the skill of Bruce. The octosyllabic couplets and the spare vocabulary, larded with formulaic devices, heavily alliterative, link *Squyer Meldrum* with the early romances—for example, this passage, which verges on parody

> The Inglis Capitane cryit hie,
> Swyith! yeild yow, doggis, or ye sall die;

cluding sermon is on the theme, 'the number of fuillis ar infinite', and *Ane Satyre* has in part the character of a French 'sottie' or fool-play. The Estates appear frequently in contemporary French drama.

> And, do ye not, I mak ane vow,
> That Scotland salbe quyte of yow.
> Than peirtlie answerit the Squyar,
> And said: O tratour Tavernar,
> I lat the wit, thow hes na micht
> This day to put us to the flicht.
> Thay derflie ay at uther dang:
> The Squyer thristit throw the thrang,
> And in the Inglis schip he lap,
> And hat the Capitane sic ane flap
> Upon his heid, till he fell doun,
> Welterand intill ane deidlie swoun.   (757–70)

and the episode continues with the English crying for mercy, which Meldrum magnanimously grants. Burlesque, in Lyndsay's writing, is not far to seek.

'Ane Supplicatioun in Contemptioun of Syde Taillis'[45] satirizes an ornamental fashion in women's garments which trail behind in the manner royal so that

> Ane mureland Meg that mylkis the yowis
> Claggit with clay abone the howis,
> In barn nor byre scho wyll not byde
> Without hir kirtyll taill be syde   (67–70)

This is a good example, together with others in *Ane Satyre*, of Lyndsay's conscious associations with the comic traditions of *Christ's Kirk*. He is far less a poet of the study than either Dunbar or Henryson, and his manifestly popular aims governed his often coarse language. As he pointed out himself:

> Because the matter bene so vyle,
> It may nocht have ane ornate style; . . .
> Of stinkand weidis maculate
> No man may mak ane rois chaiplat.   (7–8; 10–12)

and much of the content of this poem is crude, with explicit images of filth contrasting with the intended dignity of these ladies for whom the writer seems

---

[45] Written before 1542. The poet is disgusted at the needless extravagance of these long trains which drag in the dust and mud. Imitation of the Queen's Court robes seems to have been an affectation even of the servant classes, who were like others showing the effects of the nation's increased prosperity. Sir Richard Maitland wrote a poem on the same subject a few years later ('Satire on the Town Ladyes'). This was the last period of a truly Scottish fashion, since after James VI's accession and the departure of the Court for London, styles were progressively more influenced by English modes.

to have so much contempt. His jeers are cruel and humourless compared with Dunbar's, and beneath the triviality of the subject lurks a personal dislike of certain of his countrywomen who fall far short of his ideals of elegance.

The Monarche or *Ane Dialog betwix Experience and Ane Courteour* is Lyndsay's last poem, printed in 1554, the year before his death. It is a long work of 6333 lines, something of a museum-piece, on the subject of the world's misery and divine retribution on Scotland for her descent into sin. Opening with the restless poet walking in a park one May morning, 'The Prolog' proceeds according to well-worn medieval convention to describe the beauties of external Nature, which he rejects as a theme for making poetry. His inspiration, he says, is to come not from Parnassus, but from Calvary, and he prays to Christ to guide his hand. Four 'Bukes' follow, of exceeding dullness. Experience, an old man, gives the Courtier an account of the Christian interpretation of universal history, starting with the Creation, the Fall and the Flood and, in Book IV, prophesying the end of the world with extreme urgency. His plea for reform runs continuously through the entire work. The poem shows the writer's familiarity with the Bible, and *The Monarche* is to some extent redeemed from complete unreadability by the freshness of Lyndsay's attention to the making of Scots poetry out of biblical incidents, something which his predecessors had hardly attempted. The best examples of this come from his graphic description of the Deluge:

> Quhalis tumbland amang the treis,
> Wyld beistis swomand in the seis,
> Byrdis, with mony pietuous pew,
> Afferitlye in the air thay flew.
> So lang as thay had strenth to flee,
> Syne swatterit doun into the sea.
> No thyng in erth was left on lyve,
> Beistis nor foulis, man nor wyve:
> God holelye did thame distroye,
> Except thame in the Ark, with Noye,
> The quhilk lay fleittand on the flude:
> Welterand amang the stremes wode   (1449–60)

and later, from the scene after the waters have receded:

> Bot Noye had gretast displesouris,
> Behauldand the dede creatouris,
> Quhilk wes ane sycht rycht lamentabyll;
> Men, wemen, beistis, innumerabyll,
> Seyng thame ly upone the landis,
> And sum wer fleityng on the strandis:
> Quhalis and monstouris of the seis

> Stickit on stobbis, amang the treis;
> And, quhen the Flude was decressand,
> Thay wer left welteryng on the land. (1531–40)

In *The Monarche* and in Lyndsay's other writings appears the constant complaint that the clergy have neglected the Bible. In *Ane Satyre*, the figure of Truth is put into the stocks for trying, among other things, to make the New Testament available to the people at large. Flattery accuses her of heresy. In *The Tragedie of the Cardinall*, a mock confession by Beaton of his ruthless conduct in and out of ecclesiastical office, the Cardinal is made to say that he

> ... purposit tyll put to gret torment
> All favoraris of the auld and new testament   (216–7)

and later to admit that when he was consecrated Bishop he knew no more about its content than did 'ane beist berand ane precious pak' (326). Copies of Tyndale's New Testament were being read by an increasing number of people in defiance of clerical efforts to suppress its circulation,[46] and in a poem called *Kitteis Confessioun* (in the first printed edition by Charteris attributed to Lyndsay, though possibly not of his authorship), Kitty is asked by the lecherous priest if she has been guilty of heresy by having had 'Inglis bukis', that is, copies of the New Testament, read to her. Lyndsay's works are full of biblical allusions and reminiscences and, like Dunbar, he often made use of quotations from the Vulgate, as in the concluding stanza of *Squyer Meldrum*:

> My Spreit hartlie I recommend
> *In manus tuas, Domine.*
> My hoip to the is till ascend,
> *Rex, quia redemisti me.*[47]
> Fra syn *resurrexisti me*;
> Or ellis my saull had bene forlorne:
> With sapience *docuisti me*;
> Blist be the hour that thow wes borne. (246–53)

[46] Copies of the Bible came from England until the Bassendyne edition was printed in 1576–9. It deviated only slightly from the Genevan scripture, and rivalled the 'Authorized Version' of 1611 until the mid-seventeenth century. Murdoch Nisbet, an Ayrshire man inspired by Purvey's Wycliffite revision to translate the New Testament into Scots, left an unpublished attempt dated *c.* 1520 (edited by T. G. Law for the Scottish Text Society, 3 vols., 1900–4). The only version to which the Scots had access, therefore, was the Latin Vulgate, which only a small number of people could read. Popular demand for Bible teaching was one strong motive for reformation and it is clear that sixteenth-century Scottish clergy opposed any lay access to a vernacular Bible.
[47] Psalm 30, 6 (Vulgate). Other phrases recall *Proverbs* 4, 11, *Isaiah* 28, 9 and Psalm 117 (Vulgate).

or in the motto to *The Dreme*—'prophetias nolite spernere. Omnia autem probate: quod bonum est tenete.'[48] *The Complaynt of Schir David Lyndsay*, recalling poems in the same vein by Dunbar, asks the King not to forget his old servant and early aide, and reminds him of the labourers in the vineyard

> For, thocht the last men first wer servit,
> Yit gat the first that thay deservit.[49] (43–4)

while the 'papyngo' is shown as conversant with Church history and the Scriptures when he condemns Constantine's endowment of the Church, known throughout the Middle Ages from the Donation of Constantine, a forged document of considerable authority. Denial of its authenticity was considered to be heresy as late as 1533.

T. F. Henderson has called Lyndsay 'as satirist a superficial pupil of Dunbar'[50] who borrowed the allegorical machinery of his predecessors for practical rather than for aesthetic purposes. Occasionally he set himself to image, in the manner of Douglas, a natural landscape—as in this evening scene at the end of Book IV of *The Monarche*:

> The blysfull birdis bownis to the treis
> And ceissis of thare hevinlye armoneis:
> The cornecraik in the croft, I heir hir cry;
> The bak, the howlat, febyll of thare eis,
> For thare pastyme, now in the evinnyng fleis . . . (632–6)

Other passages of heavily aureate description also seem to owe their inspiration to Douglas, but the consensus of modern critical opinion echoes Lyndsay's own mock-modest insistence that he 'did never sleip on Pernaso'[51] and eschewed rhetoric in favour of 'rurall ryme'. His repetitions, pedantries, reiterated oral formulas and extensive borrowings make of him a propagandist who took his own wherever he might find it, and although he seems at first reading to bear a superficial resemblance to Skelton, Lyndsay is no deliberate innovator experimenting with language and metre. His motives for posing as a 'ragged rhymer' were of a different order from Skelton's.

Nevertheless Lyndsay, together with Douglas, marks a late and, as it happened, a final stage in the development of Scottis as a language sufficiently independent to support the weight and intricacies of meaning which contemporary poetry demanded. Though an incomplete development, and lacking the idiom of

[48] 'Despise not prophesyings. Prove all things; hold fast that which is good. (*I Thess.* 5, 20–1, Vulgate). *Cf. Ane Satyre* (1554 edn.), 269–70. The motto appears in Jascuy's 1558 text.

[49] *Matt.* 20, 16.

[50] *Scottish Vernacular Literature* (London, 1898), p. 206.

[51] *Monarche*, Prologue 226. (*cf.* Chaucer, *Franklin's Prologue*, 13.)

abstract inquiry, Scottis, as a medium for discussing political questions, was in Lyndsay's hands fairly adequate as a colloquial language designed for popular communication. The history of medieval Scots poetry is, as Kurt Wittig has remarked, 'the history of the birth of a culturally distinct Scots language'.[52] It might be added that by Lynday's time the signs of death were already writ large. Though the patriotic work of the makars continued throughout the sixteenth and even into the seventeenth century, practised by a group which included Alexander Scott, Alexander Montgomerie, James VI and a score of unnamed contributors whose relics were gathered into the Bannatyne and Maitland manuscripts, the tensions between Scottis and Inglis produced by the Reformation rapidly reduced the potency of the 'auld leid' as a vital language of serious literature.[53]

[52] *Op. cit.*, 101.

[53] Devotion to Scottis (as opposed to literary English) was represented during the period of transition by a group of enthusiastic nationalist reactionaries. John Knox, who returned to Scotland after a long absence, spoke and wrote English, thereby drawing the fire of Catholics and Protestants alike for his 'knapping of Southron'. Knox wrote as much for Englishmen as he did for Scots but reached his audience in Scotland by means of an Anglo-Scots prose. John Hamilton, the author of *Ane Catholik and Facile Treatise* (Paris, 1581) concluded this work by saying that those who caused Scottish books to be printed in London 'in contempt of our native language' were 'triple traitoris'. The influence of the English Bible helped to set up an emotional as well as a linguistic barrier between literary English and a Scots which survived as a vernacular, that is, as a group of regional spoken dialects subject to phonetic spelling. The native language became a Jacobite political symbol after the Union of the Parliaments in 1707, and the spirit of the latter period is well illustrated by the fact that the members of the Edinburgh Easy Club, which included Allan Ramsay and Thomas Ruddiman (who issued an edition of Douglas's *Aeneid* in 1710), called themselves by the names of certain of the old makars, and tried to rebuild Scots as a poetic medium.

A NOTE ON MIDDLE SCOTS

Middle Scots is a development of the so-called 'Anglian' dialect of Old English, which divided into Midland and Northumbrian during the twelfth and thirteenth centuries, and eventually became the Northern dialect of Middle English. Historians of the language usually prefer to subdivide early Scots into old, middle and late middle periods, of which Barbour, Blyn Hary and Douglas may be taken respectively as representatives; although the scribal transcription of *Bruce*, made in the 1480s, came a full century after Barbour composed it, one need not assume that it differed greatly from the original. Nevertheless, phonetic changes undoubtedly took place during the interval and the literature of the makars shows grammatical features which were not characteristic of *Bruce*.

Middle (and especially late middle) Scots drew directly upon the Latinized vocabulary which Chaucer knew only at second-hand through French transformation and which contained a much larger proportion of Latin words, together with expressions peculiar to the northern region. Both Chaucer and the makars used colloquial French terms, anglicized, which contain, in the language of linguists, a substratum of a shared literary superstratum; but whereas Chaucer's French borrowings tended to originate in central French and to reflect philosophical, academic and technical interests, those of the makars drew far more exclusively on a literary vocabulary as employed by the writers of romances, strongly Anglo-Norman in origin. In other words, borrowings from central French, through Chaucer, came at the latter end of the period 1375–1513; 'Chaucerianism' in this sense increased gradually all the time. This is why the vocabulary of *Christ's Kirk on the Grene* and that of *The Testament of Cresseid* or of Douglas's Prologues to *Aeneid* seem to differ so much and why that of Barbour's *Bruce* is distinct from that of Blyn Hary's *Wallace*, though the subject-matter of these two latter works is not dissimilar.

'Aureation', derived from Latin, is not therefore such a paramount feature of Middle Scots as is often supposed. The language of the makars is not merely that of the study, and words like *angelicall, celicall, depurit, hodiern, matutyne* and *toxicate* make up but a minor proportion of its total resources in vocabulary. Although *The Kingis Quair* and *The Goldyn Targe* represent an erudite, formal literary mode of communication imitative of Chaucerian ceremonial styles, and are packed with words not rooted in spoken Scots they do not justify the condemnation of Middle Scots as a literary language never actually spoken. It includes a powerful literary element which sometimes lapses into pedantry and even eccentricity, but this is balanced by colloquial idioms, terms of mercantile, agricultural and military origin, popular terms of ribaldry and unbridled abuse, expressive obscenities and, in contrast to the latter, the rolling formulas of the preacher, grounded in scriptural and proverbial phrases. This volume contains full illustrations of all these and more besides.

Although its practitioners were mostly drawn from the upper classes, some of these works, such as *Peblis to the Play* and *Cokelbie Sow* and others in the *Christ's Kirk* tradition were deliberately composed in a popular vein for purposes of burlesque, a literary technique in which the makars seem to have excelled. In some poems, like *The Tretis of the Twa Mariit Wemen and the Wedo* and *Schir Chantecleir and the Foxe* the vulgar combines with the aristocratic to produce an effect which even Chaucer rarely achieved. Except at their most 'aureate', the makars wrote the language of the court and of the educated classes, but supported it with the resources of the spoken Scots of their time and home soil.

Behind their efforts lay a patriotic object. They aimed to enrich their language and they succeeded, yet their 'common touch' when it appeared was rarely without at least a mild irony. As humanists on the threshold of a Renaissance they had little to offer the mob and only Henryson (and Lyndsay, a late makar) reveals genuine sympathy for the lot of the third Estate in unreformed Scotland. Dunbar, Douglas and the anonymous comic poets seem to have been constantly admiring their own images, a *double-entendre* that goes some way towards furthering later understanding of the motives which impelled them.

Orthography

Middle Scots spelling conventions differ from those of the northern dialect of Middle English. Since many of the words were not 'literary' but 'popular' and do not occur in more than one or two written works, their forms of spelling were arbitrary and could vary for a given word even in a single manuscript. Thus even a frequently-used word like *deid* may appear as *ded/dede*; *wedo* as *weido/wedow*; *dule* as *duill/dul/dool*. As in Southern English, *i/y*, *u/v/w* are interchangeable. So are *ch/gh*, as *thocht/thoght*; *bownis/bounis/bownys*; *discriue/discrive*. *Ou* and *ow* alternate, as in *loutit/lowtit*, *maugre/mawgre*. Sometimes spelling is phonetic, as *apon/upon*, *anon/onone*. The effect is one of a quaintness not unpleasing to the eye, but confusing to the reader seeking accuracy in pronunciation. The multiplication of variant forms often helps, however, towards an understanding of how the poet or at least, the scribe, sounded a word.

Features which are more or less regular and distinctive include the forms *quh-* for *wh-* (*quhose, quhat, quhelis*); *sch-* for *sh-* (*schent, schowris*); *-is* for *-es* in the plural of nouns and the third singular present indicative of verbs (*letteris, tidingis; beginnis, lurkis*); *-and* in the present participle (*bydand, doand*) and with *-it* and not *-ed* in the past participle and past tense of regular verbs (*abaisit, granit, onwemmyt*). Verbal nouns end in *-ing* (*blenking, peirsyng*) and the yogh symbol (ȝ) is represented by *ch/gh* (*lacht/laght*) more often than by *g* or *γ* (*geir, yeir*). The manuscript symbol (ß) may be transcribed *-s*, *-ss* or *-se* (*as, ass, ase; venemus, venemuss, venemuse*) though the sound intended is in all instances the same. *u/ui* for the southern *o* (*gud, guid*); and *oi* for long *o* (*moir, thairfoir*) do not change the pronunciation, for there is no diphthong sounded. Some words, like *dew/new/kneis/treis* all had diphthongs (*dëw*, *nëw*, etc.) as the metre indicates. Final *-e* was probably not pronounced at the end of a line, though the plural in *-is* usually was. The omission of *h* in *sall* (shall) is common.

The plural of *this* is *thir* and of *that* is *thay* (*I am content, quod he, to tak thay twa*) The relative pronoun *that* is often met with in Middle Scots (*how his lady, that he had bocht so deir*). *Quha, quhilk* or *the quhilk* are equivalent to 'who', 'which' and its formal version (*the quhilk throw me was sumtyme flour of love*). The literary indefinite article is *ane*, used a great deal after 1500.

A proliferation of examples, which may be augmented by consulting Gregory Smith's *Specimens of Middle Scots* or the introduction to Mackay Mackenzie's edition of Dunbar or Harvey Wood's of Henryson, only serves to underline the chaotic character of scribal orthography. Even in eighteenth-century Scotland there was no standard spelling of Scots, though some general agreement was reached among editors like Hailes and Pinkerton, mainly as a reaction against Ramsay's mingling of early Scots forms with English forms (a habit also practised by fifteenth- and sixteenth-century scribes, who would write *micht/might, thocht/thoght* interchangeably). The continuing currency of Scots as a vernacular militated against the 'normalization' of its spelling, which still tends to be phonetic and arbitrary, occasionally suggestive of English rather than Scots pronunciation. In fact, only phonetic transcription can reveal anything of the subtler differences separating the two languages considered as spoken standards. A fuller account of this may be found in the introduction to volume I of the *Scottish National Dictionary*.

Middle Scots poetry is, like all medieval poetry, designed with a view to oral recitation and the reciter should give full value to its vowels and consonants when reading aloud. There should be few slurrings and the pace should be slow and even ponderous. Many traps exist, some more obvious than others, and it is not enough simply to affect a 'braid Scots' accent—the Chaucerian influence undoubtedly affected the pronunciation of some words. But the results of the so-called 'Great Vowel Shift' of the fifteenth and sixteenth centuries, which may well have been apparent even in Chaucer's lifetime must have helped to make the makars' reading of their own works recognisably modern.

Select Bibliography

1. *Sources*

The Bannatyne Manuscript Written in Tyme Of Pest 1568, *by George Bannatyne*, edited for the Scottish Text Society by W. Tod Ritchie (Blackwoods: Edinburgh and London, 1927–30, 4 vols.).

The Maitland Folio Manuscript, edited for the Scottish Text Society by W. A. Craigie (Blackwoods: Edinburgh and London, 1919–27, 2 vols.).

Chepman and Myllar prints of Poems XI, XII and XIII (lines 104–end) (1508?).

The Testament of Cresseid/Compylit be M. Robert/Henrysone, Sculemai-/ster in Dunfer-/meling/Imprentit at Edin-/burgh be Henrie Charteris./M.D.XCIII (1593).

Virgil's 'Aeneid' Translated into Scottish Verse by Gavin Douglas Bishop of Dunkeld, edited for the Scottish Text Society by David F. C. Coldwell (Blackwoods: Edinburgh and London, 1957–64, 4 vols.).

The Kingis Quair, together with A Ballad of Good Counsel. By King James I, edited for the Scottish Text Society by the Rev. Professor W. W. Skeat (Blackwoods: Edinburgh and London, 1884, 1911).

2. *Recommended for Further Study*

The Kingis Quair, edited from the manuscript by W. Mackay Mackenzie (Faber: London, 1939).

The Poems of Robert Henryson, edited for the Scottish Text Society by G. Gregory Smith (Blackwoods: Edinburgh and London, 1906–14, 3 vols.).

The Poems and Fables of Robert Henryson, edited by H. Harvey Wood (Oliver and Boyd: London and Edinburgh, 1933, 2nd edn., 1958).

Robert Henryson: Poems, edited by Charles Elliott (Oxford, 1963).

The Asloan Manuscript, edited for the Scottish Text Society by W. A. Craigie (Blackwoods: Edinburgh and London, 1923–5, 2 vols.).

The Testament of Cresseid, edited by Denton Fox (Nelson's Medieval and Renaissance Library: London and Edinburgh, 1968).

The Poems of William Dunbar, edited by W. Mackay Mackenzie (Faber: London, 1933; reprinted 1960).

Selections from Gavin Douglas, edited by David F. C. Coldwell (Oxford, 1964).

3. *Anthologies and Selections*

Scottish Poetry from Barbour to James VI, edited by M. M. Gray (Dent: London, 1935).

The Oxford Book of Scottish Verse, edited by John MacQueen and Tom Scott (Clarendon Press: Oxford, 1967).

Selections in the Saltire Society Classics series (published by Oliver and Boyd):
  Barbour: the Bruce, edited by A. M. Kinghorn (1960).
  William Dunbar, edited by Hugh MacDiarmid (1952).
  Robert Henryson, edited by David Murison (1952).
  Gavin Douglas, edited by Sydney Goodsir Smith (1959).
  Sir David Lyndsay of the Mount, edited by Maurice Lindsay (1948).

4. *Critical Studies*

Denton Fox, 'The Scottish Chaucerians', in *Chaucer and Chaucerians*, edited by
   D. S. Brewer (Nelson, 1966), pp. 164–200.
T. F. Henderson, *Scottish Vernacular Literature*, (Edinburgh, 1898, 3rd edn., 1910).
C. S. Lewis, *English Literature in the 16th Century* (Oxford, 1954), pp. 66–119,
   'The Close of the Middle Ages in Scotland'.
J. MacQueen, *Robert Henryson* (Oxford, 1967).
John Speirs, *The Scots Literary Tradition* (London, 1940, 2nd edn., 1962).
M. W. Stearns, *Robert Henryson* (New York, 1949).
H. Harvey Wood, *Two Scottish Chaucerians* (London, 1967).

5. *Periodical Articles*

Denton Fox, 'Henryson's *Fables*', *English Literary History*, XXIX (1962), 337–56.
A. von Hendy, 'The Free Thrall: a Study of the *Kingis Quair*', *Studies in Scottish
   Literature*, II (1965), 141–51.
Isabel Hyde, 'Poetic Imagery: a point of comparison between Henryson and
   Dunbar', *Studies in Scottish Literature*, II (1965), 183–97.
Isabel Hyde, 'Primary Sources and Associations of Dunbar's Aureate Imagery',
   Modern Language Review, LI (1956), 481–92.
A. M. Kinghorn, 'The Minor Poems of Robert Henryson', *Studies in Scottish
   Literature*, III (1965), 30–40.
A. M. Kinghorn, 'Dunbar and Villon: a Comparison and a Contrast', *Modern
   Language Review*, LXII (1967), 195–208.
A. M. Kinghorn, 'The Mediaeval Makars', *University of Texas Studies in
   Literature and Language*, I (1959), 73–88.
Allan H. MacLaine, 'The *Christis Kirk* Tradition: its Evolution in Scots Poetry
   to Burns', *Studies in Scottish Literature*, II (1964–5), 3–18, 111–24, 163–82,
   234–50.
Donald MacDonald, 'Narrative Art in Henryson's *Fables*', *Studies in Scottish
   Literature*, III (1965), 101–13.
J. MacQueen, 'Tradition and the Interpretation of the *Kingis Quair*', *Review of
   English Studies*, N.S. XII (1961), 117–31.
Edwin Morgan, 'Dunbar and the Language of Poetry', *Essays in Criticism*, II,
   (1952), 138–58.

J. Preston, 'Fortunys Exiltree: a Study of the *Kingis Quair*,' *Review of English Studies*, N.S. VII (1956), 339–47.

Mary Rohrberger, '*The Kingis Quair*: an Evaluation', *University of Texas Studies in Literature and Language*, II (1960), 292–302.

6. *Historical Background*

William Croft Dickinson, *Scotland from the earliest times to* 1603, vol. I of *A New History of Scotland* (Nelson: London and Edinburgh, 1961, 2nd edn., 1965).

Gordon Donaldson, *Scottish Kings* (Batsford: London, 1967).

J. D. Mackie, *A History of Scotland* (Pelican: London, 1964).

R. L. Mackie, *King James IV of Scotland* (Oliver and Boyd: Edinburgh and London, 1958).

Note on Sources

IN the making of these texts, four principal sources have been drawn upon. These include two manuscript and two printed authorities. The former are the Bannatyne, 'written in tyme of pest 1568' and the Maitland Folio (*c.* 1580). The prints are those produced by Chepman and Myllar (*c.* 1508) and that issued by Charteris of *The Testament of Cresseid* (1593).

1. *Bannatyne Manuscript.* George Bannatyne (1545?–1608), a merchant of Edinburgh, left 800 folios of poems by fifteenth- and sixteenth-century Scotsmen, which he transcribed to pass the time while a plague was raging in the city. From Bannatyne, Allan Ramsay obtained much of the substance of his *Ever Green* (1724), but the first accurate editorial work on the collection was that of Lord Hailes (Sir David Dalrymple) whose *Ancient Scottish Poems* (1770) presented works by Henryson, Dunbar, Alexander Scott and others. The manuscript is now in the National Library of Scotland. (III, IV, V, VI, VII.)

2. *Maitland Folio Manuscript.* Sir Richard Maitland (1496–1586), lawyer, himself a poet, compiled the manuscript which bears his name with the help of his daughter Margaret. It was used for the first time during the second half of the eighteenth century by Bishop Percy and, more fully, by John Pinkerton, who edited a selection for his *Ancient Scotish Poems* (1786). It is now in the Pepys Library, Magdalene College, Cambridge. (II, IV, part of XI.)

3. Walter Chepman, a rich Edinburgh merchant, and Androw Myllar, a printer, combined financial capital and technical skill to found a printing-house, authorized by James IV in 1507

for imprenting within our realme of the bukis of our lawis, actis of parliament, croniclis, mess bukis and portuus [breviaries] after the use of our realme, with additiouns and legendis of Scottis sanctis now gaderit to be ekit [added] thairto.

The earliest prints known to issue from this press were of eleven poetical works, including poems by Henryson and Dunbar. Since Dunbar was alive at this time (1507–8), and could presumably have seen the publications and approved them, these prints have maintained an authority over corresponding manuscripts which is hard to challenge. Unfortunately, the Chepman and Myllar print of *The Twa Mariit Wemen and the Wedo* is incomplete. (IX, X, part of XI.)

4. For *The Testament of Cresseid* (VIII), the highest authority is the black-letter quarto printed by Henry Charteris in 1593. It is not the earliest text and was probably based upon another print, but in the absence of a manuscript source,

the Charteris edition, which survives in one copy only, kept in the British Museum, is accepted by editors as the best version of the poem.

Of Douglas's *Aeneid* (XII), the earliest manuscript is now in the Library of Trinity College, Cambridge. It bears no date, but the commentary which accompanies the first part of the work was almost certainly written by Douglas himself. After the last book, there is a colophon, which reads:

> Heir endis the thretteyn and final buke of Eneados quhilk is the first correk copy nixt efter the translation Wrytin be Master Matho Geddes scribe or writar to the translatar.

The probable date is 1515 and its weight, in comparison with that of manuscripts made a few years later, much greater, since it is the poet's own copy. It has recently been edited for the Scottish Text Society by Dr David F. C. Coldwell, who aimed at an accurate reproduction. This edition is the basis for the text of the two passages printed.

The fifteen stanzas taken from *The Kingis Quair* (I) have been adapted from the Scottish Text Society's edition made late last century by W. W. Skeat, and modified according to W. Mackay Mackenzie's more recent version published in 1939. The original manuscript of the *Quair*, now in the Bodleian Library, was made by two scribes *c.* 1500, but was not edited until 1783. The first to give an account of it was Thomas Warton in his *History of English Poetry* (1774–81), who quoted two stanzas (20 and 21) and identified the manuscript, calling it 'The King's Complaint'.

Other important manuscript authorities for the texts of medieval Scots poetry, for example the Asloan (early sixteenth century) and Harley 3865 (1571), and some early printed texts such as the Bassendyne (1571) are referred to in the critical apparatus but have not been used as sources.

Anonymous

I. *The Kingis Quair*

A DREAM-VISION poem in the Chaucer tradition, *The Kingis Quair* or 'King's Book' may have been the work of James I of Scotland (1394–1437). The allegorical pattern is introduced as in *The Book of the Duchess* and *The House of Fame*, by the sleepless poet's reaching for a book, in this case Boethius' *De Consolatione Philosophiae*, and reflecting that whereas Boethius fell from prosperity to adversity, he himself had undergone hardships succeeded by happiness. The writer's quasi-biographical attempt to solve youthful problems intellectually together with the possibility that he may be identified with James, contemplating his own courtship and marriage (though neither are mentioned in the narrative), have posed difficult questions for scholars.

The *Quair* contains 197 stanzas, rhyming *ababbcc*. Perhaps because of its presumed connection with James, this verse-pattern is known as 'rhyme-royal', although it was previously adopted by Chaucer in *The Parlement of Foules* and *Troilus and Criseyde*. The following extract (stanzas 152–66) describes the earthly paradise, the rich garden of love, in terms which are not entirely conventional. Just as the castle-garden, glimpsed from the poet's window, is redeemed from stereotype by a few freshly observed and expressed details—'the sharpe, grene, swete junipere' and the nightingale singing on 'smale, grene twistis'—so the dream-garden escapes from tapestry into clear northern sunlight: the blue-black sheen of fish, their glittering mailed bodies, hold the poet's gaze. One is reminded less of *Le Roman de la Rose* than of Dante's *Purgatorio*, canto xxviii. Stanzas 159–65 depict Fortune's wheel. Human kind is subject to its rising and falling and must endure in this world, but God is not influenced by it. The dreamer is freed from his real or figurative confinement by Love and Philosophy and in the end realizes that the universal order, which includes Fortune, is ruled by God. The conclusion of the *Quair* has something in common with Chaucer's philosophical conclusion to *Troilus and Criseyde* (Book V, stanzas 259–67).

MS: Arch. Selden B. 24 f.192r–f.211v. (Bodleian Summary Catalogue No. 3354) c. 1500.

Editions: W. W. Skeat, ed. cit. for the Scottish Text Society and W. Mackay Mackenzie, The Kingis Quair (London, 1939), on which the following extract is based.

First printed: William Tytler (1783).

> Quhare, in a lusty plane, tuke I my way
> Endlang a ryver, plesant to behold,

Enbroudin all with fresche flouris gay
  Quhare, throu the gravel, bryght as ony gold,
  The cristall water ran so clere and cold,   5
That in myn ere maid contynually
A maner soun, mellit with armony.

That full of lytill fischis by the brym,
  Now here, now there, with bakkis blewe as lede,
Lap and playit, and in a rout can swym   10
  So prattily, and dressit tham to sprede
  Thair curall fynnis, as the ruby rede,
That in the sonne on thair scalis bryght
As gesserant ay glitterit in my sight.

And by this ilke ryversyde alawe   15
  Ane hye way fand I like to bene,
On quhich, on every syde, a long rawe
  Off treis saw I, full of levis grene
  That full of fruyte delitable were to sene,
And also, as it come unto my mind,   20
Off bestis sawe I mony divers kynd:

The lyoun king, and his fere lyonesse;
  The pantere, like unto the smaragdyne;
The lytill squerell, full of besyness;
  The slaw as, the druggar beste of pyne;   25
  The nyce ape; the werely porpapyne;
The percyng lynx; the lufare unicorne
That voidis venym with his evour horne.

---

8. One editor (Mackenzie) points at a similarity between this stanza and a stanza in *The Parlement of Foules* (lines 183–9). The *Quair* echoes many of Chaucer's conventions and formulas, themselves part of a larger European inheritance.

23. See C. E. Bain, *English Studies*, XLVII (1966), 419–22, for an explanation of this curious comparison.

27–8. *lufare unicorne*—according to legend, this creature might be trapped only by means of a virgin decoy; *voidis*—renders innocuous. Its horn was said to be an antidote for poison. The *Parlement of Foules* was probably the inspiration for this and the succeeding two stanzas.

There sawe I dress him new out of haunt
   The fery tiger, full of felonye;   30
The dromydare; the standar oliphant;
   The wyly fox, the wedowis inemye;
   The clymbare gayte; the elk for alblastrye;
The herknere bore; the holsum grey for hortis;
The hair also, that oft gooth to the wortis.   35

The bugill, drawar by his hornis grete;
   The martrik, sable, the foynyee, and mony mo;
The chalk-quhite ermyn, tippit as the jete;
   The riall hert, the conyng, and the ro;
   The wolf, that of the murthir noght say 'ho!'   40
The lesty bever, and the ravin bare;
For chamelot the camel full of hare

With mony anothir beste divers and strange,
   That cummyth noght as now unto my mynd.
Bot now to purpos. Straucht furth the range   45
   I held a way, ourhailing in my mynd
   From quhens I come and quhare that I suld fynd
Fortune, the goddess, unto quhom in hye
Gude Hope, my gyde, has led me sodeynly.

And at the last, behalding thus asyde,   50
   A round place wallit have I found;
In myddis quhare eftsone I have spide
   Fortune, the goddess, hufing on the ground;

40. Skeat reads 'say[is]'

---

31. *standar olyphant*—the legs of elephants were supposedly jointless so that the beast had always to stand upright, and was incapable of rising from a fallen position. Many commentators refer to this belief, which emanated from Latin *Physiologus* literature and became a medieval *exemplum*.

32. *wedowis inemye*—a reference to the cock and fox fable.

33. *elk for alblastrye*—possibly an allusion to elk's hide, used to cover targets at shooting-butts. *alblastrye*—crossbows, arquebuses.

34. *grey*—badger. Badger's fat was used to make plasters. *hortis*—wounds.

42. *chamelot*—camlet, cloth made of silk, used for making cloaks. Its supposed connection with camel's hair is dubious.

And ryght before hir fete, of compas round,
A quhele, on quhich clevering I sye   55
A multitude of folk before myn eye.

And ane surcote sche werit long that tyde,
    That semyt to me of divers hewis,
Quhilum thus, quhen sche wald turn asyde,
    Stude this goddess of fortune and of glewis;   60
    A chapellet with mony fresche anewis
Sche had upon her hed; and with this hong
A mantill on hir schuldris, large and long,

That furrit was with ermyn full quhite,
    Degoutit with the self in spottis blake: 65
And quhilum in hir chier thus a lyte
    Louring sche was and thus sone it would slake,
    And sodeynly a maner smylying make,
And sche were glad; at one contenance
Sche held noght, bot ay in variance;   70

And underneth the quhele sawe I there
    Ane ugly pit, depe as ony helle,
That to behald thereon I quoke for fere;
    But o thing herd I, that quho therein fell
    Com no more up agane tidingis to telle,   75
Off quhich, astonait of that ferefull syght,
I ne wist quhat to done, so was I fricht.

Bot for to se the sudayn weltering
    Off that ilk quhele, that sloppar was to hold,
It semyt unto my wit a stronge thing,   80
    So mony I sawe that than clymben wold

60. *of glewis*—Skeat's insertion (poetical word for sport)
72. Skeat inserts *was* before *depe*

---

55. *quhele*—disyllabic. This is an Anglo-French habit since the frequent use of final -e was unknown in Northern dialects of English.
65. *self*—same (i.e. ermyn).

And failit foting and to ground were rold;
And othir eke, that sat abone on hye,
Were ouerthrawe in twinklyng of an eye.

And on the quhele was lytill void space,   85
    Wele nere ourstraught fro lawe to hye;
And they were war that long sat in that place,
    So tolter quhilum did sche it to-wrye;
    There was bot clymbe and ryght dounward hye,
And sum were eke that fallyng had so sore,   90
Therefor to clymbe thair corage was no more.

I saw also that quhere sum were slungin
    Be quhirlyng of the quhele, unto the ground,
Full sudaynly sche hath up ythrungin,
    And set thame on agane full sauf and sound: 95
    And ever I sawe a new swarm abound
That thought to clymbe upward upon the quhele,
In stede of thame that myght no langer rele.

And at the last, in presence of thame all
    That stude about, sche clepit me be name.   100
And therewith apon kneis gan I fall
    Full sodaynly hailsing, abaist for schame,
    And, smylyng thus, sche said to me in game:
'Quhat dois thou here? Quho has the hider sent?
Say on anon, and tell me thyn entent.'   105

90. *so* is Skeat's insertion
94. Skeat inserts *thaim* before *ythrungin*.
97. *Thought*—Skeat's addition

92–8. The wheel is a frequently encountered metaphor for illustrating
Fortune's inconstancy. The best portrayal of the subject in English is that in
The Parlement of Thre Ages (late fourteenth century) in which the Nine Worthies,
famous men of history and legend, spin on the wheel; Arthur's dream in *Morte
Arthure* (3218–3467) may be indebted to it.
  101. *kneis*—trisyllabic.

Anonymous

II. Christ's Kirk on the Grene

TOGETHER with *Peblis at the Play*, this poem begins a Scots comic tradition which links the medieval with the modern phase of Scottish poetry. The author's identity is in dispute. The piece was handed down in manuscript form in both Bannatyne and Maitland collections. In the former, it is assigned to James I. The tone verges on the mock-heroic, the audience was undoubtedly sophisticated, or at least not popular, and the subject is a burlesque of peasant-life seen from an upper-class viewpoint. The stanza has two quatrains and a repeated closing line; within the stanza there is a disciplined rhyme-scheme, joining the quatrains (*abab/abab/c/d*), in which *c* is called the 'bob' and the repeated closing line *d* 'the wheel'. In addition, there is heavy alliteration. The poet of *Christ's Kirk* demonstrates a meticulous concern with his craft and the work has more than once been described as a technical *tour de force*.

MSS: Maitland Folio; Bannatyne; Laing. The Maitland, on which this text is based, is the best, pp. 130–5.

Printed: 1643, 1660, 1663, 1684, 1691 (by Gibson), 1706 (by Watson), 1718 (by Ramsay). A version similar to the Laing MS (c. 1640) was used in the 1643 edn. and in Watson's Choice Collection *of 1706–11, but Ramsay's version followed Bannatyne. The Laing text, edited by Janet M. Templeton, is printed in* Studies in Scottish Literature, *IV (1967), 130–37. It is ascribed to 'James the fifth'.*

> Was never in Scotland hard nor sene
> Sic dansing nor deray,
> Nother in Falkland on the Grene,
> Nor Peblis to the Play,
> As was of wowaris as I wene   5
> At Chrystis Kirk on ane day.
> Thair come our Kittie wesching clene
> In hir new kirtill of gray,
> Full gay,
> At Chrystis Kirk on the grene.   10

3–4. Presumably 'Falkland on the Grene' was an older poem in the same tradition as 'Peblis to the Play'.

7. 'Kittie' and the other peasant-types are conventional figures, with parallels in other European literatures, e.g. South German.

To dance the damisallis thame dicht,
And lassis licht of laittis;
Thair gluvis war of the raffell richt;
Thair schone war of the straitis:
Thair kirtillis war off the lincum licht   15
Weill prest with mony plaitis.
That war so nyce quhen men tham nicht
Thay squeild lyk ony gaitis,
Ful loud
At Chrystis Kirk on the grene.   20

Sche scornit Jok and scrippit at him,
And morgeound him with mokkis;
He wald have luffit hir; sche wald nocht lat him,
For all his yallow lokkis;
He cherist hir; scho bad ga chat him,   25
Sche comptit him nocht tua clokkis;
Sa schamfullie ane schort goun sat him,
His lymmis was lyk twa rokkis,
Sche said
At Chrystis Kirk on the grene.   30

Off all thir madinis myld as meid,
Was nane sa gymp as Gillie;
As ony rose hir rude was reid,
Hir lyre was lyk the lillie;
Bot yallow yallow was hir heid,   35
And sche of luif so sillie,
Thocht all hir kin suld have bein deid,
Sche wald have bot sweit Willie,
Allane,
At Chrystis Kirk on the grein.   40

Stevin come steppand in with stendis,
No renk mycht him arrest;
Platfut he bobbit up with bendis,

---

43. *platfut*—the name of a comic dance, referred to in *The Complaynt of Scotland*, VI, 19 ('lang plat fut of gariau', i.e. Garioch, a region in N.E. Scotland).

For Mald he maid requeist;
He lap quhill he lay on his lendis,   45
Bot rysand he was prest
Quhill he hostit at bayth the endis
In honour of the feist
That day
At Chrystis Kirk on the grein.   50

Thome Lutar was thair menstrale meit;
O Lord, gif he culd lance!
He playit so schill and sang so sweit
Quhill Towsie tuik ane trance;
All auld lycht futtis he did forleyt   55
And counterfutit France;
He him avysit as man discreit
And up the moreis dance
Scho tuik
At Chrystis Kirk on the grein.   60

Than Robene Roy begouth to revell,
And Dowie to him druggit;
'Lat be!' quod Johke, and callit him gavell,
And be the taill him tuggit;
He turnit and cleikit to the cavell,   65
Bot Lord than gif thai luggit!
Thai partit thair play thane with ane nevell
Men wait gif hair wes ruggit
Betwene thame
At Chrystis Kirk on the grein.   70

Ane bend ane bow, sic sturt couth steir him;
Grit scayth war to have scard him;
He chesit ane flaine as did affeir him;
The tother said 'Dirdum Dardum!'
Throw bayth the cheikis he thocht to cheir him,   75
Or throw the chaftis have charde him

---

56. *counterfutit France*—imitated a French dancing style.
1–60. Describes a village dance and its jollities.

Bot be ane myle it come nocht neir him.
I can nocht say quhat mard him
Thair
At Chrystis Kirk on the grein. 80

With that ane freynd of his cryit, 'Fy!'
And up ane arow drew,
He forgeit it so ferslye
The bow in flenders flew;
Sa was the will of God, trow I; 85
For had the tre bene trew,
Men said that kend his archerie
That he had slane anew
That day
At Chrystis Kirk on the grein. 90

Ane haistie hensour callit Harie
Quhilk wes ane archer heynd,
Tit up ane takill but ony tarye,
That turment so him teynd;
I wait nocht quhidder his hand cud varie, 95
Or gif the man was his freynd
Bot he chapit throw the michtis of Marie
As man that na evill meynd
That tyme
At Chrystis Kirk on the grein. 100

Than Lowrie as ane lyoun lap
And sone ane flane culd fedder;
He hecht to pers him at the pape,
Thairon to wed ane wedder;
He hit him on the wambe ane wap, 105
And it bust lyk ane bledder;
But lo! as fortoun was and hap,
His doublat was of ledder
And sauft him
At Chrystis Kirk on the grein. 110

The baff so boustuousle abasit him,
To the erd he duschit doun;
The tother for dreid he preissit him
And fled out of the toun;
The wyffis come furth and up thay paisit him   115
And fand lyff in the loun
And with thre routis thay raisit him
And coverit him of swoune
Agane
At Chrystis Kirk on the grein.   120

Ane yaip young man that stude him neist
Lousit of ane schot with ire;
He etlit the berne evin in the breist,
The bout flew our the byre;
Ane cryit that he had slane ane preist   125
Ane myle beyond ane myre;
Than bow and bag fra him he caist,
And fled als fers as fyre
Of flint
At Chrystis Kirk on the grein.   130

With forkis and flalis thay leit grit flappis,
And flang togither with friggis
With bougaris of barnis thai birst blew cappis,
Quhill thay of bernis maid briggis;
The rerde rais rudlie with the rappis,   135
Quhen rungis was layd on riggis;
The wyffis come furth with cryis and clappis
'Lo quhair my lyking liggis!'
Quod scho
At Chrystis Kirk on the grein.   140

132. *with*—Bannatyne reads *lyk*.

71–130. The account of the burlesque archery contest recalls a popular sport of the time, though not a sport indulged in by peasants. On this depends the mock-heroic character of the work. The mock tournament turns up in several English and Scots satiric poems of the fifteenth and sixteenth centuries.

131–230. These eleven stanzas describe the brawl into which the contest degenerates.

Thay girnit and leit gird with granis;
Ilk gossop uther grevit;
Sum straikit stingis, sum gadderit stanis,
Sum fled and weill eschewit;
The menstrale wan within ane wanis;   145
That day full weill he previt,
For he come hame with unbrisde banis,
Quhair fechtaris war mischevit
For ever
At Chrystis Kirk on the grein.   150

Heich Huchoun with ane hissill rys
To red can throw thame rummill;
He mudlit thame doun lyk ony myse;
He was na baty bummill.
Thocht he wes wicht he wes nocht wys,   155
With sic jatouris to geummill.
For fra his thoume thay dang ane sklys
Quhill he cryit: 'Barlaw fummill!'
Ouris
At Chrystis Kirk on the grein.   160

Quhen that he saw his blude so reid,
To fle micht no man lat him;
He wend it had bene for ald feid,
The far sarar it sat him;
He gart his feit defend his heid;   165
He thocht thay cryit: 'Have at him!'
Quhill he was past out of all pleid
He suld be swyft that gat him
Throw speid
At Chrystis Kirk on the grein.   170

143. Bannatyne has *straik with*.

---

151. *hissill rys*—hazel branch.
158. *barlaw fumill*—a cry of truce (i.e. pax!) Jamieson's *Dictionary* suggests 'Parlez, foi melez' ('Let's have a truce and blend our faiths') as the origin of this exclamation. *Cf.* Beatrice White's note in Neophilologus, XXXVII (1953), 113-5.

The toun soutar in breif was boudin;
His wyf hang in his waist;
His body was in blude all browdin;
He granit lyk ony gaist;
Hir glitterand hairis that war full goldin,   175
So hard in luif him laist
That for hir saik he wes unyoldin
Sevin myle quhen he wes chaist
And mair
At Chrystis Kirk on the grein.   180

The millar was of manlie mak;
To meit him was na mowis;
Thair durst na ten cum him to tak
So nobbit he thair nowis.
The buschement haill about him brak   185
And bickert him with bowis
Syn tratourlie behind his bak
Ane hewit him on the howis
Behind
At Chrystis Kirk on the grein.   190

Twa that was herdismen of the herde
Ran upone uther lyk rammis;
Thair forsy freikis richt uneffeird
Bet on with barow trammis;
Bot quhair thair gobbis war bath ungird,   195
Thai gat upon the gammis,
Quhill bludie barkit was thair berd,
As thay had worreit lambis
Most lyk
At Chrystis Kirk on the grein.   200

The wyffis cast up ane hidduous yell,
Quhen all the youngkeiris yokkit;
Als fers as ony fyr flauchtis fell
Freikis to the feild thai flokit;
Thay cavellis with clubbis culd uther quell,   205

Quhill blude at breistis out bokkit;
So rudlie rang the commoun bell
Quhill all the steipill rokkit
For rerde
At Chrystis Kirk on the grein. 210

Quhen thai had beirit lyk batit bullis,
And brane wode brynt in balis,
Thai wox als mait as ony mulis,
That mangit war with malis,
For fantnes thay forfochin fulis 215
Fell doun lyk flauchter falis;
Fresche men com hame and halit the dulis,
And dang thame doun in dalis
Bedene
At Chrystis Kirk on the grein. 220

Quhen all wes done, Dic with ane ax
Come furth to fell ane futher;
Quod he: 'Quhair ar yon hangit smaikis
Richt now that hurt my brother?'
His wyf bad him: 'Gang hame, gud glaikis!' 225
And sua did Meg his mother,
He turnit and gaif thame bath thair paikis,
For he durst stryk na uther,
Men said
At Chrystis Kirk on the grene. 230
finis.

---

225. *gud glaikis*—you stupid fool! The poem ends with the fight still in progress. The Laing version has an extra stanza and the order of the stanzas differs from both Maitland and Bannatyne.

Robert Henryson
III. Robene and Makyne

SINCE Allan Ramsay printed it in *Ever Green* this is the poem of Henryson's most often encountered in anthologies. It is a debate in the style of an old French *pastourelle* though with no traceable source. It owes little or nothing to Chaucer, though the author shows his familiarity with stock ideals of *amour courtois*, as he does in the Cock and Fox fable.

MS: Bannatyne solus (f.365a–f.366b).
Printed: Ramsay, Ever Green (*1724*).

> Robene sat on gud grene hill,
> Kepand a flok of fe.
> Mirry Makyne said him till,
> 'Robene, thow rew on me!
> I haif the luvit lowd and still,   5
> Thir yeiris two or thre;
> My dule in dern bot gif thow dill,
> Dowtles but dreid I de.'
>
> Robene ansert: 'Be the rude,
> Nathing of lufe I knaw,   10
> Bot keipis my scheip undir yone wid,
> Lo, quhair thay raik on raw!
> Quhat hes marrit the in thy mude,
> Makyne, to me thow schaw;
> Or quhat is lufe, or to be lude?   15
> Fane wald I leir that law.'
>
> 'At luvis lair gife thow will leir,
> Tak thair ane A B C:
> Be heynd, courtass, and fair of feir,
> Wyse, hardy and fre,   20

---

3. *Makyne*—in *pastourelles*, a commonly-used girl's name, a diminutive of Matilda, Margaret, Maud, Mary, &c. Note the metrical similarity to *Christ's Kirk*.

12. *raik on raw*—wander in the fields, a convenient alliterative tag.

So that no denger do the deir
Quhat dule in dern thow dre.
Preiss the with pane at all poweir,
Be patient and previe.'

Robene anserit hir agane,   25
'I wait nocht quhat is luve.
Bot I haif mervell incertane
Quhat makis the this wanrufe:
The weddir is fair, and I am fane,
My scheip gois haill aboif;   30
And we wald play us in this plane,
They wald us bayth reproif.'

'Robene, tak tent unto my taill,
And wirk all as I reid,
And thow sall haif my hairt all haill,   35
Eik and my madinheid.
Sen God sendis bute for baill,
And for murning remeid,
I dern with the, bot gif I daill,
Dowtless I am bot deid.'   40

'Makyne, tomorne this ilk a tyde,
And ye will meit me heir,
Peraventure my scheip ma gang besyd,
Quhill we haif liggit full neir;
Bot mawgre haif I and I byd,   45
Fra thay begin to steir;
Quhat lyis on hairt I will nocht hyd;
Makyn, than mak gud cheir.'

'Robene, thow reivis me roif and rest:
I luve bot the allone.'   50
'Makyne, adew; the sone gois west,

17–24. The vocabulary is that of *amour courtois*, though the active pursuit is made by the girl.

39. *bot gif I daill*—unless I can possess you.

The day is neir hand gone.'
'Robene, in dule I am so drest,
That lufe wilbe my bone.'
'Ga lufe, Makyne, quhairevir thow list,   55
For lemman I lue none.'

'Robene, I stand in sic a styll;
I sicht, and that full sair.'
'Makyne, I haif bene heir this quhyle;
At hame god gif I wair.'   60
'My huny, Robene, talk ane quhill,
Gif thow will do na mair.'
'Makyne, sum uthir man begyle,
For hamewart I will fair.'

Robene on his wayis went,   65
Als licht as leif of tre;
Mawkin murnit in hir intent,
And trowd him nevir to se.
Robene brayd attour the bent;
Than Mawkyne cryit on hie,   70
'Now ma thow sing, for I am schent!
Quhat alis lufe at me?'

Mawkyne went home withowttin faill,
Full wery eftir cowth weip.
Than Robene in a ful fair daill   75
Assemblit all his scheip.
Be that sum pairte of Mawkynis aill
Outthrow his hairt cowd creip;
He fallowit hir fast thair till assaill,
And till hir tuke gude keip.   80

'Abyd, abyd, thow fair Makyne!
A word for ony thing!
For all my luve it sal be thyne,

56. *lue* (or *lid*) in MS—love. H. Harvey Wood (*Poems and Fables*, 2nd edn., p. 167*n*.). following Craigies, suggests *bid*— ask for.

Withowttin depairting.
All haill thy harte for till haif myne   85
Is all my cuvating;
My scheip tomorne quhill houris nyne
Will neid of no keping.'

'Robene, thow hes hard soung and say,
In gestis and storeis auld,   90
The man that will nocht quhen he may
Sall haif nocht quhen he wald.
I pray to Jesu every day
Mot eik thair cairis cauld,
That first preissis with the to play,   95
Be firth, forrest or fawld.'

'Makyne, the nicht is soft and dry,
The wedder is warme and fair,
And the grene woid rycht neir us by
To walk attour allquhair;   100
Thair ma na janglour us espy,
That is to lufe contrair;
Thairin, Makyne, bath ye and I
Unsene we ma repair.'

'Robene, that warld is all away   105
And quyt brocht till ane end,
And nevir agane theirto perfay
Sall it be as thow wend.
For of my pane thow maid it play,
And all in vane I spend: 110
As thow hes done, sa sall I say,
Murne on! I think to mend.'

'Mawkyne, the howp of all my heill,
My hairt on the is sett,
And evirmair to the be leill,   115
Quhill I may leif but lett;

91–2. Proverbial.   **96.** I.e. anywhere in the world.
116. *but lett*—without hindrance (now legal only, 'without let or hindrance').

Nevir to faill, as utheris feill,
Quhat grace that evir I gett.'
'Robene, with the I will nocht deill:
Adew, for thus we mett.'   120

Malkyne went hame blyth annewche,
Attour the holttis hair.
Robene murnit, and Malkyne lewche;
Scho sang, he sichit sair.
And so left him, bayth wo and wrewche,   125
In dolour and in cair,
Kepand his hird under a huche,
Amang the holtis hair.

---

122. *holttis hair*—gray woods, a conventional expression but in view of the context appropriate to the mood of their parting.

Robert Henryson

IV. The Thre Deid Pollis

THIS is a poem on the conventional theme of *memento mori*, brought home to the reader by means of a graphic presentation of three skulls. Death the leveller may not be eluded. In the end, human enterprise is as bare and empty as a 'deid poll'. But this is no simple churchyard message: the poet's vision of life and beauty is as strong as his vision of mortality; although there can be no reprieve, his imagination calls a brief halt, and lingers, regretfully, over these ephemeral summer creatures.

In the Bannatyne manuscript, the poem is ascribed to 'Patrik Johnistoun', mentioned in line 71 of Dunbar's 'Lament for the Makars', but the Maitland scribe and succeeding editors have added it to the Henryson canon.

MS: Bannatyne, f.57b–58b, with some borrowings from Maitland Folio, pp. 327–8. Printed: Laing (1865).

O sinfull man, into this mortall se
Quhilk is the vaill of murnyng and of cair,
With gaistly sicht behold oure heidis thre,
Oure holkit ene, oure peilit pollis bair!
As ye ar now, into this warld we wair,   5
Als fresche, als fair, als lusty to behald.
Quhan thow lukis on this suth examplair
Off thyself, man, thow may be richt unbald.

For suth it is, that every man mortall
Man thole the dethe and de, that lyfe hes tane.   10
Na erdly stait aganis deid ma prevaill.
The hour of deith and place is uncertane,
Quhilk is referrit to the hie god allane.
Heirfor haif mynd of deth, that thow mon dy!
This sair exampill to se quotidiane,   15
Sowld causs all men fra wicket vycis fle.

10. Bannatyne MS has *mon suffer deid and de*

---

3. *with gaistly sicht*—with eyes of terror.

O wantone yowth, als fresche as lusty May,
Farest of flowris, renewit quhyt and reid,
Behald our heidis! O lusty gallandis gay,
Full laichly thus sall ly thy lusty heid,   20
Holkit and how, and wallowit as the weid,
Thy crampand hair and eik thy cristall ene
Full cairfully conclud sall dulefull deid.
Thy example heir be us it may be sene.

O ladeis quhyt, in claithis corruscant,   25
Poleist with perle and mony pretius stane;
With palpis quhyt and hals so elegant,
Sirculit with gold, and sapheris mony ane.
Your fingearis small, quhyt as quhailis bane,
Arrayit with ringis and mony rubeis reid,   30
And we ly thus, so sall ye ly ilk ane,
With peilit pollis, and holkit thus your heid.

O wofull pryd, the rute of all distress,
With humill hairt upoun our pollis pens.
Man, for thy mis, ask mercy with meiknes.   35
Aganis deid na man may mak defens.
The empriour, for all his excellens,
King and quene, and eik all erdly stait,
Peure and riche, sal be but differens,
Turnit in as and thus in erd translait.   40

This questioun quha can obsolve lat see.
Quhat phisnamour or perfyt palmester?
Quha was farest or fowlest of us thre?
Or quhilk of us of kin was gentillar?
Or maist excellent in science or in lare,   45
In art, musik or in astronomye?

---

26. *poleist*—decorated.
29. *quhailis bane*—not whalebone but ivory from the walrus.
39–40. Dunbar's *All Erdly Joy Returnis in Pane, Of Manis Mortalitie* and *Of the Warldis Vanitie* contain similar references of the 'dust to dust' type.

Heir sowld be your study and repair,
And think as thus all your heidis mon be.

O febill aige ay drawand neir the dait
Of dully deid and hes thy dayis compleit,   50
Behald our heidis with murning and regrait!
Fall on thy kneis! Ask grace at God and greit.
With oritionis and haly salmes sweit,
Beseikand him on the to haif mercy.
Now of our sawlis bydand the decreit   55
Of his godheid, quhen he sall call and cry.

Als we exhort that every man mortall,
For his saik that maid of nocht all thing,
For our sawlis to pray in generall
To Jesus Chryst, of hevin and erd the king,   60
That throwch his blude we may ay leif and ring
With the hie fader be eternitie,
The sone alswa, the haly gaist conding,
Thre knit in ane be perfyt unitie.

---

49. Henryson's *The Ressoning betwix Aige and Youth* and Dunbar's *Of Manis Mortalitie* and *Lament for the Makars* also depend upon this stereotype.
57–64. This is the substance of a sermon.

Robert Henryson

V. Sum Practysis of Medecyne

HENRYSON's only known attempt at burlesque and thus not typical of his style and serious approach to life. The subject-matter is, however, consistent with his revealed interest in medical matters. In the manuscript, he is named as author.

MS: Bannatyne solus, f.141b–f.142a.
Printed: Laing (1865).

Guk guk, gud day, ser, gaip quhill ye get it!
Sic greting may gane weill gud laik in your hude.
Ye wald deir me I trow, becauss I am dottit,
To ruffill me with a ryme, na ser, be the rude,
Your saying I haif sene and on syd set it,   5
As geir of all gaddering glaikit nocht gude
Als your medicyne by mesour I haif meit met it.
The quhilk I stand ford ye nocht understude,
Bot wrett on as ye culd to gar folk wene.
For feir my lougis wes flaft ⎫   10
Or I wes dottit or daft   ⎬heir be it sene.
Gife I can ocht of the craft ⎭
Becaus I ken your cunnyng into cure
Is clowtit and clampit and nocht weill cleird,
My prettik in pottingary ye trow be als pure   15
And lyk to your lawitnes, I schrew thame that leid;
Is nowdir fevir nor fell that ouir the feild fure,
Seiknes nor sairnes in tyme gif I seid,
Bot I can lib thame and leiche thame fra lame and lesure,
With sawis thame sound mak on your saule beid,   20

18. 'in tyme gif I seid' deleted from second half of line in MS.

---

1. *gaip*—open wide.
2. *gud laik*—good fortune.
13. *cunnyng into cure*—skill at healing.
18. *seid*—see it.
19. *lib*—cure (see Dunbar's *To the Quene*). The word can also mean 'cut open'.

That ye be sicker of this sedull I send yow.
With the suthfast seggis ⎤
That glean all egeis   ⎬ of malis to mend yow.
With dia and dreggis ⎦

Dia culcakit

Cape cuk maid and crop the colleraige,   25
Ane medecyne for the maw and ye cowth mak it
With sweit satlingis and sowrokis, the sop of the sege,
The crud of my culome with your teith crakit,
Lawrean and linget seid and the luffage,
The hair of the hurcheon nocht half deill hakkit,   30
With the snowt of ane selch, ane swelling to swage;
This cure is callit in our craft 'Dia culcakkit'.
Put all thir in ane pan with pepper and pik.
Syne sottin to thiss ⎤
The count of ane cow kiss ⎬ for the collik.   35
Is nocht bettir I wiss ⎦

Dia longum

Recipe: thre ruggis of the reid ruke,
The gant of ane gray meir, the claik of ane guss,
The dram of ane drekterss, the douk of ane duke,
The gaw of ane grene dow, the leg of ane lowss,   40
Fyve unce of ane fle wing, the fyn of ane fluke,
With ane sleiffull of slak that growis in the sluss.
Myng all thir in ane mass with the mone cruke.
This untment is rycht ganand for your awin uss,
With reid nettill seid in strang wesche to steip.   45
For to bath your ba cod ⎤
Quhen ye wald nop and nod ⎬ to latt yow to sleip
Is nocht bettir, be God ⎦

22–3. This passage is corrupt. For an interpretation see G. Gregory Smith's Scottish Text Society edn., I, 73.

---

25. *cuk*—guk (line 1). Harvey Wood glosses *cukmaid* 'may be excrement'. But *cf. maith*, 'maggot, grub', current in fifteenth-century Scots.

39. *drekterss*—drake's vent.

40. According to medieval physiologists, the dove lacked a gall, which explains the parody here.

46. *ba cod*—scrotum (*ba*, testicle).

Dia glaconicon

This dia is rycht deir and denteit in daill,
Cause it is trest and trew; thairfoir that ye tak   50
Sevin sobbis of ane selche, the quhidder of ane quhaill,
The lug of ane lempet is nocht to forsaik,
The harnis of ane haddok, hakkit or haill,
With ane bustfull of blude of the scho bak,
With ane brewing caldrun full of hait caill,   55
For it wilbe the softar and sweittar of the smak.
Thair is nocht sic ane lechecraft fra Lawdian to Lundin.

It is clippit in our cannon
'Dia gleconicon'   } quhair fulis ar fundin.
For till fle awaye son   60

Dia custrum

The ferd feiskik is fyne and of ane felloun pryce;
Gud for haising and hosting or heit at the hairt.
Recipe: thre sponfull of the blak spyce,

---

49. *dia*—compounded of (pharmaceutical prefix). The remedies seem to be for the colic, for insomnia, as a purgative and for the cough. The names are almost certainly *ad hoc* improvizations, though it is possible that Henryson was directly parodying a specific medicinal manual: e.g. *dia culcakit* from *dia culum*, a popular variant of diachylum (composed of juices and making lead-plaster), or alternatively *dia colocynthio* (pumpkin); *dia longum* from *dia galenga* (galengale) or even *dia lagoum* (hare's dung); *dia glaconicon* from *gleconites* (flea-bane or penny-royal, a herb generally used to treat disorders of the stomach), or alternatively from *glaucium*, an infusion from teasel; *dia castoreum* (beaver-oil). See *NED* (edn. 1961), III, 303, and *Sydenham Society Lexicon*, on such compounds and 59n. below.

51. *quhidder*—whither, or whether (Harvey Wood: 'spouting'). A piece of nonsense, but cf. *whethering* (OED), the retention of afterbirth in cows.

54. *scho*—northern form of 'she'.

57. *Lawdian*—Lothian; *Lundin*—in Fifeshire.

59. *glecolicon*—this may be a scribal flaw but, if it is not, the poet may have been essaying a pun on 'colic'. An obscure children's complaint called the 'glack' is referred to in a mid-seventeenth-century source and there is an adjective 'glaikit' meaning senseless. (See line 6, also *Christ's Kirk on the Grene*, line 225 and *n.*) 'Culcakit' may have been suggested by 'culum' and 'cack', while 'longum' and 'custrum' might well be ribald anatomical references originating in students' Latin. (See W. A. Craigie, editor, *A Dictionary of the Older Scottish Tongue*, II, 659, 661; H. Kurath, *A Middle English Dictionary*, II, 13; J. Wright, *English Dialect Dictionary*, I, 479.)

61. *ferd*—fourth.

With ane grit gowpene of the gowk fart;
The lug of ane lyoun, the guse of ane gryce,   65
Ane unce of ane oster poik at the nether pairte,
Annoyntit with nurice doung, for it is rycht nyce
Myngit with mysdirt and with mustart.
Ye may clamp to this cure and ye will mak cost.
Bayth the bellox of ane brok ⎫   70
With thre crawis of the cok ⎬ is gud for the host.
The schadow of ane yulestok ⎭
Gud nycht, guk guk, for sa I began.
I haif no come at this tyme langer to tary,
Bot luk on this lettir and leird gif ye can   75
The prectik and poyntis of this pottingary.
Ser, minister this medecyne at evin to sum man
And or pryme be past my powder I pary
Thay sall bliss yow or ellis bittirly yow ban,
For it sall fle thame in faith out of the fary.   80
Bot luk quhen ye gadder thir gressis and gerss
Outhir sawrand or sour   ⎫
That it be in ane gud oure   ⎬ ane uthir manis erss.
It is ane mirk mirrour   ⎭

---

66. *poik*—probably stomach.
80. *out of the fary*—out of their daze or stupor.
84. *ane mirk mirrour*—old proverb, recast in coarse terms ('A mirk mirrour is a man's mind,' i.e. it is hard to know another man's thoughts).

Robert Henryson

VI. The Cock and the Fox

THIS is the familiar Aesopian theme treated by Chaucer in *The Nun's Priest's Tale*, but with an explicit *moralitas* added to explain the intended significance of the fable. Henryson's handling of the subject is less full of surprises than Chaucer's. He does not stray far from the plot, there is no 'science' or sustained burlesque of romance-styles and the personages are more obviously symbolic.

MSS: Bannatyne f.310b–f.312b on which this text is based; also in Harley 3865 (British Museum) (1571).
Printed: Charteris (1570); Bassendyne (1571).

> Thoucht brutale bestis be irrationale,
> That is to say, lakking discretioun,
> Yit ilkane in thair kyndis naturale
> Hes monye diverss inclinatioun.
> The bair bustouss, the wolf, the wyld lyoun,   5
> The fox, fenyeit, craftye and cautelouss,
> The dog to berk in nycht and keip the houss.
>
> So different thay bene in propirteis
> Unknawin unto man and infynite,
> In kynd haifand so fele diversiteis,   10
> My connyng it excedis for to dyte
> Forthy as now my purpois is to wryte
> A cass I fand quhilk fell this hinder yere
> Betuix a fox and gentill Chanteclere.
>
> A wedow duelt intill a drope thay daiss,   15
> Quhilk wan hir fude with spynning on hir rok,
> And no moir guidis, as the fable sais,
> Except of hennis scho had a joly flok
> And thame to kepe scho had a joly cok,
> Rycht curageouss unto his weidow ay.   20
> Devidand nycht, crawand befoir the day.

---

11. 'my skill is inadequate to do them justice in writing.'
14. *Chanteclere*—medieval name for a cock.

A lytill fra that foirsaid wedois houss,
A thorny schaw thair was, of grit defence,
Quhairin a fox, craftye and cawtelouss,
Maid his repair and daylie residence: 25
Quhilk to this wedow did grete violence
In piking of hir pultry day and nycht.
And be no mene revengit on him scho mycht.

This wily tod, quhen that the lark coud sing,
Full sare hungrye unto the toun him drest,   30
Quhair Chanteclere into the gray dawing,
Wery of nycht, was flowin fra his nest.
Lourence this saw and in his mynd he kest
The juperteis, the wayis and the wile
Be quhat menis he mycht this cok begile.   35

Dissimuland thus in countenance and chere,
On knees fell, and smyland thus he said:
'Gude morne, my maister, gentill Chanteclere.'
With that the cock stert backward in a braid.
'Schir, be my saull, ye neid not be affraid,   40
Nor yit for me to drede nor flee abak.
I come bot here yow service for to mak.

'Wald I nocht serve yow ser, I wer to blame,
As I have done to youre progenitouris.
Your fader oft fulfillit hes my wame,   45
And send me meit fra middingis to the muris.
At his ending I did my besy curis,
To hale his hede and gif him drinkis warme,
Syne at the last that suete suelt in my arme.'

---

29. Chaucer's widow is better off than Henryson's (see *Nun's Priest's Tale*, 1-29).

30. *toun*—farm, cottar-house and property surrounding it.

32. *Lourence*—the fox, a familiar name in Scots, probably connected with *lour*—to lurk.

34. *juperteis*—means.

37. *knees*—trissyllabic, as in *KQ*, 102, etc.

'Knew thow my fader?' quod the cok, and leuch.   50
'Yea, my fair sone, forsuth I held his hede,
Quhen that he swelt under a birkyn beuch.
Syne said the dirige quhen that he was dede.
Betuix us twa how suld thair be a fede?
Quhom suld ye trest bot me, your servitour,   55
Quhilk to your fader did sa grite honour?

Quhen I behald your fetheris fair and gent,
Youre breste, your beke, your hekill and your came,
Schir, be my saule, that blissit sacrament,
My hert warmys—methink I am at hame.   60
Yow for to serve I wald crepe on my wame,
In frost and snaw, in wederis wan and wete,
And lay my lyart lokkis under your fete.'

This feynit fox, falss and dissimilate,
Maid to the cok a cavillatioun: 65
'Methink you changit and degenerate,
Fra your fader and his conditioun:
Off crafty crawing he mycht bere the croun,
For he wald on his tais stand and crawe.
This is no lee—I stude besyde and sawe.'   70

With that, the cok upoun his tais hee
Kest up his beke and sang with all his mycht.
Quod Lourance than: 'Now ser, sa mot I thee!
Ye ar your faderis sone and air uprycht,
Bot yit ye want of his cunnyng slicht.'   75
'Quhat?' quod the cok. He wald (and haif na dout)
Bayth wink and craw and turne him thryis about.

---

53. *dirige*—first word of a line from the Office for the Dead. The fox's statement conveys an irony that is personal, since his object is to kill the cock, and also literary, for the audience is asked to picture a fox intoning an office for a dying cock. Chaucer achieves the same incongruous effect more consistently in *The Nun's Priest's Tale* by keeping the human and animal worlds separate but at all times in juxtaposition.

63. *lyart*—hoary.

69. *tais*—toes (disyllabic).

Thus inflate with the wind of fals vainegloir,
Quhilk puttis monye to confusioun,
Trestand to win a grit worschip thairfore,   80
Unwarlye winkand, walkit up and doun
And syne, to chant and craw he maid him boun.
And suddanlie, or he had sung ane note,
The fox was war, and hynt him be the throte.

Syne to the schaw but tarie with him hyit,   85
Off countermaund haifand bot lytill dout.
With that Sprowtok, Coppok and Partlot cryit,
The wedow hard, and with a cry come out.
Seand the caiss, scho said and gaif a schout:
'How, murthour, reylock!' with a hiddeous beir.   90
'Alace, have I now lost guid Chanteclere?'

As scho war wod, with monye yell and cry,
Ryvand hir hair upoun hir breist can bete,
Syne paill of hew, half in ane extasye,
Fel doun for cair in swoning and in swete.   95
With that the sillye hennis left thair mete,
And quhill, this wyfe was lyand thus in swoun,
Fell of that caiss in disputatioun.

'Alace!' quod Partlot, makand sair murning,
With teiris grete attour hir chekis fell,   100
'Yon was our drourye and our day darling,
Oure nychtingale and our horlage bell.
Oure walcryif weche us for to warne and tell
Quhen that Aurora, with hir curchis gray,
Put up hir hede betuix the nycht and day.   105

87. MS has two 'Coppoks'.
101. *day*—Harley and prints have *dayis*.
105. MS has *the day*

---

87. Sprowtok, Coppok, Partlot—hen's names, each with a literary flavour.
90. *reylock*—robber (legal term). See MacQueen, *op. cit.*, p. 195.
101. *drourye*—a personal love-token (see *Testament of Cresseid*, line 583).

'Quha sall our lemmane be? Quha sall us leid?
Quhen we ar sad, quha sall unto us sing?
With his sweit bill he wald brek us the breid
In all this warld was thair na kyndar thing.
In paramouris he wald do us plesing   110
At his power, as nature list him gyffe.
Now, eftir him, alace, how sall we lyve?'

Than Sprowtok spak: 'Seiss, sister, of your sorrow.
Ye be to made, for him sic mourning maiss.
We sall fair weill, I find, Sanct Johne to borrow: 115
The proverb sayis: "As guid luif cumis as gaiss."
I will put on my hellye dayis clais
And mak me fresch aganis this jolye May,
Syne chant this sang: "Was nevir wedow so gay."

'He was angrye, and held us in grete aw,   120
And woundit with the speir of jelosye.
Off chaumerglew, Partlot, how weill ye knaw,
Waistit he was, of nature cald and drye:
Sen he is gone, thairfore, sister, say I,
Be blyith in bale, for that is best remeid;   125
Lat quik to quik; and deid go to the deid.'

Thus Sprowtok, that feynyeit fayth befoir,
In luste, but luif, that sett al hir delyte:
'Syster, ye watte of sic as him a scoir.
May it nocht siffise to slak your appetyte.   130
I hecht yow be my hand, sen ye ar quyte,
Within a wolk, for schame and I durst speik,
To gett a berne could better claw your beke!'

133. *beke*—possibly *breik* (breeches) intended, as printed in Bassendyne.

---

115. *to borrow*—as security.
117. *hellye dayis*—holiday.
119. An ironic allusion to the season of love and growth.
123. *cold and drye*—cf. *Testament of Cresseid*, lines 316–22.

Than Coppok lyke a curate spak full crouss:
'Yone was ane verrye veangeance fra the hevin.   135
He was sa loweouss and so licherouss,
Seiss coud he nocht with kittokis mo than sevin;
Bot rychtuous God, haldand the ballaneis evin,
Smytis full soir, thocht he be patient,
Adulteraris that list thame nocht repent.   140

'Prydefull he was, and joyit of his syn,
And compit nowther of Goddis falvour nor feid,
Bot traistit ay to rax and sa furth rin,
Till at the last his synnis could him leid
To schamefull end and to yone suddane deid.   145
Thairfore I wait it was the hand of God
That causit him be wirreit with the tod!'

Quhen this was said, the wedow fra hir swoun
Stert up in haist and on hir kennatis cryid:
'How, Birkye! Burrye! Bell! Balsye Broun!   150
Rypeschaw! Ryn weill! Courtess! Nuttieclyde!
Togidder all, but gruncheing, furth ye glyid!
Reskew my nobill cok or he be slane,
Or ellis to me se ye cum nevir agane!'

With that but baid thay breddit our the bent,   155
As fyre of flynt that our the feildis flaw.
Wichtlye, iwiss, throw woddis and watteris went,
And seissit nicht Ser Lourence till thay saw.
Bot quhen he saw the raches cum on raw,

137. MS has *sissockis*. Bassendyne prints *kittokis*—paramours.
151. MS has 'cutt and clyid'.

---

137. *mo than sevin*—in plenty. But see MacQueen, *op cit.*, 195–6.
150–1. Dog's names, some still current in Scotland. *Nuttieclyde* is printed in Bassendyne. *Bawsy Brown* occurs in Dunbar's *Dance of the Sevin Deidly Synnis*, line 30; *Curtes* in *Reynard The Fox*.
152. *but gruncheing*—without complaining.
159. *raches*—i.e. the pursuing dogs; *on raw*—cf. *Robene and Makyne*, line 12.

Unto the cok he said in mynde: 'God sen,   160
That I and thow wer liftit in my den.'

Than spak the cok, with sum guid spreit inspyrit:
'Do my counsale, and I sall warrand the:
Hungrie thow art and for grit travell tyrit,
Rycht fant of force and may nocht forder flee.   165
Swyith turne agane and say that I and ye
Freindis ar maid, and fallowis for a yeir;
Than will thay stynt. I stand for it and nocht steir.'

This fox, thocht he was fals and frivelouss,
And hes fraudis his quarrellis to defend,   170
Dissavit was throw mynis marvellous,
For falsheid failyeis at the latter end.
He turnit about and cryit, as he was kend.
With that the cok brade into a buche.
Now reid ye sall quhairat Ser Lowrence luche: 175

Begylit thus, the tod under a tree
On knees fell, and said: 'Gude Chanteclere,
Cum doun agane and I but mete or fee
Salbe your man and servand for ane yeir.'
'Nay, murther, theif and rivere. Stand on reir!   180
My bludye hekkill and my bek so bla
Hes pairtit lowe for evir betwene us twa.

'I was unwyis that winkit at thy will,
Quhairthrow allmaist I lossit had my heid.
I was moir full,' quod he, 'could nocht be still,   185
Bot spake to put my pray unto pleid.
Fair on, fals theif! God keip me fra thy feid!'

160-1. Ms has *god then*/*Sen I and thow wer liftit*. The present text
follows Bassendyne.

---

167. *for a yeir*—indefinite period.
168. *I stand for it and nocht steir*—'I will stand still and not move while you
do it.'

With that, the coke our feildis tuke the flicht:
In at the wedowis lewar coud he licht.

Moralitas

Now, worthy folk, suppois this be a fable,   190
And ourhelit with typis figurall,
Yit may ye find a sentence rycht greabill
Under the fenyeit termys textuall.
Till oure purpois this cok wele may we call
A nyce proud man, void and vanegloriouss,   195
Off kyn or gude quhilk is presumptuouss.

Fy, pompouss pryd! Thow art rycht poysonable.
Quha favouris the of force man have a fall.
Thy strength is nocht. Thy stule standis unstable.
Tak witness of the feindis infernall   200
Quhilk huntit war, doun fro the hevinly all
To hellis hole and to that hidous houss,
Becaus of pryde thay war presumptuouss.

This feynit fox may wele be figurate
To flatteraris with plesand wirdis quhite.   205
With fals menyng and mouth mellifluate,
To loife and lee quhilk settis thair delyte.
All worthy folk at sic suld hafe dispyte,
For quhair is moir perilouss pestilence
Than giff to liaris haistelye credence?   210

This wikkit wind of adulatioun
Of swete socour haifand a similitude.
Bittir of gall and full of fell poysoun.
Quha tastis it; and clerelye understude
Forthy as now, schortly for to conclude: 215
Thir twa synnis, flattery and vaineglore
Ar venemouss! Guid folk, fle thame thairfore!

190–217. *Cf*. Chaucer's ending to *The Nun's Priest's Tale*, which enjoins the reader to extract for himself the 'fruyt' of the narrative. Though Henryson has written a comic tale, quite unlike that of the moralistic Aesop, he is invariably guided in selection of material by a didactic purpose not so apparent in Chaucer.

Robert Henryson

VII. Orpheus and Eurydice

ONE of Henryson's major narrative poems, possibly an early work. His plot is founded on Boethius's account of the legend but is circumscribed by the necessity to interpret its personages and action allegorically. The *moralitas* (paraphrased below) follows Trivet's commentary closely.

MSS: Bannatyne, Asloan. The former adds a moralitas *45 lines longer but the interpretation in both cases follows Trivet's. The present version is based on Bannatyne, f.317b–f.325a with some debt to Asloan and the early print.*

First printed: Chepman and Myllar (1508) but the only known copy (in the National Library of Scotland) is incomplete (lines 59–175 missing). Asloan agrees closely with it and may have been a copy.

The nobilnes and grit magnificens
Of prince and lord, quhai list to magnifie,
His ancestre and lineall discens
Suld first extoll, and his genolegie,
So that his harte he mycht inclyne thairby   5
The moir to vertew and to worthiness,
Herand reherss his elderis gentilness.

It is contrair the lawis of nature
A gentill man to be degenerat,
Nocht following of his progenitour   10
The worthe rewll and the lordly estait;
A ryall rynk for to be rusticat
Is bot a monsture in comparesoun,
Had in dispyt and full derisioun.

I say this be the grit lordis of Grew,   15
Quhich set thair hairt and all thair haill curage,
Thair faderis steppis justly to persew,
Eiking the wirschep of thair he lenage.
The anseane and sadwyse men of age
Wer tendouris to yung and insolent,   20
To mak thame in all vertewis excellent.

14. Chepman and Myllar has *foule*.

---

15. *Grew*—Greece.

Lyk as a strand of watter of a spring
Haldis the sapour of the fontell well;
So did in Grece ilk lord and worthy king.
Of forbearis thay tuk knawlege and smell,   25
Amang the quhilk of ane I think to tell:
Bot first his gentill generatioun
I sall rehers, with your correctioun.

Upone the mont of Elecone,
The most famous of all Arrabea,   30
A goddes dwelt, excellent in bewte,
Gentill of blude, callit Memoria,
Quhilk Jupiter that goddess to wyfe can ta
And carnaly hir knew and eftir syne
Apone a day bare him fair dochteris nyne.   35

The first in Grew wes callit Euterpe,
In our language gud delectatioun;
The secound maid clippit Melpomyne,
As hony sueit in modelatioun;
Thersycore is gud instructioun   40
Of everything—the thrid sister, I wis
Thus out of Grew in Latyne translait is.

Caliope, that madin mervalous,
The ferd sistir, of all musik maistress,
And mother to the king schir Orpheous,   45
Quilk throw his wyfe wes efter king of Trais;
Clio, the fyift, that now is a goddess,
In Latyne callit meditatioun,
Of everything that hes creatioun.

The sext sister is callit Herato,   50
Quhilk drawis lyk to lyk in everything;
The sevint lady was fair Polimio,

25. *knawlege*—Chepman and Myllar has *tarage*—smell, which appears
more consistent, though this could be a wrong setting of *curage*. Asloan
has *carage*.

Quhilk cowth a thowsand sangis sueitly sing;
Talia syne, quhilk can our saulis bring
In profound wit and grit agilite,   55
Till undirstand and haif capacitie.

Urania, the nynt and last of all,
In Greik langage, quha cowth it rycht expound,
Is callit armony celestiall,
Rejosing men with melody and sound.   60
Amang thir nyne Calliope wes cround
And maid a quene be michty god Phebus,
Of quhome he gat this prince schir Orpheous.

No wondir wes thocht he wes fair and wyse,
Gentill and gud, full of liberalitie,   65
His fader god, and his progenetryse
A goddess, finder of all armony:
Quhen he wes borne scho set him on hir kne,
And gart him souk of hir twa paupis quhyte
The sueit lecour of all musik perfyte.   70

Incressand sone to manheid up he drew,
Of statur large, and frely fair of face;
His noble fame so far it sprang and grew,
Till at the last the michty quene of Trace
Excelland fair, haboundand in riches,   75
A message send unto that prince so ying,
Requyrand him to wed hir and be king.

Euridices this lady had to name
And quhene scho saw this prince so glorius,
Hir erand to propone scho thocht no schame,   80
With wordis sueit, and blenkis amorous,

29–63. The descent of Orpheus from Jupiter represents the descent of human from divine intellect, through Memory, Apollo and the Muses. In the Middle English *Sir Orfeo*, the hero is given only faint divine origins and emerges as a substantially human medieval knight. Henryson's Orpheus is 'degenerat' (line 9) because he did not try to live up to his inheritance.

Said, 'Welcum lord and lufe schir Orpheus,
In this provynce ye salbe king and lord!'
Thay kissit syne, and thus thay can accord.

Betuix Orpheus and fair Erudices,   85
Fra thai wer weddit, on fra day to day
The low of lufe cowth kyndill and incress,
With mirth, and blythnes, solace and with play
Of wardly joy; allace, quhat sall I say?
Lyk till a flour that plesandly will spring   90
Quhilk fadis sone and endis with murnyng.

I say this be Erudices the quene,
Quhilk walkit furth into a May mornyng,
Bot with a madyn, untill a medow grene,
To tak the air, and se the flouris spring;   95
Quhair in a schaw, neir by this lady ying,
A busteous hird callit Arresteus,
Kepand his beistis, lay under a bus.

And quhen he saw this lady solitar,
Bairfut, with schankis quhyter than the snaw,   100
Preckit with lust, he thocht withoutin mair
Hir till oppress, and to his cave hir draw:
Dreidand for evil scho fled, quhen scho him saw;
And as scho ran, all bairfute on a bus
Scho strampit on a serpent vennemus.   105

This crewall venome wes so penetrife,
As natur is of all mortall pusoun,
In peisis small this quenis harte can rife,
And scho annone fell on a deidly swoun.
Seand this caiss, Proserpyne maid hir boun,   110
Quhilk clepit is the goddes infernall,
Ontill hir court this gentil quene can call.

---

105. Virgil, *Georgics*, Lib. IV, 485–6; Ovid, *Metamorphoses*, X, 50–2;
Boethius, *De Consolatione Philosophiae*, III, xii.

D

And quhen scho vaneist was and unvisible,
Her madyn wepit with a wofull cheir,
Cryand with mony schowt and voce terrible,   115
Quhill at the last king Orpheus can heir,
And of hir cry the caus sone cowth he speir.
Scho said: 'Allace! Euridices your quene
Is with phary tane befoir my ene.'

This noble king inflammit all in yre,   120
And rampand as a lyoun rewanus,
With awfull luke, and ene glowand as fyre,
Sperid the maner, and the maid said thus:
'Scho strampit on a serpent venemus,
And fell on swoun; with that the quene of fary   125
Clawcht hir upsone, and furth with hir cowth cary.'

Quhen scho had said, the king sichit full soir,
His hart neir brist for verry dule and wo;
Half out of mynd, he maid no tary moir,
Bot tuk his harp, and on to wod cowth go,   130
Wrinkand his handis, walkand to and fro,
Quhill he mycht stand, syne sat doun on a stone,
And till his harp thusgait he maid his mone.

The Complaint of Orpheus

'O dulful herp, with mony dully string,
Turne all thy mirth and musik in murning,   135
And seis of all thy sutell songis sweit.
Now weip with me, thy lord and cairfull king,
Quhilk lossit hes in erd all his lyking;
And all thy game thow change in gole, and greit.
Thy goldin pynnis with mony teiris weit,   140
And all my pane for till report thow preis,
Cryand with me, in every steid and streit,
"Quhair art thow gone, my luve Ewridices?"'

---

121. An heraldic reference.
138. *lyking*—all he held dear.
140. *pynnis*—pegs of a harp.

Him to rejoss yit playit he a spring,
Quhill that the fowlis of the wid can sing, 145
And treis dansit with thair levis grene,
Him to devod from his grit womenting.
Bot all in vane, that wailyeit no thing;
His hairt wes so upoun his lusty quene,
The bludy teiris sprang out of his ene, 150
Thair wes no solace mycht his sobbing ses,
Bot cryit ay, with cairis cauld and kene,
'Quhair art thow gone, my luf Euridices?'

'Fair weill my place, fair weill plesandis and play,
And wylcum woddis wyld and wilsum way, 155
My wicket werd in wildirnes to ware,
My rob ryell, and all my riche array
Changit sal be in rude russet and gray;
My dyademe in till a hate of hair;
My bed sal be with bever, brok and bair, 160
In buskis bene with mony busteous bes,
Withowttin song, sayand with siching sair,
"Quhair art thow gone, my luve Euridices?"

'I the beseik, my fair fadir Phebus,
Haif pety of thy awin sone Orpheus; 165
Wait thow nocht weill I am thy sone and chyld?
Now heir my plaint, peinfull and peteuss:
Direk me fro this deid so dolorus,
Quhilk gois thus withouttin gilt begyld;
Lat nocht thy face with cluddis to be oursyld; 170
Len me thy lycht and lat me nocht go leis,
To find that fair in fame that was nevir fyld,
My lady quene and lufe Euridices.

'O Jupiter, thow god celestiall,
And grantser to myself, on the I call 175
To mend my murning and my drery mone.
Thow gif me fors, that I nocht fant nor fall,
Till I hir fynd; forsuth seik hir I sall,

And nowthir stint nor stand for stok nor stone.
Throw thy godheid grant me quhair scho is gone,   180
Gar hir appeir, and put my hairt in pes.'
King Orpheus thus, with his harp allone,
Soir weipand for his wyfe Euridices.

Quhen endit wer thir songis lamentable,
He tuke his harp and on his breist can hing,   185
Syne passit to the hevin, as sayis the fable,
To seik his wyfe, bot that welyeid no thing:
By wedlingis streit he went but tareing,
Syne come doun throw the speir of Saturne ald,
Quhilk fadir is to all the stormis cald.   190

Quhen scho wes socht ourthrow that cauld regioun,
Till Jupiter his grandser can he wend,
Quhilk rewit soir his lamentatioun,
And gart his spheir be socht fro end to end.
Scho was nocht thair and doun he can descend   195
Till Mars, the god of battell and of stryfe,
And socht his spheir, yit gat he nocht his wyfe.

Than went he doun till his fadir Phebus,
God of the sone, with bemis brycht and cleir;
Bot quhen he saw his awin sone Orpheus   200
In sic a plicht, that changit all his cheir,
And gart annone ga seik throw all his spheir;
Bot all in vane, his lady come nocht thair.
He tuk his leif and to Venus can fair.

Quhen he hir saw, he knelit and said thus: 205
'Wait ye nocht weill I am your awin trew knycht?
In luve none leler than ser Orpheus;
And ye of luve goddes and most of micht,
Of my lady help me to get a sicht.'

---

188. *wedlingis streit*—Watling Street (the Milky Way). *Cf.* Douglas, *Aen.*,
III, viii, 22 and *House of Fame*, II, 427 *et seq.*, though the reference was familiar
in medieval writing.

'Forsur,' quod scho, 'ye mone seik nedirmair.'   210
Than fra Venus he tuk his leif but mair.

Till Mercury but tary is he gone,
Quhilk callit is the god of eloquens,
Bot of his wyfe thair gat he knawledge none.
With wofull hairt he passit doun frome thens   215
On to the mone; he maid no residens.
Thus frome the hevin he went onto the erd,
Yit be the way sum melody he lerd.

In his passage amang the planeitis all,
He hard a hevinly melody and sound,   220
Passing all instrumentis musicall,
Causit be rollyn of the speiris round;
Quhilk armony of all this mappamound,
Quhill moving seis unyt perpetuall,
Quhilk of this warld Pluto the saule can call.   225

Thair leirit he tonis proportionat,

223–5. The near repetitions in these lines suggest corruption.

226ff. The following note on this difficult passage has been written by Mr Edward Maddrell. A vibrating string (or a column of air in a pipe) produces a note of musical pitch. If its vibrating length is halved, by stopping the string half-way, it produces a note one octave higher. The interval of an octave was thus said to result from the 'proportion' 2:1. Other proportions give other intervals, on the same principle. The proportions referred to by Henryson are:
duplare: 2:1, diapason (octave);
triplare: 3:1, disdiapente (twelfth, i.e. octave plus fifth);
emetricus: 4:3, diatesseron (fourth); the correct term is *epitritus*;
enolius: 3:2, diapente (fifth); the correct term is *emiolus*;
eppodeus: 9:8, tonus (whole tone); the correct term is *epogdous*;
quadruplait: 4:1, disdiapason or duplex diapason (two octaves).

Five of these intervals are mentioned as perfect consonances in 232–5; note, however, that although *disdiapason* ('dyapasone . . . dowplait') means two octaves, *disdiapente* ('dyapenty componyt with the dyss') means a twelfth and not two fifths. *Dyss* should not be emended to *byss*.

Henryson displays some knowledge of technical terms in this little cadenza, but no clear understanding of their meaning. His modesty in lines 240–2 is very proper. Douglas makes a similar confession in *The Palace of Honour*, I, 493–6, 517–8.

As duplare, triplare and emetricus,
Enolius and eik the quadruplait,
Epoddeus rycht hard and curius;
Off all thir sex, sueit and delicius,   230
Rycht consonant fyfe hevinly symphonys
Componyt ar, as clerkis can devyse.

First diatesserone, full sueit, I wiss,
And dyapasone, semple and dowplait,
And dyapenty, componyt with the dys;   235
Thir makis fyve of thre multiplicat:
This mirry musik and mellefluat,
Compleit and full of nummeris od and evin,
Is causit be the moving of the hevin.

Off sic musik to wryt I do bot doit,   240
Thairfoir of this mater a stray I lay,
For in my lyfe I cowth nevir sing a noit.
Bot I will tell how Orpheus tuk the way,
To seik his wyfe attour the gravis gray,
Hungry and cauld, with mony wilsum wone,   245
Withouttin gyd, he and his harp allone.

He passit furth the space of twenty dayis,
Fer and full fer, and ferrer than I can tell,
And ay he fand streitis and reddy wayis.
Till at the last unto the yet of hell   250
He come, and thair he fand a porter fell,
With thre heidis, wes callit Serberus
A hound of hell, a monstour mervellus.

Than Orpheus began to be agast,
Quhen he beheld that ugly hellis hound   255
He tuk his harp and on it playit fast,

191–239. Orpheus appeals to his forbears, both genealogical and musical.
The terms used are Latin and Greek, taken probably from Boethius' *De Musica*
and *De Arithmetica*, and the technical effect is one of consonance. See J. Mac-
Queen, *Robert Henryson* (Oxford, 1967), 41–2.

Till at the last, throw sueitnes of the sound,
This dog slepit and fell doun on the ground.
Than Orpheus attour his wame install,
And neddirmair he went, as ye heir sall.   260

He passit furth ontill a ryvir deip,
Our it a brig, and on it sisteris thre,
Quhilk had the entre of the brig to keip,
Electo, Mygra, and Thesaphone,
Turnit a quheill wes ugly for to se,   265
And on it spred a man hecht Exione,
Rolland about rycht windir wo begone.

Than Orpheus playd a joly spring,
The thre susteris full fast thay fell on sleip,
The ugly quheill seisit of hir quhirling.   270
Thus left wes none the entre for to keip.
Thane Exione out of the quheill gan creip,
And stall away; and Orpheus annone,
Without stopping, atour the brig is gone.

Nocht far from thyne he come unto a flude,   275
Drubly and deip, and rythly doun can rin,
Quhair Tantelus nakit full thirsty stude.
And yit the wattir yeid aboif his chin;
Quhen he gaipit thair wald no drop cum in;
Quhen he dowkit the watter wald discend;   280
Thus gat he nocht his thrist to slake nor mend.

Befoir his face ane naple hang also,
Fast at his mowth upoun a twynid threid,
Quhen he gaipit it rollit to and fro,
And fled, as it refusit him to feid.   285
Quhen Orpheus thus saw him suffir neid,
He tuk his harp and fast on it can clink:
The wattir stud, and Tantalus gat a drink.

---

264. The Eumenides or Furies.

Syne our a mure, with thornis thik and scherp,
Wepand allone, a wilsum way he went,   290
And had nocht bene throw suffrage of his harp,
With pikis he had bene schorne and schent.
As he blenkit, besyd him on the bent
He saw lyand speldit a wofull wycht,
Nalit full fast and Titius he hecht.   295

And on his breist thair sat a grisly grip,
Quhilk with his bill his belly throw can boir,
Both maw, myddret, hart, lever and trip
He ruggit out—his panis was the moir.
Quhen Orpheus thus saw him suffir soir,   300
He tuke his herp and maid sueit melody—
The grip is fled and Titius left his cry.

Beyond this mure he fand a feirfull streit,
Myrk as the nycht, to pass rycht dengerus,
For sliddrenes skant mycht he hald his feit,   305
In quhilk thair wes a stynk rycht odius,
That gydit him to hiddouss hellis hous
Quhair Rodomantus and Proserpina
Wer king and quene; and Orpheus in can ga.

O dully place, and grundles deip dungeoun,   310
Furness of fyre and stink intollerable,
Pit of dispair, without remissioun,
Thy meit wennome, thy drink is pusonable,
Thy grit panis and to compte unnumerable;
Quhat creature cumis to dwell in the   315
Is ay deand and nevirmoir sall de.

Thair fand he mony cairfull king and quene,
With croun on heid, with brass full birnand,
Quhilk in thair lyfe full maisterfull had bene;
And conquerouris of gold, riches and land.   320
Hector of Troy and Priame, thair he fand,
And Alexander for his wrang conqueist;
Antiochus als for his foull incest.

And Julius Cesar for his foull crewaltie;
And Herod with his brudiris wyfe he saw;   325
And Nero for his grit iniquitie;
And Pilot for his breking of the law.
Syne undir that he lukit and cowth knaw
Cresus, that king none mychtiar on mold
For cuvatyse, yet full of birnand gold.   330

Thair saw he Pharo, for the oppressioun
Of godis folk on quhilk the plaigis fell;
And Sawll, for the grit abusioun
Was justice to the folk of Israell;
Thair saw he Acob and quene Jesabell,   335
Quhilk silly Nabot, that wes a propheit trew,
For his wyne yaird withouttin mercy slew.

Thair saw he mony paip and cardynall,
In haly kirk quhilk did abusioun,
And bishopis in thair pontificall,   340
Be symonie and wrang intrusioun;
Abbottis and all men of religioun,
For evill disponyng of thair place and rent,
In flame of fyre wer bittirly torment.

Syne neddirmair he went quhair Pluto was,   345
And Proserpyne, and hiddirwart he drew,
Ay playand on his harp quhair he cowth pass;
Till at the last Erudices he knew,
Lene and deidlyk, and peteouss paill of hew,
Rycht warsche and wane and walluid as the weid,   350
Hir lilly lyre wes lyk unto the leid.

289-344. The road to hell is here seen as a rough Scottish moorland track, though later hell proper is conceived in Dantesque terms (lines 310–6). Within its confines, allegorically interpreted as the realm of unslaked and unbridled appetite, are two main groups of personages, tyrannical princes and corrupt ecclesiastics (see Dante, *Inferno*, xix).

350. *walluid as the weid*—see *The Thre Deid Pollis*, line 21. In the ME *Sir Orfeo* Herodis retained her vital beauty while captive.

D*

Quod he, 'My lady leill, and my delyt,
Full woe is me to se yow changit thus;
Quhair is your rude as ross with cheikis quhyte,
Your cristell ene with blenkis amorus,   355
Your lippis reid to kiss delicius?'
Quod scho, 'as now I der nocht tell, perfay;
Bot ye sall wit the causs ane uthir day.'

Quod Pluto, 'Schir, thocht scho be lyk ane elf,
Scho hes no causs to plenye, and for quhy?   360
Scho fairis alsweill daylie as dois my self,
Or King Herod for all his chevelry:
It is langour that putis hir in sic ply;
War scho at hame in hir cuntre of Trace,
Scho wald refet full sone in fax and face.'   365

Than Orpheus befoir Pluto sat doun
And in his handis quhit his herp can ta,
And playit mony sueit proportioun,
With baiss tonis in Ipotdorica,
With gemilling in Yporlerica;   370
Quhill at the last for rewth and grit petie,
Thay weipit soir, that cowth him heir or se.

Than Proserpene and Pluto bad him ass
His waresoun—And his wald haif rycht nocht
Bot licience with his wyfe away to pass   375
To his cuntre, that he so far had socht.
Quod Proserpyne: 'Sen I hir hiddir brocht,
We sall nocht pairte without conditioun.'
Quod he: 'Thairto I mak promissioun.'

'Euridices than be the hand thow tak,   380

365. Bannatyne reads *rewert*; print has *refete*; text follows Asloan.
370. Print has *gemynyng. Cf.* Douglas, *Palace of Honour*, I 501.

369–70. Greek musical terms.
370. *gemilling*—a simple form of two-part harmony.

And pass thi way, bot undirneth this pane:
Gife thow turnis or blenkis behind thy bak,
We sall hir haif to hell for evir agane.'
Thocht this was hard, yit Orpheus was fane,
And on thay went, talkand of play and sport,   385
Till thay almost come to the outwart port.

Thus Orpheus, with inwart lufe repleit,
So blindit was with grit effectioun,
Pensyfe in hart apone his lady sueit,
Remembrit nocht his hard conditioun.   390
Quhat will ye moir? In schort conclusioun,
He blent bakwart, and Pluto come annone,
And on to hell with hir agane is gone.

Allace! It wes grit pety for to heir
Of Orpheus the weping and the wo,   395
How his lady, that he had bocht so deir,
Bot for a luk so sone wes tane him fro.
Flatlingis he fell and micht no fordir go,
And lay a quhile in swoun and extasy.
Quhen he ourcome, this out of lufe gan cry: 400

'Quhat art thow, luve? How sall I the defyne?
Bittir and sueit, crewall and merciable,
Plesand to sum, to uthir plent and pyne,
Till sum constant, to uthir wariable;
Hard is thy law, thy bandis unbrekable;   405
Quho servis they, thocht thay be nevir so trew,
Perchance sum tyme thay sall haif causs to rew.

'Now find I weill this proverb trew,' quod he,
'"Hart on the hurd, and handis on the soir;
Quhair luve gois, on forss mone turne the E."   410
I am expart, and wo is me thairfoir,
Bot for a luke my lady is forloir.'

---

400. *ourcome*—recovered.

Thus chydand on, with luve our burne and bent,
A wofull wedo hamewart is he went.

---

414. *wedo*—widower.

415–633. *Moralitas.* Phoebus is the god of sapience, Calliope of eloquence and their offspring: Orpheus represents the intellectual part of man's soul; Eurydice is appetitive power; Aristaeus is virtue; the serpent's sting is deadly sin, which oppresses the soul with worldly lust. Cerberus, the triple-headed dog, stands for the death of young, middle-aged and old, while the three sisters, the Fates, are respectively wicked thought, word and deed. Between them they turn Fortune's wheel; on the wheel are Ixion, who tried to violate Juno, Tantalus, who slew his son and fed him to the god of riches, and Tityus, who sought to divine the future, thus usurping the prerogative of Apollo, who were condemned to undergo punishments of thirst and torture. All three represent abuses of fleshly appetite, conscience and human knowledge. Orpheus, playing his harp, satisfies appetite by means of intellect. The union of Orpheus and Eurydice signifies the harmony between desire and reason, leading to contemplation. When this takes place, abuses will be banished. But to look back at appetite, as Orpheus did when he led Eurydice out of the underworld, is to embrace worldly lust and vain prosperity. Reason is in this way made a widow.

Robert Henryson

VIII. The Testament of Cresseid

THIS is Henryson's best-known poem. It represents the high point of achievement among the makars. Unlike Chaucer's *Troilus and Criseyde*, of which it claims to be a continuation, *The Testament of Cresseid* is austerely didactic and its personages are little more than symbols, having no 'psychology' or comprehensible motives which demand analysis in the light of human experience. Its compelling severity and remorseless movement towards an inevitable end are relieved only by the poet's stern compassion for Cresseid and by his sober optimism concerning the effect of her 'schort conclusioun' upon the other members of her sex. It is, indeed, appropriate that Henryson should have begun a work so clear-sighted and direct of aim in the cold moonlight of a Scottish spring, when 'the northin wind had purifyit the air.'

MSS: No early manuscripts extant. The Kinaston and Cambridge University Library manuscripts are both late sixteenth century.

Printed texts: Thynne's edition of Chaucer (1532) printed the poem after Troilus and Criseyde *but the best for editorial purposes is the unique Charteris text of 1593 on which the following version is based. (British Museum C. 21, c.14).*

Ane doolie sessoun to ane cairfull dyte
Suld correspond and be equivalent:
Richt sa it wes quhen I began to wryte
This tragedie, the wedder richt fervent,
Quhen Aries, in middis of the Lent,   5
Schouris of haill can fra the north discend,
That scantlie fra the cauld I micht defend.

Yit nevertheless within myne oratur
I stude, quhen Titan had his bemis bricht
Withdrawin doun, and sylit under cure.   10
And fair Venus, the bewtie of the nicht,

---

4. *tragedie*—a change in fortune from happiness to misery.

5. *Aries*—helps to date the scene in late March. *Cf.* Chaucer, *Prologue to C.T.*, line 8.

1–7. After the *sententia*, which predicts the character of the work (1–2), the spring-time setting usually depicted by Southern poets is ironically presented in realistic Scottish terms, that is, with showers of hail coming from the North.

sunset

Uprais and set unto the west full richt
Hir goldin face in oppositioun
Of God Phebus direct discending doun.

Throwout the glas hir bemis brast sa fair   15
That I micht se on everie syde me by
The northin wind had purifyit the air
And sched the mistie cloudis fra the sky.
The froist freisit, the blastis bitterly
Fra Pole Artick come quhisling loud and schill,   20
And causit me remufe aganis my will.

For I traistit that Venus, luifis quene,
To quhome sum tyme I hecht obedience,
My faidit hart of lufe scho wald mak grene,
And thereupon, with humbill reverence   25
I thocht to pray hir hie magnificence.
Bot for greit cald as than I lattit was
And in my chalmer to the fyre can pas.

Thocht lufe be hait, yit in ane man of age
It kendillis nocht sa sone as in youtheid,   30
Of quhome the blude is flowing in ane rage,
And in the auld the curage doif and deid,
Of quhilk the fyre outward is best remeid,
To help be phisike quhair that nature faillit
I am expert, for baith I have assailit.   35

I mend the fyre and beikit me about,
Than tuik ane drink my spreitis to comfort
And armit me weill fra the cauld thairout.
To cut the winter nicht and mak it schort
I tuik ane quair, and left all uther sport,   40

15–21. See Introduction, p. 4. Ayala (*op. cit.*) refers to glazing in Scottish
houses in a letter dated 25th July, 1498. *Cf. Book of the Duchess*, 336–43.
24. The common metaphor of fading and growth is used to develop the
poem (see *Orpheus and Eurydice*, 90–1). In *The Testament* the poet is too old to
be warmed by the fires of love and has to resort to other external devices.

Writtin be worthie Chaucer glorious
Of fair Cresseid, and worthie Troylus.

And thair I fand, efter that Diomeid
Ressavit had that lady bricht of hew,
How Troilus neir out of wit abraid   45
And weipit soir with visage paill of hew,
For quhilk wanhope his teiris can renew
Quhill Esperus rejoisit him agane:
Thus quhyle in joy he levit, quhyle in pane.

Of hir behest he had greit comforting,   50
Traisting to Troy that scho suld make retour,
Quhilk he desyrit maist of eirdly thing
Forquhy scho was his only paramour.
Bot quhen he saw passit baith day and hour
Of hir ganecome, than sorrow can oppres   55
His wofull hart in cair and hevines.

Of his distres me neidis nocht reheirs,
For worthie Chauceir in the samin buik
In gudelie termis and in joly veirs
Compylit hes his cairis, quha will luik.   60
To brek my sleip ane uther quair I tuik,
In quhilk I fand the fatall destenie
Of fair Cresseid, that endit wretchitlie.

Quha wait gif all that Chauceir wrait was trew?
Nor I wait nocht gif this narratioun   65
Be authoreist, or fenyeit of the new
Be sum poeit, throw his inventioun
Maid to report the lamentatioun
And wofull end of this lustie Creisseid,
And quhat distress scho thoillit, and quhat deid.   70

---

48. *Esperus*—happy evening star.
50. *hir*—Criseyde (*Troilus and Criseyde*, V, 1423 *et seq.*).
61–70. *ane uther quair*—possibly a poetic fiction. But see Harvey Wood's note, *Poems and Fables*, 2nd edn., XXXIX–XL.

Quhen Diomeid had all his appetyte,
And mair, fulfillit of this fair ladie,
Upon ane uther he set his haill delyte
And send to hir ane lybell of repudie,
And hir excludit fra his companie.   75
Than desolait scho walkit up and doun
And (sum men sayis) into the court, commoun.   *courtesan*

O fair Creisseid, the flour and A per se
Of Troy and Grece, how was thou fortunait!
To change in filth all thy feminitie   80
And be with fleschlie lust sa maculait,   *stained*
And go amang the Greikis air and lait
Sa gigotlike, takand thy foull plesance.
I have pietie thou suld fall sic mischance.

Yit nevertheless quhat ever men deme or say   85
In scornefull langage of thy brukkilnes,   *frailty*
I sall excuse, als far furth as I may,
Thy womanheid, thy wisdome and fairnes,
The quhilk Fortoun hes put to sic distress
As hir pleisit, and nathing throw the gilt   90
Of the, throw wickit langage to be spilt.

This fair lady, in this wyse destitute
Of all comfort and consolatioun,
Richt privelie, but fellowschip on fute
Disagysit passit far out of the toun   95
Ane myle or twa, unto ane mansioun,
Beildit full gay, quhair hir father Calchas
Quhilk than amang the Greikis dwelland was.

Quhen he hir saw, the caus he can inquyre
Of hir cumming: scho said, siching full soir,   100

---

74. *ane lybell of repudie*—a bill of divorcement.
77. *into the court, commoun*—become the common property of the court, i.e. a courtesan; *commoun*—promiscuous.
79. *how was thou fortunait*—how ill-fortuned you were.

'Fra Diomeid had gottin his desyre
He wox werie, and wald of me no moir'.
Quod Calchas: 'Douchter, weip thou not thairfoir.
Peraventure all cummis for the best.
Welcum to me, thou art full deir ane gest'.   105

This auld Calchas, efter the law was tho,
Wes keiper of the tempill as ane preist,
In quhilk Venus and hir sone Cupido
War honourit, and his chalmer was thame neist;
To quhilk Cresseid with baill aneuch in breist   110
Usit to pas, hir prayeris for to say,
Quhill at the last, upon ane solempne day

As custome was, the pepill far and neir
Befoir the none unto the tempill went
With sacrifice, devoit in thair maneir: 115
Bot still Cresseid, hevie in hir intent,
Into the kirk wald not hirself present
For giving of the pepill ony deming
Of hir expuls fra Diomeid the king.

Bot past into ane secreit orature   120
Quhair scho micht weip hir wofull desteny,
Behind hir bak scho cloisit fast the dure
And on hir kneis bair fell doun in hy.
Upon Venus and Cupide angerly   *curses gods*
Scho cryit out, and said on this same wyse,   125
'Allace that ever I maid you sacrifice.

'Ye gave me anis ane devine responsaill
That I suld be the flour of luif in Troy.
Now am I maid ane unworthie outwaill,
And all in cair translatit is my joy.   130
Quha sall me gyde? Quha sall me now convoy

106–9. *after the law was tho*—according to contemporary custom. Chaucer's Calchas is a priest of Apollo, as in the classical story; Henryson places him in a temple of love.

Sen I fra Diomeid and nobill Troylus
Am clene excludit as abject odious?

'O fals Cupide, is nane to wyte bot thow,
And thy mother, of lufe the blind goddes.   135
Ye causit me alwayis understand and trow
The seid of lufe was sawin in my face,
And ay grew grene throw your supplie and grace.
Bot now allace that seid with froist is slane
And I fra luifferis left and all forlane.'   140

Quhen this was said, doun in ane extasie,
Ravischit in spreit, intill ane dreame scho fell
And be apperance hard, quhair scho did ly,
Cupide the king ringand ane silver bell,
Quhilk men micht heir fra hevin unto hell.   145
At quhais sound befoir Cupide appeiris
The seven planetis descending fra thair spheiris

Quhilk hes power of all thing generabill
To reull and steir be thair greit influence,
Wedder and wind, and coursis variabill: 150
And first of all Saturne gave his sentence,
Quhilk gave to Cupide litill reverence,
Bot, as ane busteous churle on his maneir,
Come crabitlie with auster luik and cheir.

His face fronsit, his lyre was lyke the leid,   *old ruler*   155
His teith chatterit, and cheverit with the chin;
His ene drowpit, how sonkin in his heid,
/ Out of his nois the meldrop fast can rin,
With lippis bla and cheikis leine and thin;
The iceschoklis that fra his hair doun hang   160
Was wonder greit, and as ane speir als lang.

155. Charteris reads *frosnit* but other authorities agree on a variant of
fronsit—wrinkled. See Fox, *ed. cit.* p. 98n.

---

135. This transference of blindness from Cupid to Venus is rare. See D. Fox,
editor, *The Testament of Cresseid* (London and Edinburgh, 1968), p. 95n.

Atouir his belt his lyart lokkis lay
Felterit unfair, ouirfret with froistis hoir,
His garmound and his gyte full gay of gray,
His widderit weid fra him the wind out woir; 165
Ane busteous bow within his hand he boir;
Under his girdill ane flasche of felloun flanis
Fedderit with ice, and heidit with hailstanis.

*(young)
new ruler*

Than Juppiter richt fair and amiabill,
God of the starnis in the firmament, 170
And nureis to all thing generabill,
Fra his father Saturne far different,
With burelie face and browis bricht and brent,
Upon his heid ane garland, wonder gay,
Of flouris fair, as it had bene in May. 175

His voice was cleir, as cristall wer his ene,
As goldin wyre sa glitterand was his hair;
His garmound and his gyte full [gay] of grene,
With golden listis gilt on everie gair;
Ane burelie brand about his midill bair. 180
In his richt hand he had ane groundin speir,
Of his father the wraith fra us to weir.

Nixt efter him come Mars, the god of ire,
Of strife, debait, and all dissensioun,
To chide and fecht, als feirs as ony fyre; 185
In hard harnes, hewmound and habirgeoun,
And on his hanche ane roustie fell fachioun,
And in his hand he had ane roustie sword;
Wrything his face with mony angrie word.

Schaikand his sword, befoir Cupide he come 190
With reid visage, and grislie glowrand ene;

164. *gyte*—cloak is probably correct though one editor (Elliott) prefers
gyis—guise, attire, which is the Charteris reading. *Cf.* lines 178, 260
and *Wife of Bath's Prologue*, line 559.

And at his mouth ane bullar stude of fome
Lyke to ane bair quhetting his tuskis kene,
Richt tuilyeour-lyke, but temperance in tene:
Ane horne he blew, with mony bosteous brag   195
Quhilk all this warld with weir hes maid to wag.

Than fair Phebus, lanterne and lamp of licht
Of man and beist, baith frute and flourisching,
Tender nureis and banischer of nicht,
And of the warld causing, be his moving   200
And influence, lyfe in all eirdlie thing,
Without comfort of quhome, of force to nocht
Must all ga die that in this warld is wrocht.

As king royall he raid upon his chair
The quhilk Phaeton gydit sum tyme unricht;   205
The brichtnes of his face quhen it was bair
Nane micht behald for peirsing of his sicht.
This goldin cart with fyrie bemis bricht
Four yokkit steidis full different of hew,
But bait or tyring, throw the spheiris drew.   210

The first was soyr, with mane als reid as rois,
Callit Eoye into the orient.
The secund steid to name hecht Ethios,
Quhitlie and paill, and sum deill ascendent.
The thrid Peros, richt hait and richt fervent;   215
The feird was blak and callit Philologie
Quhilk rollis Phebus doun into the sey.

Venus was thair present, that goddes [gay],
Hir sonnis querrell for to defend and mak
Hir awin complaint, cled in ane nyce array,   220

---

194. *tuilyeour*—a swaggerer or bravo.
211. The horses' names are from Ovid, *Metamorphoses*, II, 153–5. *Philologie* (216) is properly *Phlegon*, but see Fox, *edn. cit.* pp. 103–5nn.

The ane half grene, the uther half sabill black.
Quhyte hair as gold kemmit and sched abak,
Bot in hir face semit greit variance,
Quhyles perfyte treuth, and quhyles inconstance.

*being a victim
of such a god!
– no wonder Cris.
curse her*

225

Under smyling scho was dissimulait,
Provocative, with blenkis amorous,
And suddanely changit and alterait,
Angrie as ony serpent vennemous,
Richt pungitive, with wordis odious;
Thus variant scho was, quha list tak keip,   230
With ane eye lauch, and with the uther weip.

In taikning that all fleschelie paramour
Quhilk Venus hes in reull and governance,
Is sum type sweit, sum tyme bitter and sour,
Richt unstabill and full of variance,   235
Mingit with cairfull joy and fals plesance,
Now hait, now cauld, now blyith, now full of wo,
Now grene as leif, now widderit and ago.

With buik in hand than come Mercurius,
Richt eloquent and full of rethorie,   240
With polite termis and delicious,
With pen and ink to report al reddie;
Setting sangis and singand merilie.
His hude was reid, heklit atouir his croun,
Lyke to ane poeit of the auld fassoun.   245

Boxis he bair with fine electuairis,
And sugerit syropis for digestioun,
Spycis belangand to the pothecairis,
With mony hailsum sweit confectioun.
Doctour in phisick, cled in ane skarlot goun   250
And furrit weill, as sic ane aucht to be,

218–38. Venus is here associated with the twists of Fortune.

Honest and gude, and not ane word culd le.

Nixt efter him come Lady Cynthia, (Moon)
The last of all and swiftest in hir spheir,
Of colour blak, buskit with hornis twa,   255
And in the nicht scho listis best appeir.
Haw as the leid, of colour nathing cleir;
For all hir licht scho borrowis at hir brother
Titan, for of hirself scho hes nane uther.

Hir gyte was gray, and full of spottis blak,   260
And on hir breist ane churle paintit full evin,
Beirand ane bunche of thornis on his bak,
Quhilk for his thift micht clim na nar the hevin.
Thus quhen thay gadderit war, thir Goddes sevin,
Mercurius thay cheisit with ane assent   265
To be foirspeikar in the parliament.

Quha had bene thair and liken for to heir
His facound toung and termis exquisite,
Of rethorick the prettick he micht leir,
In breif sermone and pregnant sentence wryte.   270
Befoir Cupide, veiling his cap a lyte,
Speiris the caus of that vocatioun,
And he anone schew his intentioun.

'Lo!' (quod Cupide) 'quha will blaspheme the name
Of his awin god, outher in word or deid,   275
To all goddis he dois baith lak and schame,
And suld have bitter panis to his meid.
I say this by yone wretchit Cresseid,

239–52. Mercury is presented according to astrological tradition as a sophisticated scholar. The Romans associated him with medicine (250) and Henryson here stresses his many-sidedness, as musician and as deity of liars and thieves (243, 252), as well as of traders (the ironic allusion to his honesty and truthfulness in 252). *Cf.* Fox, *op. cit.*, 107*n.*

253. *Cynthia* (the moon) represents change, a sign of corruption and thus of evil.

The quhilk throw me was sum tyme flour of lufe,
Me and my mother starklie can reprufe,   280

'Saying of hir greit infelicitie
I was the caus, and my mother Venus,
Ane blind goddes hir cald, that micht not se,
With sclander and defame injurious.
Thus hir leving unclene and lecherous   285
Scho wald returne on me and my mother
To quhome I schew my grace abone all uther.

'And sen ye ar all sevin deificait,
Participant of devyne sapience,
This greit injure done to our hie estait   290
Me think with pane we suld mak recompence.
Was never to goddes done sic violence.
As weill for yow, as for my self I say,
Thairfoir ga help to revenge I yow pray.'

Mercurius to Cupide gave answeir,   295
And said: 'Schir king, my counsall is that ye
Refer yow to the hiest planeit heir,
And tak to him the lawest of degre,
The pane of Cresseid for to modifie.
As god Saturne, with him tak Cynthia.'   300
'I am content' (quod he) 'to tak thay twa.'

Than thus proceidit Saturne and the Mone
Quhen thay the mater rypelie had degest,
For the dispyte to Cupide scho had done,
And to Venus oppin and manifest,   305
In all hir lyfe with pane to be opprest

290. *injure*—preferred to *injurie* as metrically superior and better Middle Scots. *injurie* is an English form not adopted during Henryson's lifetime. *Cf. injure, Troilus and Criseyde*, III, 1018.

---

287. *quhome*—i.e. Cresseid.
297. *Saturn*—pre-eminent among the gods. He does not speak in the debate but together with Cynthia pronounces sentence on Cresseid.

And torment sair, with seiknes incurabill,
And to all lovers be abhominabill.

This duleful sentence Saturne tuik on hand
And passit doun quhair cairfull Cresseid lay,   310
And on hir heid he laid ane frostie wand.
Than lawfullie on this wyse can he say:
'Thy greit fairnes and all thy bewtie gay,
Thy wanton blude, and eik thy goldin hair,
Heir I exclude fra the for evermair.   315

'I change thy mirth into melancholy
Quhilk is the mother of all pensivenes.
Thy moisture and thy heit in cald and dry,
Thyne insolence, thy play and wantones
To greit diseis; thy pomp and thy riches   320
In mortal neid, and greit penuritie
Thou suffer sall, and as ane beggar die.'

O cruell Saturne, fraward and angrie!
Hard is thy dome and to malitious.
On fair Cresseid quhy hes thou na mercie,   325
Quhilk was sa sweit, gentill and amorous?
Withdraw thy sentence and be gracious
As thou was never; so schawis thow thy deid,
Ane wraikfull sentence gevin on fair Cresseid.

Than Cynthia quhen Saturne past away,   330
Out of hir sait discendit doun belyve,
And red ane bill on Cresseid quhair scho lay,
Contening this sentence diffinityve:
'Fra heit of bodie I the now depryve

316–22. Henryson uses astrological tradition cleverly; the details of cold and dryness are rooted in medieval physiology (see Elliott, *ed. cit.* 152*n.*). *Cf. Cock and Fox*, line 123.

326. *amorous*—affectionate.

332. *red ane bill*—passed sentence, reading from a formal document.

And to thy seiknes sal be na recure, 335
Bot in dolour thy dayis to indure.

'Thy cristall ene minglit with blude I mak,
Thy voice sa cleir, unplesand hoir and hace,
Thy lustie lyre ourispred with spottis blak,
And lumpis haw appeirand in thy face. 340
Quhair thou cumis ilk man sal fle the place.
This sall thou go begging fra hous to hous
With cop and clapper lyke ane lazarous.'

This doolie dreame, this uglye visioun
Brocht to ane end, Cresseid fra it awoik, 345
And all the court and convocatioun
Vanischit away, than rais scho up and tuik
Ane poleist glas, and hir schaddow culd luik.
And quhen scho saw hir face sa deformait,
Gif scho in hart was wa aneuch, God wait. 350

Weiping full sair, 'Lo quhat it is' (quod sche)
'With fraward langage for to mufe and steir
Our craibit goddis, and sa is sene on me:
My blaspheming now have I bocht full deir.
All eirdlie joy and mirth I set areir. 355
Allace this day, allace this wofull tyde,
Quhen I began with my goddis for to chyde.'

Be this was said ane chyld come fra the hall
To warne Cresseid the supper was reddy:
First knokkit at the dure and syne culd call: 360
'Madame, your father biddis yow cum in hy;
He has mervell sa lang on grouf ye ly,
And sayis your prayers bene to lang sum deill.
The goddis wait all your intent full weill.'

---

342. *This*—thus.   **362.** *on grouf*—grovelling.
334–43. Henryson depicts the symptoms of leprosy with great care. Though
not especially contagious, it was feared as a visitation of the devil and some of
this fear lingers on to this day. *Cf.* Introduction, p. 30 and *nn.* 30, 31.

Quod scho: 'Fair chyld, ga to my father deir   365
And pray him cum to speik with me anone.'
And sa he did, and said: 'Douchter quhat cheir?'
'Allace' (quod scho) 'Father, my mirth is gone.'
'How sa?' (quod he) and scho can all expone
As I have tauld, the vengeance and the wraik   370
For hir trespass, Cupide on hir culd tak.

He luikit on hir uglye lipper face,
The quhilk befor was quhite as lillie flour,
Wringand his handis oftymes he said allace
That he had levit to se that wofull hour!   375
For he knew weill that thair was na succour
To hir seiknes, and that dowblit his pane.
Thus was thair cair aneuch betuix thame twane.

Quhen that togidder murnit had full lang,
Quod Cresseid: 'Father, I wald not be kend.   380
Thairfoir in secreit wyse ye let me gang
Into yon hospitall at the tounis end,
And thidder sum meit for cheritie me send
To leif upon, for all mirth in this eird
Is fra me gane—sic is my wickit weird!'   385

Than in ane mantill and ane bawer hat
With cop and clapper wonder prively,
He opnit ane secreit yet and out thair at
Convoyit hir, that na man suld espy,
Into ane village half ane myle thairby,   390
Delyverit hir in at the spittaill hous,
And daylie sent hir part of his almous

Sum knew her weill, and sum had na knawledge
Of hir, becaus scho was sa deformait,

---

386. The description could refer to Calchas, who wishes to leave un-
recognized. Change of hat was a sign of change of fortune, though it seems
unlikely that he and not Cresseid carried the cap and clapper through the
gate.

With bylis blak ouirspred in hir visage 395
And hir fair colour faidit and alterait.
Yit thay presumit for her hie regrait
And still murning, scho was of nobill kin.
With better will thairfoir they tuik hir in.

The day passit and Phebus went to rest. 400
The cloudis blak ouirquhelmit all the sky.
God wait gif Cresseid was ane sorrowfull gest,
Seeing that uncouth fair and harbery!
But meit or drink scho dressit hir to ly
In ane dark corner of the hous allone. 405
An on this wyse, weiping, scho maid her mone:

The Complaint of Cresseid

'O sop of sorrow, sonkin into cair!
O cative Creisseid, for now and ever mair,
Gane is thy joy and all thy mirth in eird.
Of all blyithnes now art thou blaiknit bair; 410
Thair is na salve may saif the of thy sair.
Fell is thy fortoun, wickit is thy weird;
Thy blys is baneist and thy baill on breird,
Under the eirth God gif I gravin wer
Quhair nane of Grece nor yit of Troy micht heird. 415

'Quhair is thy chalmer wantounlie besene?
With burely bed and bankouris browderit bene,
Spycis and wyne to thy collatioun,
The cowpis all of gold and silver schene;
The sweit meitis, servit in plaittis clene, 420
With saipheron sals of ane gud sessoun?
Thy gay garmentis with mony gudely goun,
Thy plesand lawn pinnit with goldin prene?
All is areir, thy greit royall renoun.

---

413. *breird*—first shoots. *thy baill on breird*—your misery is about to begin.

'Quhair is thy garding with thir greissis gay   425
And fresche flowris, quhilk the quene Floray
Had paintit plesandly in everie pane?
Quhair thou was wont full merilye in May,
To walk and tak the dew be it was day,
And heir the merle and mawis mony ane,   430
With ladyis fair in carrolling to gane,
And se the royall rinkis in thair array,
In garmentis gay garnischit on everie grane.

'Thy greit triumphand fame and hie honour,
Quhair thou was callit of eirdlye wichtis flour,   435
All is decayit, thy weird is welterit so:
Thy hie estait is turnit in darknes dour.
This lipper ludge tak for thy burelie bour,
And for thy bed tak now ane bunche of stro.
For waillit wyne and meitis thou had tho,   440
Tak mowlit breid, peirrie and ceder sour.
Bot cop and clapper, now is all ago.

'My cleir voice, and courtlie carrolling,
Quhair I was wont with ladyis for to sing,
Is rawk as ruik, full hiddeous, hoir and hace,   445
My plesand port all utheris precelling;
Of lustines I was hald maist conding.
Now is deformit the figour of my face;
To luik on it na leid now lyking hes.
Sowpit in syte, I say with sair siching,   450
Ludgeit amang the lipper leid, "allace!"

'O ladyis fair of Troy and Grece, attend
My miserie, quhilk nane may comprehend;
My frivoll fortoun, my infelicitie,
My greit mischeif quhilk na man can amend.   455
Be war in tyme, approchis neir the end,

438–41. As in the ME *Sir Orfeo*, change of fortune is explained in terms of a marked contrast in living conditions, a device brought to perfection in *King Lear*.

And in your mynd ane mirrour mak of me.
As I am now, peradventure that ye
For all your micht may cum to that same end,
Or ellis war, gif ony war may be. 460

'Nocht is your fairnes bot ane faiding flour,
Nocht is your famous laud and hie honour
Bot wind inflat in uther mennis eiris.
Your roising reid to rotting sall retour.
Exempill mak of me in your memour, 465
Quhilk of sic thingis wofull witnes beiris.
All welth in eird, away as wind it weiris.
Be war thairfoir, approchis neir the hour:
Fortoun is fikkill, quhen scho beginnis and steiris.'

Thus chydand with hir drerie destenye, 470
Weiping, scho woik the nicht fra end to end.
Bot all in vane! Hir dule, hir cairfull cry,
Micht not remeid, nor yit hir murning mend.
Ane lipper lady rais and till hir wend
And said: 'Quhy spurnis thow aganis the wall, 475
To sla thyself, and mend nathing at all?

'Sen thy weiping dowbillis bot thy wo,
I counsall the mak vertew of ane neid,
To leir to clap thy clapper to and fro,
And leif efter the law of lipper leid.' 480
Thair was na buit, bot furth with thame scho yeid,
Fra place to place, quhill cauld and hounger sair
Compellit hir to be ane rank beggair.

That samin tyme of Troy the garnisoun,
Quhilk had to chiftane worthie Troylus, 485
Throw jeopardie of weir had strikken doun
Knichtis of Grece in number mervellous.
With greit tryumphe and laude victorious

---

480. Some editors prefer *leir* to *leif*.

Agane to Troy richt royallie they raid
The way quhair Cresseid with the lipper baid.   490

Seing that companie, thai come all with ane stevin;
Thay gaif ane cry and schuik coppis gude speid.
Said 'Worthie lordis, for goddis lufe of hevin,
To us lipper part of your almous deid.'
Than to thair cry nobill Troylus tuik heid,   495
Having pietie, neir by the place can pas
Quhair Cresseid sat, not witting quhat scho was.

Than upon him scho kest up baith hir ene,
And with ane blenk it come into his thocht
That he sumtime hir face befoir had sene,   500
But scho was in sic plye he knew hir nocht.
Yit than hir luik into his mynd it brocht
The sweit visage and amorous blenking
Of fair Cresseid, sumtyme his awin darling.

Na wonder was, suppois in mynd that he   505
Tuik hir figure sa sone, and lo now, quhy?
The idole of ane thing in cace may be
Sa deip imprentit in the fantasy
That it deludis the wittis outwardly,
And sa appeiris in forme and lyke estait,   510
Within the mynd as it was figurait.

Ane spark of lufe than till his hart culd spring
And kendlit all his bodie in ane fyre.
With hait fewir ane sweit and trimbling
Him tuik, quhill he was reddie to expyre.   515
To beir his scheild, his breist began to tyre;

---

498. Cresseid does not recognize him, possibly because she is partially blinded by the disease, a harshly ironic association with the blindness of Venus (and of Cupid).

505-11. An Aristotelian theory (see M. W. Stearns, *Robert Henryson* (New York 1947), 98–105).

510-11. And so the image appears just as it had been formed in the memory.

Within ane quhyle he changit mony hew,
And nevertheless not ane ane uther knew.

For knichtlie pietie and memoriall
Of fair Cresseid, ane gyrdill can he tak, 520
Ane purs of gold, and mony gay jowall,
And in the skirt of Cresseid doun can swak:
Than raid away and not ane word he spak
Pensive in hart, quhill he come to the toun,
And for greit care oftsyis almaist fell doun. 525

The lipper folk to Cresseid than can draw,
To se the equall distribution
Of the almous, bot quhen the gold they saw,
Ilk ane to uther prevelie can roun,
And said: 'Yone lord hes mair affectioun, 530
How ever it be, unto yone lazarous,
Than to us all; we knaw be his almous.'

'Quhat lord is yone' (quod scho), 'have ye na feill,
Hes done to us so greit humanitie?'
'Yes' (quod a lipper man), 'I knaw him weill. 535
Schir Troylus it is, gentill and fre.'
Quhen Cresseid understude that it was he,
Stiffer than steill, thair stert ane bitter stound
Throwout hir hart and fell doun to the ground.

Quhen scho ouircome, with siching sair and sad, 540
With mony cairfull cry and cald ochane:
'Now is my breist with stormie stoundis stad,
Wrappit in wo, ane wretch full will of wane.'
Than swounit scho oft or scho culd refrane
And ever in hir swouning cryit scho thus: 545
'O fals Cresseid and trew knicht Troylus.

'Thy lufe, thy lawtie, and thy gentilnes,

---

540. *ouircome*—recovered. *Cf. Orpheus and Eurydice*, 400.
541. *ochane*—alas! (a Gaelic expression of sorrow).

I countit small in my prosperitie,
Sa elevait I was in wantones,
And clam upon the fickill quheill sa hie.   550
All faith and lufe I promissit to the,
Was in the self fickill and frivolous.
O fals Cresseid, and trew knicht Troilus!

'For lufe of me thou keipt gude continence,
Honest and chaist in conversatioun,   555
Of all wemen protectour and defence
Thou was, and helpit thair opinioun.
My mynd in fleschelie foull affectioun
Was inclylynit to lustis lecherous.
Fy, fals Cresseid, O trew knicht Troylus!   560

'Lovers, be war and tak gud heid about
Quhome that ye lufe, for quhome ye suffer paine.
I lat yow wit, thair is richt few thairout
Quhome ye may traist to have trew lufe agane.
Preif quhen ye will, your labour is in vaine.   565
Thairfoir, I reid, ye tak thame as ye find,
For thay ar sad as widdercock in wind.

'Becaus I knaw the greit unstabilnes
Brukkill as glas, into myself I say,
Traisting in uther als greit unfaithfulnes,   570
Als unconstant, and als untrew of fay.
Thocht sum be trew, I wait richt few ar thay.
Quha findis treuth lat him his lady ruse.
Nane but myself as now I will accuse.'

Quhen this was said, with paper scho sat doun,   575
And on this maneir maid hir testament.

---

550. A reference to the wheel of fortune, recalling *Troilus and Criseyde*, IV, 323–4.

567. *sad*—stable, predictable. A frequently-used simile. *Cf. Clerk's Tale*, line 939.

570. *traisting in uther*—'expecting to find in others'.

'Heir I beteiche my corps and carioun
With wormis and with taidis to be rent.
My cop and clapper and myne ornament,
And all my gold the lipper folk sall have,   580
Quhen I am deid, to burie me in grave.

'This royal ring, set with this rubie reid,
Quhilk Troylus in drowrie to me send,
To him agane I leif it quhen I am deid,
To mak my cairfull deid unto him kend.   585
Thus I conclude schortlie and mak ane end:
My spreit I leif to Diane quhair scho dwellis,
To walk with hir in waist woddis and wellis.

'O Diomeid, thou hes baith broche and belt
Quhilk Troylus gave me in takning   590
Of his trew lufe'—and with that word scho swelt.
And sone ane lipper man tuik of the ring,
Syne buryit hir withouttin tarying.
To Troylus furthwith the ring he bair,
And of Cresseid the deith he can declair.   595

Quhen he had hard his greit infirmitie,
Hir legacie and lamentatioun,
And how scho endit in sic povertie,
He swelt for wo and fell doun in ane swoun.
For greit sorrow his hart to brist was boun.   600
Siching full sadlie, said: 'I can no moir:
Scho was untrew and wo is me thairfoir.'

Sum said he maid ane tomb of merbell gray,
And wrait hir name and superscriptioun,
And laid it on hir grave quhair that scho lay   605
In goldin letteris, conteining this ressoun:

582–3. Troilus's gift, according to Chaucer, was a brooch (V, 1040, 1660–94).
588. *wellis*—streams. Gregory Smith suggested 'fountains', associated with Diana, but this seems incongruous in the context.

E

'Lo, fair ladyis, Cresseid, of Troyis toun,
Sumtyme countit the flour of womanheid,
Under this stane, lait lipper, lyis deid.'

Now worthie wemen, in this ballet short   610
Made for your worschip and instructioun,
Of cheritie, I monische and exhort:
Ming not your lufe with fals deceptioun:
Beir in your mynd this schort conclusioun
Of fair Cresseid—as I have said befoir.   615
Sen scho is deid I speik of hir no moir.

Finis

614. *schort conclusioun*—Thynne's 1532 edition has 'sore', which
avoids the repetition from line 610, but is for that reason less character-
istic of Henryson.

610–6. Cresseid is the universal figure of suffering womanhood as well as a
symbol of the mistrusted Eve castigated by popular preachers in the St Jerome
tradition. In her dual role she is an example to other women of the results of
infidelity, for she is endowed with just enough humanity to maintain their
sympathies.

William Dunbar

IX. *Lament for the Makars*

THOUGH not especially typical of Dunbar, this is his best-known poem. In the *ubi sunt* tradition of complaint, the substance is that of a medieval sermon on vanity. The refrain, a line from the Office for the Dead, is not a personal comment; it emphasizes the remorselessness of the procession to the grave.

MSS: Bannatyne (f.109a–f.110a); Maitland Folio 190–2.
Printed in Dunbar's lifetime by Chepman and Myllar (1508), on which the following
    version is based.

I that in heill wes and gladnes,
Am trublit now with gret seiknes,
And feblit with infermite:
Timor mortis conturbat me.

Our plesance heir is all vane glory,
This fals warld is bot transitory,
The flesch is brukle, the fend is sle:
Timor mortis conturbat me.

The stait of man dois change and vary
Now sound, now seik, now blith, now sary   10
Now dansand mery, now like to dee:
Timor mortis conturbat me.

No stait in erd heir standis sickir;
As with the wynd wavis the wickir,
Wavis this warldis vanite: 15
Timor mortis conturbat me.

On to the ded gois all estatis,
Princis, prelotis, and potestatis,
Baith riche and pur of al degre:
Timor mortis conturbat me.   2

15. Print has *vainte*.

He takis the knychtis into the feild,
Anarmyt under helme and scheild;
Victour he is at all mellie:
Timor mortis conturbat me.

That strang unmercifull tyrand   25
Takis, on the moderis breist sowkand,
The bab full of benignite:
Timor mortis conturbat me.

He takis the campion in the stour,
The capitane closit in the tour,   30
The lady in bour full of bewte:
Timor mortis conturbat me.

He sparis no lord for his piscence,
Na clerk for his intelligence;
His awfull strak may no man fle: 35
Timor mortis conturbat me.

Art, magicianis, and astrologgis,
Rethoris, logicianis, and theologgis,
Thame helpis no conclusionis sle:
Timor mortis conturbat me.   40

In medicyne the most practicianis,
Lechis, surrigianis, and phisicianis,
Thame self fra ded may not supple:
Timor mortis conturbat me.

I se that makaris amang the laif   45
Playis heir ther pageant, syne gois to graif;
Sparit is nocht ther faculte:
Timor mortis conturbat me.

21. Print has *knythis*. Bannatyne inserts *the* before *feild*.
Maitland reads *in the*.
47. Print has *naught* (similarly 62, 94).

33. *for*—in respect of.

He has done petuously devour,
The noble Chaucer, of makaris flour,   50
The Monk of Bery, and Gower, all thre:
Timor mortis conturbat me.

The gud Syr Hew of Eglintoun,
And eik Heryot, and Wyntoun,
He has tane out of this cuntre: 55
Timor mortis conturbat me.

That scorpion fell has done infek
Maister Johne Clerk, and James Afflek,
Fra balat making and trigide:
Timor mortis conturbat me.   60

Holland and Barbour he has berevit;
Allace! that he nocht with us levit
Schir Mungo Lokert of the Le:
Timor mortis conturbat me.

Clerk of Tranent eik he has tane,   65
That maid the Anteris of Gawane;

59. Both MSS have *tragidie.*

---

51. *the monk of Bery*—Lydgate, d. 1449; Lydgate also used the 'Timor mortis' refrain in a poem on the same subject.

53. *Sir Hew of Eglintoun*—d. 1377 but not known as a poet.

54. *Heryot*—unknown; *Wyntoun*—author of the *Orygynale Cronikil*, d. *c.* 1423.

58. *Johne Clerk*—unknown, though the Bannatyne MS contains some poems by a 'Clerk'. The name was common *Affiek* (Auchinleck?)—unknown.

61. *Holland*—d. *c.* 1482, author of *The Buke of the Howlat*. *Barbour*—d. *c.* 1395, author of *Bruce.*

63. *Schir Mungo Lockert of the Le*—a knight of this name d. 1489.

65. *Clerk of Tranent*—unknown.

66. *Anteris of Gawane*—Wyntoun refers to such a poem as the work of Huchown of the Awle Ryall, so that it is possible that Clerk and Huchown are the same person. One MS (Maitland) reads 'the clerk' of Tranent in line 65. By earlier scholars *The Adventures of Gawain* was thought to be *Sir Gawain and the Green Knight* or possibly *Gologros and Gawane*, which was also printed by Chepman and Myllar.

Schir Gilbert Hay endit has he:
Timor mortis conturbat me.

He has Blind Hary and Sandy Traill
Slaine with his schour of mortall haill,   70
Quhilk Patrik Johnestoun mycht nocht fle:
Timor mortis conturbat me.

He has reft Merseir his endite,
That did in luf so lifly write,
So schort, so quyk, of sentence hie: 75
Timor mortis conturbat me.

He has tane Roull of Aberdene,
And gentill Roull of Corstorphin;
Two bettir fallowis did no man se:
Timor mortis conturbat me.   80

In Dumfermelyne he has done roune
With Maister Robert Henrisoun;
Schir Johne the Ros enbrast has he:
Timor mortis conturbat me.

---

67. *Schir Gilbert Hay*—d. 1456, translated *The Buke of Alexander* and other works from the French.

69. *Blind Hary*—d. *c.* 1480, author of *Wallace*. *Sandy Traill*—unknown.

71. *Patrik Johnestoun*—d. *c.* 1405, actor and writer of interludes. In the Bannatyne MS *The Thre Deid Pollis* is ascribed to him. See p. 71 above.

73. *Merseir*—unknown, though both Bannatyne and Maitland MSS assign some poems to a 'Mersar' or 'Marsar'. *Endite* here means 'talent for composition'.

77. *Roull of Aberdene*—unknown.

78. *Roull of Corstorphin*—the poem known in the Bannatyne MS as *The cursing of Sir Johine Rowlis* may be his but otherwise he is unknown.

82. *Maister Robert Henrisoun*—Dunbar's contemporary, so described in the print and MSS. He died, presumably in 1505, too early to oversee the prints of his poems.

83. *Schir Johne the Ros*—mentioned in *The Flyting of Dunbar and Kennedie*, line 1, and thought by earlier scholars to have been author of *Wallace*, but otherwise unknown.

And he has now tane, last of aw, 85
Gud gentill Stobo and Quintyne Schaw,
Of quham all wichtis has pete:
Timor mortis conturbat me.

Gud Maister Walter Kennedy
In poynt of dede lyis veraly, 90
Gret reuth it wer that so suld be:
Timor mortis conturbat me.

Sen he has all my brether tane,
He will nocht lat me lif alane,
On forse I man his nyxt pray be: 95
Timor mortis conturbat me.

Sen for the ded remeid is none,
Best is that we for dede dispone,
Eftir our deid that lif may we:
Timor mortis conturbat me. 100

quod Dunbar quhen he wes sek.

---

86. *Stobo*—d. 1505. Royal secretary to James II, III and IV. Mentioned in *The Flyting*, line 331. His real name was John Reid, Stobo his village of origin. *Quintyne Schaw*—probably an Ayrshire landowner, the 'Quinting' or 'Quintene' referred to in *The Flyting*, lines 2, 34, who died *c.* 1505.

89. *Maister Walter Kennedy*—Dunbar's opponent in *The Flyting* described as in the Bannatyne and Maitland MSS which contain his poems. He and Dunbar are the only two living makars on the list.

95. *man*—must. Dunbar did not die at this time. External evidence suggests that the poem was written during the second half of 1505. As it was printed in 1508, he must have joined the procession many years after its composition. It has been suggested that he died at Flodden, though there is no evidence for this and he may have survived until 1521. The last recorded payment to him is that of 14th May, 1513, four months before Flodden.

97-100. A conventional ending. Compare Henryson's *The Thre Deid Pollis, In Prais of Aige, The Abbay Walk* and Dunbar's *Of Manis Mortalitie.*

William Dunbar

X. The Goldyn Targe

WITH *The Thressill and the Rois*, this is Dunbar's most ambitious composition in French allegorical form. In line 259 he refers to Chaucer's and his own language as 'oure Inglisch', and the stanza is that used by Chaucer in the 'Compleynt of Anelida the quene upon fals Arcite'. The Prologue to the dream (lines 1-45) has been called Chaucerian in manner; some indebtedness is clear. But this dazzling landscape, against which the light of sunrise splinters, is quite alien to Chaucer. So, too, is the poet's wild verbal intoxication, as the May morning explodes upon his literary senses in a shower of roses, singing-birds and jewels.

MSS: *Bannatyne MS f.345a–348b, Maitland Folio 64–81, and in the contents list of Asloan, of which the relevant portion is lost.*
Printed by Chepman and Myllar (1508), the basis of the following version.

> Ryght as the stern of day begouth to schyne,
> Quhen gone to bed war Vesper and Lucyne,
>   I raise, and by a rosere did me rest;
> Up sprang the goldyn candill matutyne,
> With clere depurit bemes cristallyne,   5
>   Glading the mery foulis in thair nest;
>   Or Phebus was in purpur cape revest
> Up raise the lark, the hevyns menstrale fyne
> In May, in till a morrow myrthfullest.
>
> Full angellike thir birdis sang thair houris   10
> Within thair courtyns grene, in to thair bouris
>   Apparalit quhite and red wyth blomes suete;

---

2. *Vesper*—evening; *Lucyne*—moon.

4-5. These lines demonstrate how 'aureation', at its best, is not mere ornament, but an extension of language in the service of the imagination. The use of the Latinate 'matutyne' and 'cristallyne' emphasizes the shining ritual of sunrise: the juxtaposition of 'sprang', 'goldyn' and 'clere' reminds us of the instinctive response to natural beauty.

7. *purpur*—dark red rather than purple (similarly 26, 41).

10. *houris*—*horae* or day-hours of the Church.

Anamalit was the felde wyth all colouris,
The perly droppis schake in silvir schouris,
   Quhill all in balme did branch and levis flete: 15
   To part fra Phebus did Aurora grete,
Hir cristall teris I saw hyng on the flouris,
   Quhilk he for lufe all drank up wyth his hete.

For mirth of May, with skippis and wyth hoppis,
The birdis sang upon the tender croppis,   20
   With curiouse note, as Venus chapell clerkis:
The rosis yong, new spreding of their knopis,
War powderit brycht with hevinly beriall droppis,
   Throu bemes rede birnyng as ruby sperkis;
   The skyes rang for schoutyng of the larkis,   25
The purpur hevyn, ourscailit in silvir sloppis,
   Ourgilt the treis, branchis, lef, and barkis.

Doune throu the ryce a ryvir ran wyth stremys,
So lustily agayn thai lykand lemys,
   That all the lake as lamp did leme of licht,   30
Quhilk schadowit all about wyth twynkling glemis;
That bewis bathit war in secund bemys
   Throu the reflex of Phebus visage brycht;
   On every syde the hegies raise on hicht,
The bank was grene, the bruke was full of bremys,   35
   The stanneris clere as stern in frosty nycht.

The cristall air, the sapher firmament,
The ruby skyes of the orient,
   Kest beriall bemes on emerant bewis grene;
The rosy garth, depaynt and redolent,   40
With purpur, azure, gold, and goulis gent
   Arayed was, by Dame Flora the quene,
   So nobily, that joy was for to sene;

---

13. *anamalit*—enamelled. The reference to the decorative arts points the highly-wrought nature of the poetry. *Cf.* 251, 257.
20. *tender croppis*—a Chaucerian echo.
35. *bremys*—bream, a freshwater fish.

E*

The roch agayn the rivir resplendent
  As low enlumynit all the leves schene.   45

Quhat throu the mery foulys armony,
And throu the ryveris soune rycht ran me by,
  On Florais mantill I slepit as I lay,
Quhare sone in to my dremes fantasy
I saw approch, agayn the orient sky,   50
  A saill, als quhite as blossum upon spray,
  Wyth merse of gold, brycht as the stern of day,
Quhilk tendit to the land full lustily,
  As falcoune swift desyrouse of hir pray.

And hard on burd unto the blomyt medis,   55
Amang the grene rispis and the redis,
  Arrivit sche, quhar fro anone thare landis
Ane hundreth ladyes, lusty in to wedis,
Als fresch as flouris that in May up spredis,
  In kirtillis grene, withoutyn kell or bandis: 60
  Thair brycht hairis hang gletering on the strandis
In tressis clere, wyppit with goldyn thredis;
  With pappis quhite, and mydlis small as wandis.

Discrive I wald, bot quho coud wele endyte
How all the feldis wyth thai lilies quhite   65
  Depaynt war brycht, quhilk to the hevyn did glete:
Noucht thou, Omer, als fair as thou coud wryte,
For all thine ornate stilis so perfyte;
  Nor yit thou, Tullius, quhois lippis suete
  Off rethorike did in to termes flete: 70
Your aureate tongis both bene all to lyte,
  For to compile that paradise complete.

Thare saw I Nature and Venus, quene and quene,
The fresch Aurora, and lady Flora schene,
  Juno, Appollo, and Proserpyna,   75

---

69. *Tullius*—Cicero.

Dyane the goddesse chaste of woddis grene,
My lady Cleo, that help of makaris bene,
   Thetes, Pallas, and prudent Minerva,
   Fair feynit Fortune, and lemand Lucina,
Thir mychti quenis in crounis mycht be sene,   80
   Wyth bemys blith, bricht as Lucifera.

There saw I May, of myrthfull monethis quene,
Betuix Aprile and June, her sistir schene,
   Within the gardyng walking up and doun,
Quham of the foulis gladdith al bedene;   85
Scho was full tender in hir yeris grene.
   Thare saw I Nature present hir a goune
   Rich to behald and nobil of renoune,
Off eviry hew under the hevin that bene
   Depaynt, and broud be gude proporcioun.   90

Full lustily thir ladyes all in fere
Enterit within this park of most plesere,
   Quhare that I lay ourhelit wyth levis ronk;
The mery foulis, blisfullest of chere,
Salust Nature, me thoucht, on thair manere,   95
   And eviry blome on branch, and eke on bonk,
   Opnyt and spred thair balmy levis donk,
Full low enclynyng to thair quene so clere,
   Quham of thair nobill norising thay thonk.

Syne to dame Flora, on the samyn wyse,   100
Thay saluse, and thay thank a thousand syse;
   And to dame Venus, lufis mychti quene,
Thay sang ballettis in lufe, as was the gyse,
With amourouse notis lusty to devise,
   As thay that had lufe in thair hertis grene;   105
   Thair hony throtis, opnyt fro the splene,
With werblis suete did perse the hevinly skyes,
   Quhill loud resownyt the firmament serene.

---

106. *splene*—heart.

Ane othir court thare saw I consequent,
Cupide the king, wyth bow in hand ybent,   110
   And dredefull arowis grundyn scharp and square;
Thare saw I Mars, the god armypotent,
Aufull and sterne, strong and corpolent;
   Thare saw I crabbit Saturn ald and haire,
   His luke was lyke for to perturb the aire;   115
Thare was Mercurius, wise and eloquent,
   Of rethorike that fand the flouris faire;

Thare was the god of gardingis, Priapus;
Thare was the god of wildernes, Phanus;
   And Janus, god of entree delytable;   120
Thare was the god of fludis, Neptunus;
Thare was the god of wyndis, Eolus,
   With variand luke, rycht lyke a lord unstable;
   Thare was Bacus, the gladder of the table;
Thare was Pluto, the elrich incubus,   125
   In cloke of grene, his court usit no sable.

And eviry one of thir, in grene arayit,
On harp or lute full merily thai playit,
   And sang ballettis with michty notis clere:
Ladyes to dance full sobirly assayit,   130
Endlang the lusty ryvir so thai mayit,
   Thair observance rycht hevynly was to here;
   Than crap I throu the levis, and drew nere,
Quhare that I was rycht sudaynly affrayit,
   All throu a luke, quhilk I have boucht full dere.   135

And schortly for to speke, be lufis quene
I was aspyit, scho bad hir archearis kene
   Go me arrest; and thay no time delayit;
Than ladyes fair lete fall thair mantillis grene,
With bowis big in tressit hairis schene,   140

---

126. Green signified the presence of faëry.

136. Unlike the eavesdropper in *The Twa Mariit Wemen and the Wedo*, he is quickly detected.

All sudaynly thay had a felde arayit;
  And yit rycht gretly was I noucht affrayit,
The party was so plesand for to sene,
  A wonder lusty bikkir me assayit.

And first of all, with bow in hand ybent,   145
  Come dame Beautee, rycht as scho wald me schent;
    Syne folowit all hir dameselis yfere,
With mony diverse aufull instrument,
Unto the pres, Fair Having wyth hir went
  Fyne Portrature, Plesance, and lusty Chere.   150
    Than come Resoun, with schelde of gold so clere,
In plate and maille, as Mars armypotent,
  Defendit me that nobil chevallere.

Syne tender Youth come wyth hir virgyns ying,
  Grene Innocence, and schamefull Abaising,   155
    And quaking Drede, wyth humble Obedience;
The Goldyn Targe harmyt thay no thing;
Curage in thame was noucht begonne to spring;
  Full sore thay dred to done a violence:
    Suete Womanhede I saw cum in presence,   160
Of artilye a warld sche did in bring,
  Servit wyth ladyes full of reverence.

Sche led wyth hir Nurture and Lawlynes,
Contenence, Pacience, Gude Fame, and Stedfastnes,
  Discrecioun, Gentrise, and Considerance,   165
Levefell Company, and Honest Besynes,
Benigne Luke, Mylde Chere, and Sobirnes:
  All thir bure ganyeis to do me grevance;
    But Resoun bure the Targe wyth sik constance,
Thair scharp assayes mycht do no dures   170
  To me, for all thair aufull ordynance.

Unto the pres persewit Hie Degree,

---

157. *targe*—round shield.

Hir folowit ay Estate, and Dignitee,
　Comparisoun, Honour, and Noble Array,
Will, Wantonnes, Renoun, and Libertee, 175
Richesse, Fredome, and eke Nobilitee:
　　Wit ye thay did thair baner hye display;
　　A cloud of arowis as hayle schour lousit thay.
And schot, quhill wastit was their artilye.
　　Syne went abak reboytit of thair pray. 180

Quhen Venus had persavit this rebute,
Dissymilance scho bad go mak persute,
　At all powere to perse the Goldyn Targe;
And scho, that was of doubilnes the rute,
Askit hir choise of archeris in refute. 185
　　Venus the best bad hir go wale at large;
　　Scho tuke Presence, plicht ankers of the barge,
And Fair Callyng, that wele a flayn coud schute,
　　And Cherising for to complete hir charge.

Dame Hamelynes scho tuke in company, 190
That hardy was and hende in archery,
　And broucht dame Beautee to the felde agayn;
With all the choise of Venus chevalry
Thay come and bikkerit unabaisitly:
　　The schour of arowis rappit on as rayn; 195
　　Perilouse Presence, that mony syre has slayne,
The bataill broucht on bordour hard us by,
　　The salt was all the sarar suth to sayn.

Thik was the schote of grundyn dartis kene;
Bot Resoun, with the Scheld of Gold so schene, 200
　Warly defendit quho so evir assayit;
The aufull stoure he manly did sustene,
Quhill Presence kest a pulder in his ene,

201. Print has *assayes*; Bannatyne and Maitland MSS read *assayit*.

---

187. *plicht ankers*—sheet anchors.
190. *Hamelynes*—familiarity (*cf.* Lyndsay's *Thre Estaits*).

And than as drunkyn man he all forvayit:
Quhen he was blynd, the fule with hym thay playit,   205
And banyst hym amang the bewis grene;
   That sory sicht me sudaynly affrayit.

Than was I woundit to the deth wele nere,
And yoldyn as a wofull prisonnere
   To lady Beautee, in a moment space;   210
Me thoucht scho semyt lustiar of chere,
Efter that Resoun tynt had his eyne clere,
   Than of before, and lufliare of face:
   Quhy was thou blyndit, Resoun? Quhi, allace!
And gert ane hell my paradise appere,   215
   And mercy seme, quhare that I fand no grace.

Dissymulance was besy me to sile,
And Fair Calling did oft apon me smyle,
   And Cherising me fed wyth wordis fair;
New Acquyntance enbracit me a quhile,   220
And favouryt me, quhill men mycht go a myle,
   Syne tuk hir leve, I saw hir nevirmare:
   Than saw I Dangere toward me repair,
I coud eschew hir presence be no wyle.
   On syde scho lukit wyth ane fremyt fare.   225

And at the last departing coud hir dresse,
And me delyverit unto Hevynesse
   For to remayne, and scho in cure me tuke.
Be this the Lord of Wyndis, wyth wodenes.
God Eolus his bugill blew I gesse,   230
   That with the blast the levis all to-schuke;
   And sudaynly, in the space of a luke,
All was hyne went, thare was bot wildernes,
   Thare was no more bot birdis, bank, and bruke.

145–225. This is the central part of the poem—the conflict between Reason and the poet on one side, and the disciples of Venus, the Queen of Love, on the other, appropriated from *The Romaunt of the Rose. fare*—expression.

In twynkling of ane eye to schip thai went,   235
And swyth up saile unto the top thai stent,
   And with swift course atour the flude thay frak;
Thay fyrit gunnis with powder violent,
Till that the reke raise to the firmament,
   The rochis all resownyt wyth the rak,   240
   For rede it semyt that the raynbow brak;
Wyth spirit affrayde apon my fete I sprent
   Amang the clewis, so carefull was the crak.

And as I did awake of my sueving,
The joyfull birdis merily did syng   245
   For myrth of Phebus tendir bemes schene;
Suete war the vapouris, soft the morowing,
Halesum the vale, depaynt wyth flouris ying;
   The air attemperit, sobir, and amene;
   In quhite and rede was all the felde besene,   250
Throu naturis nobil fresch anamalyng,
   In mirthfull May, of eviry moneth Quene.

O reverend Chaucere, rose of rethoris all,
As in oure tong ane flour imperiall,
   That raise in Britane evir, quho redis rycht,   255
Thou beris of makaris the tryumph riall;
Thy fresch anamalit termes celicall
   This mater coud illumynit have full brycht:
   Was thou noucht of oure Inglisch all the lycht,
Surmounting eviry tong terrestriall,   260
   Alls fer as Mayis morow dois mydnycht?

O morall Gower, and Ludgate laureate,
Your sugurit lippis and tongis aureate,
   Bene to oure eris cause of grete delyte;
Your angel mouthis most mellifluate   265
Oure rude langage has clere illumynate,
   And fair ourgilt oure speche, that imperfyte

241-3. A nightmarish ending to the vision.

Stude, or your goldyn pennis schupe to write;
This ile before was bare and desolate
   Off rethorike or lusty fresch endyte. 270

Thou lytill quair, be evir obedient,
Humble, subject, and symple of entent,
   Before the face of eviry connyng wicht:
I knaw quhat thou of rethorike hes spent;
Off all hir lusty rosis redolent 275
   Is none in to thy gerland sett on hicht;
   Eschame tharof, and draw the out of sicht.
Rude is thy wede, disteynit, bare, and rent,
   Wele aucht thou be aferit of the licht.

274. Maitland MS has *may spend*; text here follows Bannatyne MS.

253–79. A conventional salutation to English poets in the Chaucerian tradition, cast in terms of excessive adulation (*cf. Kingis Quair*, stanza 197; *Aeneid*, Prologue to Book I, 339–43).

William Dunbar

XI. *The Tretis of the Twa Mariit Wemen and the Wedo*

THIS is Dunbar's longest poem and the only one cast in an alliterative un-rhymed metre, which it at times burlesques, as for example in the opening ten lines, where the conventions of the allegorical rose garden are exaggerated and indeed caricatured. The satire, both literary and social, is pungent and the scatological elements in Dunbar's humour, like Villon's, look forward to Swift in English and Burns in Scots. Unlike Swift, however, Dunbar means to amuse rather than to disgust. *The Tretis* presents a side of James IV's court not revealed in *The Goldyn Targe* and invites comparison and contrast with the latter poem. (An attempt at a translation into modern colloquial English has been made by Eric Linklater: *New Saltire*, no. 9 (September 1963), 7–20.)

MS: Maitland Folio, 82–96.
Printed by Chepman and Myllar (1508) on which the following version is based. The print has lines 1–103 missing, which are supplied from Maitland Folio, as are certain words omitted or obscure in the rest of the poem.

Apon the Midsummer evin, mirriest of nichtis,
I muvit furth allane, neir as midnicht wes past,
Besyd ane gudlie grein garth, full of gay flouris,
Hegeit, of ane huge hicht, with hawthorne treis;
Quhairon ane bird, on ane bransche, so birst out hir notis   5
That never ane blythfullar bird was on the beuche harde:
Quhat throw the sugarat sound of hir sang glaid,
And throw the savour sanative of the sueit flouris,
I drew in derne to the dyk to dirkin efter mirthis;
The dew donkit the daill and dynnit the feulis.   10
     I hard, under ane holyn hevinlie grein hewit,
Ane hie speiche, at my hand, with hautand wourdis;
With that in haist to the hege so hard I inthrang
That I was heildit with hawthorne and with heynd leves:
Throw pykis of the plet thorne I presandlie luikit,   15
Gif ony persoun wald approche within that plesand garding.
     I saw thre gay ladeis sit in ane grein arbeir,
All grathit in to garlandis of fresche gudlie flouris;

So glitterit as the gold wer thair glorius gilt tressis,
Quhill all the gressis did gleme of the glaid hewis;   20
Kemmit was thair cleir hair, and curiouslie sched
Attour thair schulderis doun schyre, schyning full bricht;
With curches cassin thair abone, of kirsp cleir and thin:
Thair mantillis grein war as the gress that grew in May sessoun,
Fetrit with thair quhyt fingaris about thair fair sydis: 25
Off ferliful fyne favour war thair faceis meik,
All full of flurist fairheid, as flouris in June;
Quhyt, seimlie, and soft, as the sweit lillies
New upspred upon spray, as new spynist rose;
Arrayit ryallie about with mony rich vardour,   30
That nature full nobillie annamalit with flouris
Off alkin hewis under hevin, that ony heynd knew,
Fragrant, all full of fresche odour fynest of smell.
Ane cumlie tabil coverit wes befoir tha cleir ladeis,
With ryalle cowpis apon rawis, full of ryche wynis.   35
And of thir fair wlonkes, tua weddit war with lordis,
Ane wes ane wedow, I wis, wantoun of laitis.
And, as thai talk at the tabill of many taill sindry,
Thay wauchtit at the wicht wyne and waris out wourdis;
And syne thai spak more spedelie, and sparit no matiris.   40

'Bewrie,' said the Wedo, 'ye woddit wemen ying,
Quhat mirth ye fand in maryage, sen ye war menis wyffis;
Reveill gif ye rewit that rakles conditioun?
Or gif that ever ye luffit leyd upone lyf mair
Nor thame that ye your fayth hes festinit for ever?   45
Or gif ye think, had ye chois, that ye wald cheis better?
Think ye it nocht ane blist band that bindis so fast,
That none undo it a deill may bot the deith ane?'

Than spak ane lusty belyf with lustie effeiris:
'It, that ye call the blist band that bindis so fast,   50
Is bair of blis, and bailfull, and greit barrat wirkis.

---

31. *annamalit*—*cf. Goldyn Targe*, lines 13, 257.
36. *wlonkes*—trisyllabic.
48. *ane*—alone.

Ye speir, had I fre chois, gif I wald cheis better?
Chenyeis ay ar to eschew; and changeis ar sueit:
Sic cursit chance till eschew, had I my chois anis,
Out of the chenyeis of ane churle I chaip suld for evir.   55
God gif matrimony were made to mell for ane yeir!
It war bot merrens to be mair, bot gif our myndis pleisit:
It is agane the law of luf, of kynd, and of nature,
Togidder hairtis to strene, that stryveis with uther:
Birdis hes ane better law na bernis be meikill,   60
That ilk yeir, with new joy, joyis ane maik,
And fangis thame ane fresche feyr, unfulyeit, and constant,
And lattis thair fulyeit feiris flie quhair thai pleis.
Cryst gif sic ane consuetude war in this kith haldin!
Than weill war us wemen that evir we war fre;   65
We suld have feiris as fresche to fang quhen us likit,
And gif all larbaris thair leveis, quhen thai lak curage.
Myself suld be full semlie in silkis arrayit,
Gymp, jolie, and gent, richt joyus, and gent[ryce].
I suld at fairis be found new faceis to se;   70
At playis, and at preichingis, and pilgrimages greit,
To schaw my renone, royaly, quhair preis was of folk,
To manifest my makdome to multitude of pepill,
And blaw my bewtie on breid, quhair bernis war mony;
That I micht cheis, and be chosin, and change quhen me lykit.   75
Than suld I waill ane full weill, our all the wyd realme,
That suld my womanheid weild the lang winter nicht;
And when I gottin had ane grome, ganest of uther,
Yaip, and ying, in the yok ane yeir for to draw;
Fra I had preveit his pitht the first plesand moneth,   80
Than suld I cast me to keik in kirk, and in markat,
And all the cuntre about, kyngis court, and uther,

65. Last word in MS is indecipherable. Pinkerton (1786) suggested the final word, reminiscent of *Bruce*, I, line 219, which Pinkerton was editing at the time
66. Maitland MS has *freiris*.
69. MS—last word obliterated. Mackay Mackenzie suggested last syllable.

78. *ganest of uther*—the lustiest available.

Quhair I ane galland micht get aganis the nixt yeir,
For to perfurneis furth the werk quhen failyeit the tother;
A forthy fure, ay furthwart, and forsy in draucht,   85
Nother febill, nor fant, nor fulyeit in labour,
But als fresche of his forme, as flouris in May;
For all the fruit suld I fang, thocht he the flour burgeoun.

'I hafe ane wallidrag, ane worme, ane auld wobat carle,
A waistit wolroun, na worth bot wourdis to clatter;   90
Ane bumbart, ane dron bee, ane bag full of flewme,
Ane skabbit skarth, ane scorpioun, ane scutarde behind;
To see him scart his awin skyn grit scunner I think.
Quhen kissis me that carybald, than kyndillis all my sorrow;
As birs of ane brym bair, his berd is als stif,   95
Bot soft and soupill as the silk is his sary lume;
He may weill to the syn assent, bot sakles is his deidis.
With goreis his tua grym ene ar gladderrit all about,
And gorgeit lyk twa gutaris that war with glar stoppit;
Bot quhen that glowrand gaist grippis me about,   100
Than think I hiddowus Mahowne hes me in armes;
Thair ma na sanyne me save fra that auld Sathane;
For, thocht I croce me all cleine, fra the croun doun,
He wil my corse all beclip, and clap me to his breist.
Quhen schaiffyne is that ald schalk with a scharp rasour,   105
He schowis one me his schevill mouth and schedis my lippis;
And with his hard hurcheone skyn sa heklis he my chekis,
That as a glemand gleyd glowis my chaftis;
I schrenk for the scharp stound, bot schout dar I nought,
For schore of that auld schrew, schame him betide!   110
The luf blenkis of that bogill, fra his blerde ene,
As Belzebub had on me blent, abasit my spreit;
And quhen the smy one me smyrkis with his smake smolet,
He fepillis like a farcy aver that flyrit one a gillot.

85. *forthy*—MS has *forky*, which makes no sense
104. *me* inserted from Maitland MS. This is the first line in the print.

---

89. *worme*—reptile, low form of life; *wobat*—hairy caterpillar.
114. *farcy aver*—diseased old cart-horse. *Cf.* 387.

Quhen that the sound of his saw sinkis in my eris,   115
Than ay renewis my noy, or he be neir cumand:
Quhen I heir nemmyt his name, than mak I nyne crocis,
To keip me fra the cummerans of that carll mangit,
That full of eldnyng is and anger and all evill thewis.
I dar nought luke to my luf for that lene gib,   120
He is sa full of jelusy and engyne fals;
Ever ymagynyng in mynd materis of evill,
Compasand and castand casis a thousand
How he sall tak me, with a trawe, at trist of ane othir:
I dar nought keik to the knaip that the cop fillis,   125
For eldnyng of that ald schrew that ever one evill thynkis;
For he is waistit and worne fra Venus werkis,
And may nought beit wortht a bene in bed of my mystirs.
He trowis that young folk I yerne yeild, for he gane is,
Bot I may yuke all this yer, or his yerd help.   130
   Ay quhen that caribald carll wald clyme one my wambe,
Than am I dangerus and daine and dour of my will;
Yit leit I never that larbar my leggis ga betueene,
To fyle my flesche, na fumyll me, without a fee gret;
And thoght his pene purly mc payis in bed,   135
His purse pays richely in recompense efter:
For, or he clym on my corse, that carybald forlane,
I have conditioun of a curche of kersp allther fynest,
A goun of engranyt claith, right gaily furrit,
A ring with a ryall stane, or other riche jowell,   140
Or rest of his rousty raid, thoght he wer rede wod:
For all the buddis of Johne Blunt, quhen he abone clymis,
Me think the baid deir aboucht, sa bawch ar his werkis;
And thus I sell him solace, thoght I it sour think:
Fra sic a syre, God yow saif, my sueit sisteris deir!'   145
   Quhen that the semely had said her sentence to end,
Than all thai leuch apon loft with latis full mery,
And raucht the cop round about full of riche wynis,
And ralyeit lang, or thai wald rest, with ryatus speche.

---

118. *carll mangit*—old dotard.
125. *to*—at.
142. *for all the buddis of Johne Blunt*—i.e. for all the tea in China.

The wedo to the tothir wlonk warpit ther wordis: 150
'Now, fair sister, fallis yow but fenyeing to tell,
Sen man ferst with matrimony yow menskit in kirk,
How haif ye farne be your faith? Confese us the treuth:
That band to blise, or to ban, quhilk yow best thinkis?
Or how ye like lif to leid in to leill spousage?   155
And syne myself ye exeme one the samyn wise,
And I sall say furth the south, dissymyland no word.

The plesand said, 'I protest, the treuth gif I schaw,
That of your toungis ye be traist.' The tothir twa grantit;
With that sprang up hir spreit be a span hechar.   160
'To speik,' quoth scho, 'I sall nought spar; ther is no spy neir:
I sall a ragment reveil fra rute of my hert,
A roust that is sa rankild quhill risis my stomok;
Now sall the byle all out brist, that beild has so lang;
For it to beir one my brist wes berdin our hevy: 165
I sall the venome devoid with a vent large,
And me assuage of the swalme, that suellit wes gret.
'My husband wes a hur maister, the hugeast in erd,
Tharfoir I hait him with my hert, sa help me our Lord!
He is a young man ryght yaip, bot nought in youth flouris;   170
For he is fadit full far and feblit of strenth:
He wes as flurising fresche within this few yeris,
Bot he is falyeid full far and fulyeid in labour;
He has bene lychour so lang quhill lost is his natur,
His lume is waxit larbar, and lyis in to swonne: 175
Wes never sugeorne werse na one that snaill tyrit,
For efter vii oulkis rest, it will nought rap anys;
He has bene waistit apone wemen, or he me wif chesit,
And in adultre, in my tyme, I haif him tane oft:
And yit he is als brankand with bonet one syde,   180
And blenkand to the brichtest that in the burgh duellis,

155. *leill*, Maitland MS; print has *lell*.
176. Print has *wer set*.

161. Ironic, since the poet hears every word.
170-1. An ironic usage of the metaphor of the fading flower (see *Orpheus and Eurydice*, 90-1, etc.).

Alse curtly of his clething and kemmyng of his hair,
And he that is mare valyeand in Venus chalmer;
He semys to be sumthing worth, that syphyr in bour,
He lukis as he wald luffit be, thocht he be litill of valour;   185
He dois as dotit dog that damys on all bussis,
And liftis his leg apone loft, thoght he nought list pische;
He has a luke without lust and lif without curage;
He has a forme without force and fessoun but vertu,
And fair wordis but effect, all fruster of dedis;   190
He is for ladyis in luf a right lusty schadow,
Bot in to derne, at the deid, he salbe drup fundin;
He ralis, and makis repet with ryatus wordis,
Ay using him of his radis and rageing in chalmer;
But God wait quhat I think quhen he so thra spekis,   195
And how it settis him so syde to sege of sic materis.
Bot gif him self, of sum evin, myght ane say amang thaim,
Bot he nought ane is, bot nane of naturis possessoris.
  Scho that has ane auld man nought all is begylit;
He is at Venus werkis na war na he semys: 200
I wend I josit a gem, and I haif geit gottin;
He had the glemyng of gold, and wes bot glase fundin.
Thought men be ferse, wele I fynd, fra falye ther curage,
Thar is bot eldnyng or anger ther hertis within.
Ye speik of berdis one bewch: of blise may thai sing,   205
That one Sanct Valentynis day ar vacandis ilk yer;
Hed I that plesand prevelege to part quhen me likit,
To change, and ay to cheise agane, than, chastite, adew!
Than suld I haif a fresch feir to fang in myn armes:
To hald a freke, quhill he faynt, may foly be calit.   210
  'Apone sic materis I mus, at mydnyght, full oft,
And murnys so in my mynd I murdris my selfin;
Than ly I walkand for wa, and walteris about,
Wariand oft my wekit kyn, that me away cast
To sic a craudoune but curage, that knyt my cler bewte,   215
And ther so mony kene knyghtis this kenrik within:

---

186. 'He carries on like a silly dog that urinates on every bush.' *Cf.* Chaucer, *Parson's Tale*, line 858.

205–6. *Cf. Parlement of Foules* where the scene is set on 14 February.

Than think I on a semelyar, the suth for to tell,
Na is our syre be sic sevin; with that I sych oft:
Than he ful tenderly dois turne to me his tume person,
And with a yoldin yerd dois yolk me in armys,   220
And sais: "My soverane sueit thing, quhy sleip ye no betir?
Me think ther haldis yow a hete, as ye sum harme alyt."
Quoth I: "My hony, hald abak, and handill me nought sair;
A hache is happinit hastely at my hert rut."
With that I seme for to swoune, thought I na swerf tak;   225
And thus beswik I that swane with my sueit wordis:
I cast on him a crabit E, quhen cleir day is cummyn,
And lettis it is a luf blenk, quhen he about glemys,
I turne it in a tender luke, that I in tene warit,
And him behaldis hamely with hertly smyling.   230
    I wald a tender peronall, that myght na put thole,
That hatit men with hard geir for hurting of flesch,
Had my gud man to hir gest; for I dar God suer,
Scho suld not stert for his straik a stray breid of erd.
And syne, I wald that ilk band, that ye so blist call,   235
Has bund him so to that bryght, quhill his bak werkit;
And I wer in a beid broght with berne that me likit,
I trow that bird of my blis suld a bourd want.'

    Onone, quhen this amyable had endit hir spreche,
Loudly lauchand the laif allowit hir mekle: 240
Thir gay wiffis maid game amang the grene leiffis;
Thai drank and did away dule under derne bewis;

240. Print has 'Luly rauthand,' a wrong setting. Maitland MS has 'loud lauchand'.

217-8. 'Then I think about just such a one, seven times more suitable, you may be sure, than our fine gentlemen.'

220. *yoldin yerd*—flaccid member.

236. *quhill his bak werkit*—as long as he went on living.

237. 'And I had gone to another bed with a fellow that suited me.' *a* is emphatic here.

239. *amyable*—i.e. the second wife.

Thai swapit of the sueit wyne, thai swanquhit of hewis,
Bot all the pertlyar in plane thai put out ther vocis.

 Than said the Weido, 'Iwis ther is no way othir;   245
Now tydis me for to talk; my taill it is nixt:
God my spreit now inspir and my speche quykkin,
And send me sentence to say, substantious and noble;
Sa that my preching may pers your perverst hertis,
And mak yow mekar to men in maneris and conditiounis. 250
 'I schaw yow, sisteris in schrift, I wes a schrew evir,
Bot I wes schene in my schrowd, and schew me innocent;
And thought I dour wes and dane, dispitous, and bald,
I wes dissymblit suttelly in a sanctis liknes:
I semyt sober, and sueit, and sempill without fraud, 255
Bot I couth sexty dissaif that suttilar wer haldin.
 'Unto my lesson ye lyth, and leir at me wit,
Gif you nought list be forleit with losingeris untrew:
Be constant in your governance, and counterfeit gud maneris,
Thought ye be kene, inconstant, and cruell of mynd; 260
Thought ye as tygris be terne, be tretable in luf,
And be as turtoris in your talk, thought ye haif talis brukill;
Be dragonis baith and dowis ay in double forme,
And quhen it nedis yow, onone, note baith ther stranthis;
Be amyable with humble face, as angellis apperand, 265
And with a terrebill tail be stangand as edderis;
Be of your luke like innocentis, thoght ye haif evill myndis;
Be courtly ay in clething and costly arrayit,
That hurtis yow nought worth a hen; yowr husband pays for all.
 'Twa husbandis haif I had, thai held me baith deir, 270
Thought I dispytit thaim agane, thai spyit it na thing:
Ane wes ane hair hogeart, that hostit out flewme;
I hatit him like a hund, thought I it hid preve:
With kissing and with clapping I gert the carll fone;

256. Maitland MS has *desave*.

---

 252. *schene in my shrowd*—a stock alliterative phrase, lit. 'beautiful in my gown'.
 261. *as tygris be terne*—see *Clerk's Tale*, Envoy, 1198–9.

Weil couth I keyth his cruke bak, and kemm his cowit noddill, 275
And with a bukky in my cheik bo on him behind,
And with a bek gang about and bler his ald E,
And with a kynd contynance kys his crynd chekis;
In to my mynd makand mokis at that mad fader,
Trowand me with trew lufe to treit him so fair. 280
This cought I do without dule and na dises tak,
Bot ay be mery in my mynd and myrth full of cher.
    'I had a lufsummar leid my lust for to slokyn,
That couth be secrete and sure and ay saif my honour,
And sew bot at certayne tymes and in sicir placis; 285
Ay when the ald did me anger, with akword wordis,
Apon the galland for to goif it gladit me agane.
I had sic wit that for wo weipit I litill,
Bot leit the sueit ay the sour to gud sesone bring.
Quhen that the chuf wald me chid, with girnand chaftis, 290
I wald him chuk, cheik and chyn, and cheris him so mekill,
That his cheif chymys I had chevist to my sone,
Suppos the churll wes gane chaist, or the child wes gottin:
As wis woman as I wrought and not as wod fule,
For mar with wylis I wan na wichtnes of handis. 295

    'Syne maryit I a marchand, myghti of gudis:
He was a man of myd eld and of mene statur;
Bot we na fallowis wer in frendschip or blud,
In fredome, na furth bering, na fairnes of persoune,
Quhilk ay the fule did foryhet, for febilnes of knawlege, 300
Bot I sa oft thoght him on, quhill angrit his hert,
And quhilum I put furth my voce and Pedder him callit:
I wald ryght tuichandly talk be I wes tuyse maryit,
For endit wes my innocence with my ald husband:
I wes apperand to be pert within perfit eild; 305

275. *cowit* supplied from Maitland MS. Print has *kewt. keyth* has been explained as a paleographical error for *krych*—scratch. Maitland MS has *claw*.
303. Print has *tinchandly*; Maitland MS has *twichand in*.

292. *cheif*—principal; *to*—for, on account of.

Sa sais the curat of our kirk, that knew me full ying:
He is our famous to be fals, that fair worthy prelot;
I salbe laith to lat him le, quhill I may luke furght.
I gert the buthman obey, ther wes no bute ellis;
He maid me ryght hie reverens, fra he my rycht knew: 310
For, thocht I say it myself, the severance wes mekle
Betuix his bastard blude and my birth noble.
That page was never of sic price for to presome anys
Unto my persone to be peir, had pete nought grantit.
Bot mercy in to womanheid is a mekle vertu,   315
For never bot in a gentill hert is generit ony ruth.
I held ay grene in to his mynd that I of grace tuk him,
And for he coutht ken himself I curtasly him lerit:
He durst not sit anys my summondis, for, or the secund charge,
He wes ay redy for to ryn, so rad he wes for blame.   320
Bot ay my will wes the war of womanly natur;
The mair he loutit for my luf, the les of him I rakit;
And eik, this is a ferly thing, or I him faith gaif,
I had sic favour to that freke, and feid, syne for ever,

  'Quhen I the cure had all clene and him ourcummyn haill,   325
I crew abone that craudone, as cok that wer victour;
Quhen I him saw subject and sett at myn bydding,
Than I him lichtlyit as a lowne and lathit his maneris.
Than woxe I sa unmerciable to martir him I thought,
For as a best I broddit him to all boyis laubour: 330
I wald haid ridden him to Rome with raip in his heid,
Wer not ruffill of my renoune and rumour of pepill.

  'And yit hatrent I hid within my hert all;
Bot quhilis it hepit so huge, quhill it behud out:
Yit tuk I nevir the wosp clene out of my wyde throte,   335
Quhill I oucht wantit of my will or quhat I wald desir.
Bot quhen I severit had that syre of substance in erd,
And gottin his biggingis to my barne, and hie burrow landis,
Than with a stew stert out the stoppell of my hals,

313–4. An ironic treatment of a courtly virtue. 'That poor creature never had the nerve to demand his marital rights till I showed I was sorry for him.'
338. *hie burrow landis*—houses in a principal burgh.

That he all stunyst throu the stound, as of a stele wappin.   340
Than wald I, efter lang, first sa fane haif bene wrokin,
That I to flyte wes als fers as a fell dragoun.
I had for flattering of that fule fenyeit so lang,
Mi evidentis of heritagis or thai wer all selit,
My breist, that wes gret beild, bowdyn wes sa huge,   345
That neir my baret out brist or the band makin.
Bot quhen my billis and my bauchles wes all braid selit,
I wald na langar beir on bridill, bot braid up my heid;
Thar mycht na molet mak me moy, na hald my mouth in:
I gert the renyeis rak and rif into sondir;   350
I maid that wif carll to werk all womenis werkis,
And laid all manly materis and mensk in this eird.
Than said I to my cumaris in counsall about,
"Se how I cabeld yone cout with a kene brydill!
The cappill, that the crelis kest in the caf mydding,   355
Sa curtasly the cart drawis, and kennis na plungeing,
He is nought skeich, na yit sker, na scippis nought one syd:"
And thus the scorne and the scaith scapit he nothir.
    'He wes no glaidsum gest for a gay lady,
Tharfor I gat him a game that ganyt him bettir;   360
He wes a gret goldit man and of gudis riche;
I leit him be my lumbart to lous me all misteris,
And he wes fane for to fang fra me that fair office,
And thoght my favoris to fynd through his feill giftis.
He grathit me in a gay silk and gudly arrayis,   365
In gownis of engranyt claith and gret goldin chenyeis,
In ringis ryally set with riche ruby stonis,
Quhill hely raise my renoune amang the rude peple.
Bot I full craftely did keip thai courtly wedis,
Quhill efter dede of that drupe, that dotht nought in chalmir: 370
Thought he of all my clathis maid cost and expense,
Ane othir sall the worschip haif, that weildis me eftir;
And thoght I likit him bot litill, yit for luf of othris,
I wald me prunya plesandly in precius wedis,
That luffaris mycht apone me luke and ying lusty gallandis,   375

---

346. *or the band makin*—'before the deal was signed and sealed.'

That I held more in daynte and derer be ful mekill
Ne him that dressit me so dink: full dotit wes his heyd.
Quhen he wes heryit out of hand to hie up my honoris,
And payntit me as pako, proudest of fedderis,
I him miskennyt, be Crist, and cukkald him maid;   380
I him forleit as a lad and lathlyit him mekle:
I thoght myself a papingay and him a plukit herle;
All thus enforsit he his fa and fortifyit in strenth,
And maid a stalwart staff to strik him selfe doune.

'Bot of ane bowrd in to bed I sall yow breif yit: 385
Quhen he ane hail year was hanyt, and him behuffit rage,
And I wes laith to be loppin with sic a lob avoir,
Alse lang as he wes on loft, I lukit on him never,
Na leit never enter in my thoght that he my thing persit,
Bot ay in mynd ane other man ymagynit that I haid;   390
Or ellis had I never mery bene at that myrthles raid.
Quhen I that grome geldit had of gudis and of natur,
Me thought him graceless one to goif, sa me God help:
Quhen he had warit all one me his welth and his substance,
Me thoght his wit wes all went away with the laif;   395
And so I did him despise, I spittit quhen I saw
That super spendit evill spreit, spulyeit of all vertu.
For weill ye wait, wiffis, that he wantis riches
And valyeandnes in Venus play, is ful vile haldin:
Full fruster is his fresch array and fairnes of personne,   400
All is bot frutlese his effeir and falyeis at the upwith.

'I buskit up my barnis like baronis sonnis,
And maid bot fulis of the fry of his first wif.
I banyst fra my boundis his brethir ilkane;
His frendis as my fais I held at feid evir;   405
Be this, ye belief may, I luffit nought him self,
For never I likit a leid that langit till his blude:
And yit thir wisemen, thai wait that all wiffis evill
Ar kend with ther conditionis and knawin with the samin.

'Deid is now that dyvour and dollin in erd: 410

---

393. *graceless one to goif*—unsavoury to look at, an unattractive sight.
410. Cf. *Wife of Bath's Prologue*, 587–92 and Sprutok in *The Taill of Schir Chantecleir and the Foxe*, lines 117 *et seq*.

With him deit all my dule and my drey thoghtis;
Now done is my dolly nyght, my day is upsprungin,
Adew dolour, adew! my daynte now begyinis:
Now am I a wedow, I wise and weill am at ese;
I weip as I were woful, but wel is me for ever;   415
I busk as I wer bailfull, bot blith is my hert;
My mouth it makis murnyng, and my mynd lauchis;
My clokis thai ar caerfull in colour of sabill,
Bot courtly and ryght curyus my corse is ther undir:
I drup with a ded luke in my dule habit,   420
As with manis daill [I] had done for dayis of my lif.
   'Quhen that I go to the kirk, cled in cair weid,
As foxe in a lambis fleise fenye I my cheir;
Than lay I furght my bright buke one breid one my kne,
With mony lusty letter ellumynit with gold;   425
And drawis my clok forthwart our my face quhit,
That I may spy, unaspyit, a space me beside:
Full oft I blenk by my buke, and blynis of devotioun,
To se quhat berne is best brand or bredest in schulderis,
Or forgeit is maist forcely to furnyse a bancat   430
In Venus chalmer, valyeandly, withoutin vane ruse:
And, as the new mone all pale, oppressit with change,
Kythis quhilis her cleir face through cluddis of sable,
So keik I through my clokis, and castis kynd lukis
To knychtis, and to cleirkis, and cortly personis.   435
   'Quhen frendis of my husbandis behaldis me one fer,
I haif a watter spunge for wa, within my wyde clokis,
Than wring I it full wylely and wetis my chekis,
With that watteris myn ene and welteris doune teris.
Than say thai all that sittis about: "Se ye nought, allace!   440
Yone lustlese led so lelely scho luffit hir husband:
Yone is a pete to enprent in a princis hert,
That sic a perle of plesance suld yone pane dre!"
I sane me as I war ane sanct, and semys ane angell;
At langage of lichory I leit as I war crabit: 445
I sich, without sair hert or seiknes in body;

---

422. *cair weid*—mourning clothes.

According to my sable weid I mon haif sad maneris,
Or thai will se all the suth; for certis, we wemen
We set us all fra the syght to syle men of treuth:
We dule for na evill deid, sa it be derne haldin.   450
  'Wise wemen has wayis and wonderfull gydingis
With gret engyne to bejaip ther jolyus husbandis;
And quyetly, with sic craft, convoyis our materis
That, under Crist, no creatur kennis of our doingis.
Bot folk a cury may miscuke, that knawlege wantis,   455
And has na colouris for to cover thair awne kindly fautis;
As dois thir damysellis, for derne dotit lufe,
That dogonis haldis in dainte and delis with thaim so lang,
Quhill all the cuntre knaw ther kyndnes and faith:
Faith has a fair name, bot falsheid faris bettir: 460
Fy one hir that can nought feyne her fame for to saif!
Yit am I wise in sic werk and wes all my tyme:
Thoght I want wit in warldlynes, I wylis haif in luf,
As ony happy woman has that is of hie blude,
Hutit be the halok las a hunder yeir of eild!   465
  'I have ane secrete servand, rycht sobir of his toung,
That me supportis of sic nedis, quhen I a syne mak:
Thoght he be sympill to the sicht, he has a tong sickir;
Full mony semelyar sege wer service dois mak:
Thought I haif cair, under cloke, the cleir day quhill nyght,   470
Yit haif I solace, under serk, quhill the sone ryse.
  'Yit am I haldin a haly wif our all the haill schyre,
I am sa peteouse to the pur, quhen ther is personis mony.
In passing of pilgrymage I pride me full mekle,
Mair for the prese of peple na ony perdoun wynyng.   475
  'Bot yit me think the best bourd, quhen baronis and knychtis,
And othir bachilleris, blith blumyng in youth,
And all my luffaris lele, my lugeing persewis,
And fyllis me wyne wantonly with weilfair and joy:

---

449. 'We all take it upon ourselves to hide truth from men's sight.'
465. An obscure line. The sense seems to be that a sophisticated woman is always disliked by a foolish one.
473. *personis mony*—many persons present.

Sum rownis, and sum ralyeis, and sum redis ballatis,   480
Sum raiffis furght rudly with riatus speche,
Sum plenis, and sum prayis, sum prasis mi bewte,
Sum kissis me, sum clappis me, sum kyndnes me proferis,
Sum kerffis to me curtasli, sum me the cop giffis,
Sum stalwardly steppis ben, with a stoute curage,   485
And a stif standand thing staiffis in mi neiff;
And mony blenkis ben our, that but full fer sittis,
That mai, for the thik thrang, nought thrif as thai wald.
Bot, with my fair calling, I comfort thaim all:
For he that sittis me nict, I nip on his finger;   490
I serf him on the tothir syde on the samin fasson;
And he that behind me sittis, I hard on him lene;
And him befor, with my fut fast on his I stramp;
And to the bernis far but sueit blenkis I cast:
To every man in speciall speke I sum wordis   495
So wisely and so womanly, quhill warmys ther hertis.
    'Thar is no liffand leid so law of degre
That sall me luf unluffit, I am so loik hertit;
And gif his lust so be lent into my lyre quhit,
That he be lost or with me lig, his lif sall nocht danger.   500
I am so mercifull in mynd, and menys all wichtis,
My sely saull salbe saif, quhen sa bot all jugis.
Ladyis leir thir lessonis and be no lassis fundin:
This is the legeand of my lif, thought Latyne it be nane.'
    Quhen endit had her ornat speche, this eloquent wedow,   505
Lowd thai lewch all the laif, and loffit hir mekle;
And said thai suld exampill take of her soverane teching,
And wirk efter hir wordis, that woman wes so prudent.
Than culit thai thair mouthis with confortable drinkis;
And carpit full cummerlik with cop going round.   510

    Thus draif thai our that deir nyght with danceis full noble,

502. *sa bot* makes no sense, but the MS reads *sall not*, faintly inserted, perhaps
by a puzzled printer.

---

504. *legeand*—an ironic reference to Latin legends of the Saints, scarcely
appropriate in this context.

F

Quhill that the day did up daw, and dew donkit flouris;
The morrow myld wes and meik, the mavis did sing,
And all remuffit the myst, and the meid smellit;
Silver schouris doune schuke as the schene cristall,   515
And berdis schoutit in schaw with ther schill notis;
The goldin glitterand gleme so gladit ther hertis,
Thai maid a glorius gle amang the grene bewis.
The soft sowch of the swyr and soune of the stremys,
The sueit savour of the sward and singing of foulis,   520
Myght confort ony creatur of the kyn of Adam,
And kindill agane his curage, thocht it wer cald sloknyt.
    Than rais thir ryall roisis, in ther riche wedis,
And rakit hame to ther rest through the rise blumys;
And I all prevely past to a plesand arber,   525
And with my pen did report thair pastance most mery.

    Ye auditoris most honorable, that eris has gevin
Oneto this uncouth aventur, quhilk airly me happinnit;
Of thir thre wantoun wiffis, that I haif writtin heir,
Quhilk wald ye waill to your wif, gif ye suld wed one?   530

511–26. These lines take the audience back to the original vernal scene before firing a parting shot.

Gavin Douglas

XII. Translation of Virgil's Aeneid

THE Prologues to each of thirteen books of the *Aeneid* (one additional book from a fifteenth-century continuation by Maffeo Vegio) are original additions and many of them reflect Douglas's own views on life and literature. The language of the Prologues is more directly related to the aureate diction of Dunbar's allegorical and devotional poetry than to the language of the actual translation. The following extracts (lines 1–146; 339–451) from the Prologue to Book I reveal Douglas's skill in aureation, his enthusiasm for Virgil and his scorn for Caxton's redaction, together with some conventional praise of Chaucer. The significant part is that dealing with Douglas's methods of translation; in it, he states a humanist's dilemma—whether to present a free or a word-for-word rendering, a problem which had engaged scholars since Gregory the Great. Douglas's conservatism is shown in his unequivocal certainty that English was inadequate for daring poetic flights, a view not held by more progressive humanists, but which persisted until the eighteenth century. Nevertheless, Douglas succeeded in making a translation of Virgil which comes close to Goethe's ideal—a substitute for the original work.

MS: Trinity College, Cambridge (c. 1515) the colophon of which describes it as 'the first correk copy nixt after the translation'. This was made by Douglas's own secretary and bears annotations possibly by the poet himself.

Other MSS: Elphynstoun (c. 1520) University of Edinburgh; Ruthven (n.d.) University of Edinburgh; Lambeth (1545) Lambeth Palace; Bath (1547) Longleat House; three fragments of Book I (early sixteenth century); Bannatyne, Prologues IV, V, part of IX.

Edition: D. F. C. Coldwell, editor, Virgil's 'Aeneid' translated into Scottish Verse by Gavin Douglas, Bishop of Dunkeld (Scottish Text Society, Edinburgh and London, 4 vols., 1957–64); based on Cambridge MS.

First printed: William Copland (London, 1553), from which Bannatyne is copied with some corrections.

BOOK I

Incipit Prologus in Virgilii Eneados

Lawd, honour, praysyngis, thankis infynyte
To the and thy dulce ornat fresch endyte,
Maist reverend Virgill, of Latyn poetis prynce,

Gem of engyne and flude of eloquens,
Thow peirless perle, patroun of poetry,   5
Roys, regester, palm, lawrer and glory,
Chosyn charbukkill, cheif flour and cedyr tre,
Lantarn, laid stern, myrrour and A per se,
Maister of masteris, sweit sours and spryngand well
Wyde quhar our all rung is thyne hevynyly bell   10
I meyn thy crafty warkis curyus
Sa quyk, lusty and maist sentencyus,
Plesand, perfyte and feilabill in all degre,
As quha the mater beheld tofor thar e,
In every volume quhilk the lyst do wryte   15
Surmontyng fer all other maner endyte,
Lyke as the royss in June with hir sweit smell
The maryguld or dasy doith excell.
Quhy suld I than with dull forhed and vayn,
With rude engyne and barrand emptyve brayn,   20
With bad, harsk spech and lewit barbour tong
Presume to write quhar thy sweit bell is rung
Or contyrfate sa precyus wordys deir?
Na, na, noth swa, but kneill quhen I thame heir.
For quhat compair betwix mydday and nycht?   25
Or quhat compair betwix myrknes and lycht?
Or quhat compar is betwix blak and quhyte?
Far grettar difference betwix my blunt endyte
And thy scharp sugurate sang Virgiliane,
Sa wysly wrocht with nevir a word in vane.   30
My waverand wyt, my cunnyng febill at all,
My mynd mysty, thir may nocht myss a fall
Stra for thys ignorant blabryng imperfyte
Besyde thy polyst termys redymyte.

---

7. *charbukkill*—the carbuncle was said to shine in the dark. Precious stones were commonly-employed symbols of excellence.

8. *laid stern*—lodestar.

1–18. A fine example of late medieval adulation of Virgil, recalling phrases from praise of the Virgin.

29. *scharp*—clear.

33. *stra*—straw (thing of no value): cf. *Squire's Tale*, 695.

And netheles with support and correctioun, 35
For naturall lufe and frendely affectioun
Quhilkis I beir to thy warkis and endyte
All thocht God wait tharin I knaw full lyte
And that thy facund sentence mycht be song
In our langage alsweill as Latyn tong 40
Alsweill? Na, na, impossibill war, per de
Yit with thy leif, Virgile, to follow the,
I wald into my rurall vulgar gros
Wryte sum savoryng of thyne Eneados.
But sair I dreid for to disteyn the quyte 45
Throu my corruppit cadens imperfyte
Disteyn the? Nay forsuyth, that may I nocht;
Weill may I schaw my burall bustuus thocht
Bot thy wark sall endur in lawd and glory
But spot or falt condyng etern memory. 50
Thocht I offend, onwemmyt is thy fame;
Thyne is the thank and myne salbe the schame.
Quha may thy versis follow in all degre
In bewtie, sentence and in gravite?
Nane is, nor was, ne yit salbe, trow I, 55
Had, hass or sal have sic craft in poetry.
Of Helicon so drank thou dry the flude
That of thy copioss fouth or plenitude
All mon purches drynk at thy sugurit tun;
So lamp of day thou art and schynand son 60
All otheris on forss mon thar lycht beg or borrow;
Thou art Vesper and the day stern at morow,
Thow Phebus lightnar of the planetis all
I not quhat dewly I the clepe sall,
For thou art all and sum, quhat nedis more, 65
Of Latyn poetis that sens was, or befor.
Of the writis Macrobius sans faill
In hys gret volume clepit Saturnaill.
Thy sawys in sic eloquens doith fleit,

---

41. *per de*—a mild expletive (par Dieu).
67. *Macrobius*—a fourth-century commentator, author of *Saturnalia*.

So inventive of rethorik flowris sweit   70
Thou art, and hass so hie profund sentens
Tharto, perfyte but ony indigens,
That na lovyngis ma do incress thy fame,
Nor na reproche dymynew thy gud name.
Bot sen I am compellit the to translait,   75
And not only of my curage, God wait,
Durst interpryd syk owtrageus foly,
Quhar I offend the less reprefe serve I;
And that ye knaw at quhais instans I tuke
Forto translait this maist excellent buke,   80
I meyn Virgillis volume maist excellent,
Set this my wark full febill be of rent,
At the request of a lord of renown
Of ancistry nobill and illustir baroun,
Fader of bukis, protectour to sciens and lair,   85
My speciall gud Lord Henry, Lord Sanct Clair,
Quhilk with gret instance diverss tymys seir
Prayt me translait Virgill or Homeir,
Quhais plesour suythly as I undirstude
As neir conjunct to hys lordschip in blude   90
So that me thocht hys request ane command,
Half disparit this wark I tuke on hand
Nocht fully grantand nor anys sayand yee,
Bot only to assay quhou it mycht be.
Quha mycht gaynsay a lord so gentill and kynd   95
That ever had only curtasy in thar mynd,
Quhilk besyde hys innatyve pollecy,
Humanyte, curage, fredome and chevalry,
Bukis to recollect, to reid and se,
Has gret delyte as ever had Ptholome?   100
Quharfor to hys nobilite and estait,

---

82. *febill be of rent*—of poor quality (a conventional self-denigration).

86. *Lord Henry, Lord Sanct Clair*—a distant relative of Douglas, killed at Flodden, who may have suggested the translation to him, as he says.

88. *Homeir*—Douglas was not a Greek scholar; his acquaintance with Homer came about through existing Latin renderings, such as Valla's. (See note to line 127.)

Quhat so it be, this buke I dedicait,
Written in in the langage of Scottis natioun,
And thus I mak my protestatioun:
Fyrst I protest, beaw schirris, be your leif,   105
Beis weill avisit my wark or yhe repreif,
Consider it warly, reid oftar than anys;
Weill at a blenk sle poetry nocht tayn is,
And yit forsuyth I set my bissy pane
And that I couth to mak it braid and plane,   110
Kepand na sudron bot our awyn langage,
And spekis as I lernyt quhen I was page.
Nor yit sa cleyn all sudron I refus,
Bot sum word I pronunce as nyghtbouris doys:
Lyke as in Latyn beyn Grew termys sum,   115
So me behufyt quhilum or than be dum
Sum bastard Latyn, French or Inglys oyss
Quhar scant was Scottis—I had nane other choys.
Nocht for our tong is in the selwyn skant
Bot for that I the fowth of langage want   120
Quhar as the cullour of his properte
To kepe the sentens tharto constrenyt me,
Or than to mak my sayng schort sum tyme,
Mair compendyus, or to lykly my ryme.
Tharfor, gude frendis, for a gymp or a bourd,   125
I pray you note me nocht at every word.
The worthy clerk hecht Lawrens of the Vaill,
Amang Latynys a gret patron sans faill,
Grantis quhen twelf yheris he had beyn diligent
To study Virgill, skant knew quhat he ment.   130
Than thou or I, my frend, quhen we best weyn

120–4. A comment on the problem of finding adequate rhymes.

---

108. *sle poetry*—cunningly composed, technically skilful verse.

115. *Grew*—Greek. *Cf. Orpheus and Eurydice*, line 15.

116. *or than*—or else.

118. *Scottis*—Scots as distinguished from any other language, a novel literary reference since in the fifteenth century 'Scots' implied 'Gaelic'.

119. *for*—because; *in the selwyn*—in itself.

127. *Lawrens of the Vaill*—Laurentius Valla (1407–57), Professor of Rhetoric at Rome, author of *Elegantiae Linguae Latinae*, an authority for later humanists.

To have Virgile red, understand and seyn,
The rycht sentens perchance is fer to seik.
This wark twelf yheris first was in makyng eyk
And nocht correct quhen the poet gan decess;   135
Thus for small faltis, my wyss frend, hald thy pess.
Adherdand to my protestatioun,
Thocht Wilyame Caxtoun, of Inglis natioun,
In proyss hes prent ane buke of Inglys gross,
Clepand it Virgill in Eneadoss,   140
Quhilk that he says of Franch he dyd translait,
It hass no thing ado tharwith, God wait,
Ne na mair lyke than the devill and Sanct Austyne.
Have he na thank tharfor, bot loyss his pyne
So schamefully that story did pervert.   145
I red his wark with harmys at my hart.

[lines 339–451]

Thoght venerabill Chauser, principal poet but peir,
Hevynly trumpat, orlege and reguler,
In eloquens balmy, cundyt and dyall,
Mylky fontane, cleir strand and royss ryall,
Of fresch endyte, throu Albion iland braid,   5
In hys legend of notabill ladeis said
That he couth follow word by word Virgill,
Wisar than I may faill in lakar stile.
Sum tyme the text mon have ane expositioun,
Sum tyme the collour will caus a litill additioun,   10
And sum tyme of a word I mon mak thre
In witnes of this term 'oppetere'.

---

135. Virgil's death before he had completed corrections on *Aeneid* was traditional. Douglas himself translated the work in eighteen months.

138–43. Caxton's *Eneydos* (1490) was a translation of the prose *Livre des Eneydes*; in spite of Douglas's attack on it, it is a fact that Caxton's adaptation caught much more of the spirit of Virgil than any previous vernacular versions: see L. B. Hall, 'Caxton's "Eneydos" and the Redactions of Virgil' (*Mediaeval Studies*, XXII, 136–47).

1–5. Conventional praise of Chaucer, *cf.* similar address to Virgil in passage 1.

6. *Legend of Good Woman*, 1002–3.

12. *oppetere*—Lat. to go to meet (death).

Eik weill I wait syndry expositouris seir
Makis on a text sentens diverss to heir,
As thame apperis, accordyng thar entent,   15
And for thar part schawis ressonys evident.
All this is ganand, I will weill it swa be,
Bot a sentens to follow may suffice me.
Sum tyme I follow the text als neir I may,
Sum tyme I am constrenyt ane other way.   20
Besyde Latyn our langage is imperfite
Quhilk in sum part is the causs and the wyte
Quhy that of Virgillis verss the ornate bewte
Intill our tung may nocht observyt be,
For thar be Latyn wordis mony ane   25
That in our leyd ganand translatioun hass nane
Less than we mynyss thar sentens and gravyte
And yit scant weill exponyt. Quha trewys nocht me,
Lat thame interprit 'animal' and 'homo'
With many hundreth other termys mo   30
Quhilkis in our language suythly as I weyn
Few men can tell me cleirly quhat thai meyn.
Betweyn 'genus', 'sexus' and 'species'
Diversyte in our leid to seik I cess.
For 'objectum' or 'subjectum' alsswa   35
He war expert couth fynd me termys twa,
Quhilkis ar als ryfe amangis clerkis in scuyll
As evir fowlis plungit in laik or puyll.
Logicianys knawys heirin myne entent,
Undir quhais boundis lurkis mony strange went   40
Quharof the process as now we mon lat be.
Bot yit twychyng our tungis penuryte,
I meyn into compar of fair Latyn
That knawyn is maste perfite langage fyne,
I mycht also percace cum lyddir speid   45
For 'arbor' and 'lignum' intill our leid
To fynd different proper termys twane
And tharto put circumlocutioun nane.
Richt so by aboutspech oftyn tymys
And semabill wordis we compile our rymys.   50

F*

God wait, in Virgill ar termys mony a hundir
Fortill expone maid me a felloun blundir.
To follow alanerly Virgilis wordis, I weyn,
Thar suld few undirstand me quhat thai meyn.
The bewte of his ornate eloquens   55
May nocht al tyme be kepit with the sentens.
Sanct Gregor eik forbyddis us to translait
Word efter word bot sentence follow algait:
'Quha haldis,' quod he, 'of wordis the properteis
Full oft the verite of the sentens fleys.'   60
And to the sammyn purpos we may apply
Horatius in hys Art of Poetry:
'Pres nocht,' says he, 'thou traste interpreter,
Word eftir word to translait thi mater.'
Lo, he reprevis and haldis myssemyng   65
Ay word by word to reduce ony thing.
I say nocht this of Chauser for offens,
Bot till excus my lewyt insufficiens,
For as he standis beneth Virgill in gre,
Undir hym alsfer I grant myself to be.   70
And netheless into sum place, quha kend it,
My mastir Chauser gretly Virgill offendit.
All thoch I be to bald hym to repreif,
He was fer baldar, certis, by hys leif,
Sayand he followit Virgillis lantern toforn,   75
Quhou Eneas to Dydo was forsworn.
Was he forsworn? Than Eneas was fals—
That he admittis and callys hym traytour als.
Thus, wenyng allane Ene to have reprevit,
He hass gretly the prynce of poetis grevit,   80
For, as said is, Virgill dyd diligens
But spot of cryme, reproch or ony offens

57–66. Gregory the Great's views on translation and Horace's are in accord;
Douglas adds a lengthy marginal note explaining the examples he has given.

69. *gre*—rank, order of merit.

76. *Legend of Good Women* (Dido, 925–7). Chaucer praised Dido and blamed
Aeneas both in *The Legend* and in *The Hous of Fame*.

79. *Ene*—Aeneas.

Eneas for to loif and magnyfy,
And gif he grantis hym maynsworn fowlely,
Than all hys cuyr and crafty engyne gais quyte,   85
Hys twelf yheris laubouris war nocht worth a myte.
Certis Virgill schawys Ene dyd na thing
From Dydo of Cartage at hys departyng
Bot quhilk the goddis commandit hym beforn,
And gif that thar command maid hym maynsworn,   90
That war repreif to thar divinyte
And na reproch onto the said Enee.
Als in the first, quhar Ilioneus
Spekis to the queyn Dido, says he nocht thus,
Thar curss by fait was set tyll Italy?   95
Thus mycht scho not pretend na just causs quhy
Thocht Trojanys eftir departis of Cartage,
Sen thai befor declaryt hir thar vayage.
Reid the ferd buke quhar Queyn Dido is wraith,
Thar sal yhe fynd Ene maid nevir aith,   100
Promyt nor band with hir fortill abyde:
Thus hym to be maynsworn may nevir betyde,
Nor nane onkyndnes schew forto depart
At the bydding of Jove with reuthfull hart,
Sen the command of God obey suld all   105
And undir his charge na wrangwyss deid may fall.
   Bot sikkyrly of resson me behufis
Excuss Chauser fra all maner repruffis:
In lovyng of thir ladeis lylly quhite
He set on Virgill and Eneas this wyte,   110
For he was evir (God wait) all womanis frend.
I say na mair, but, gentil redaris heynd,
Lat all my faltis with this offens pass by.

87–106. Douglas notes here that the argument does not excuse the infidelity or perjury of Aeneas since Juno and Venus were not goddesses of Fortune and Aeneas himself acted with free-will, as God permitted.

109. *lovyng* (Fr. *louer*) may imply both affection and praise, in this case the latter.

Glossary

THE makars are difficult to read, mainly because they are linguistically self-conscious poets who achieve their precise effects with words the meanings of which are nowadays elusive even for a Scotsman. An extensive glossary is thus an indispensable aid to the crudest literal interpretation. Unfortunately no glossary can do justice to works like *Christ's Kirk*, *Peblis to the Play*, *The Tretis of the Twa Mariit Wemen and the Wedo* and other poems in the burlesque tradition which are heavily idiomatic, closely related to contemporary speech and packed with 'Scottis' words and expressions for which exact modern equivalents in English scarcely exist. In many instances, such equivalents are but a rough guide to nuances and connotations which the original audiences must have grasped immediately.

Such a glossary as this is to be regarded as no more than a crutch and the student is urged not to accept its authority without first bringing his own discretion to bear on the particular problem of translation involved. Standard full-dress dictionaries, for example, the *Dictionary of the Older Scottish Tongue* and *The Scottish National Dictionary*, so far as they have been completed, Kurath's *Middle English Dictionary*, likewise incomplete, and Stratmann's one-volume glossary, together with the *Oxford English Dictionary*, should be consulted, Wright's *English Dialect Dictionary* is a also a valuable adjunct, since a large part of the late medieval Scotsman's vocabulary was shared with his southern neighbour. An informative article on Scottish lexicography is A. J. Aitken's 'Completing the Record of Scots', *Scottish Studies*, VIII (1964), 129–40.

abasit *v.pres.t.* 3 *sing.* and *pl.* depressed, confounded, cast down, *CK* 111; *TMW* 112

abject *n.* thing cast off, outcast, *TC* 133

aboutspech *n.* circumlocution, *Aen* Prol. I, 387 (passage ii, 49)

abraid *v.past p.* 3 *sing.* started, *TC* 45

affeir *v.inf.* frighten, *CK* 73; **afferitlye** *adv.* in fear, *introd.* p. 41

affrayit *v.past t.* 3 *sing.* frightened, *GT* 207.

ago *v.past p.* gone, *TC* 238, 442

alanerly *adv.* only, exclusively, *Aen* Prol. I, 391 (passage ii, 53)

alawe *adv.* down, *KQ* 15

alkin *adj.* every kind of, *TMW* 32

almous-(deid) *n.* charity, *TC* 494, 532

alsfer *adv.* just as far, *Aen* Prol. I, 408 (passage ii, 70)

a lyte *adv.* to a slight extent, a little, *TC* 271

amene *adj.* pleasant, *GT* 249

amorus *n.pl.* (*adj.* as *n.*) wooers, amorous (ones), *introd.* p. 36

aneuch *adv.* enough, *TC* 110; **annewche**, *RM* 121

anewis *n.pl.* small wreaths, *KQ* 61

angelicall *adj.* angel-like, *introd.* p. 22

anis *adv.* once, *TC* 127; *TMW* 177; at any time, *TMW* 313, 319, etc.

ankers *n.pl.* anchors, *GT* 187*n.*

anseane *adj.* venerable, *OE* 19

A per se *n.* paragon, something unique, *TC* 78; *Aen* Prol. I, 8

areir *adv.* behind, *TC* 44, 355

armony *n.* harmony, *OE* 67, 223; *pl.* **armoneis**, *introd.* p. 43

artilye *n.* artillery, missiles, *GT* 161, 179

as *n.* ass, *KQ* 25

as *n.* ash, dust, *TDP* 40

ass *v.inf.* ask, *OE* 373

assailit *v.past p.* attempted, *TC* 35

assayit *v.past t.* 3 *sing.* attacked, *GT* 201

attour *prep.* over, down, *RM* 69, 100, 122; *CF* 100; *OE* 244, 259; *TMW* 22; **atouir,** *TC* 162, 244

aureate *adj.* golden, *GT* 71, 263

authoreist *v.past p.* authenticated, *TC* 66

aver *n.* cart-horse, *TMW* 114, 387

avisit *v.past t.* 3 *sing.* advised, counselled, *CK* 57; *Aen* Prol. I, *past p.* 106

avoir *see* **aver**

babil-beirers *n.pl.* jesters, *lit.* 'baublecarriers', *introd.* p. 38

baff *n.* blow (with something soft), *CK* 111

baid *v.past t.* 3 *sing.* was living, *TC* 490

baid *n.* waiting, delay, *CF* 155; *TMW* 143

baill *n.* sorrow, *introd.* pp. 7, 36; *TC* 110; *adj.* **bailful,** *TMW* 51

bair *adj.* desolate, hopeless, *TC* 410; *TMW* 51

bairds *n.pl.* bards, *introd.* p. 38

bait *n.* feed (for horses), *TC* 210

bak *n.* bat, *SPM* 54

balis *n.pl.* bonfires, *CK* 212

ballaneis *n.* balance, *CF* 138

ballox *n.pl.* testicles, *SPM* 70

ban *v.inf.* curse, *SPM* 79; *TMW* 154

bancat *n.* banquet, *TMW* 430

band *n.* bond, union *TMW* 47, 235; agreement, *TMW* 346 *n.pl.* fetters, *OE* 405; *introd.* p. 7; headbands, *GT* 60

bankouris *n.pl.* seat coverings, *TC* 417

barbour *adj.* barbarous, outlandish, *Aen* Prol. I, 21

baret *n.* vexation, *TMW* 346; **barrat,** *TMW* 51

barkit *v.past p.* clotted, *CK* 197

barnis *n.pl.* barns, *CK* 133

basnetis *n.pl.* light headpieces, *introd.* p. 6

batit *v.past p.* as *adj.* baited, *CK* 211

bauchles *n.pl.* (?—perhaps corruption of text), *TMW* 347

bawch *adj.* feeble, worthless, *TMW* 143

bawer *n.* as *adj.* beaver, *TC* 386

bay *n.* singing of birds, *introd.* p. 36

baythe *adv.* as well, *introd.* p. 6

beclip *v.inf.* embrace, *TMW* 104

bedene, bedeyn *adv.* forthwith, *introd.* p. 35, etc.

bedowyn *v.past p.* immersed, *introd.* p. 36

begouth *v.past t.* 3 *sing.* began, *GT* 1

behud *v.past t.* 3 *sing.* behoved, had to, *TMW* 334; **behuffit,** *TMW* 386

beid *v.pres.subj.* be it, *SPM* 20

beid *n.* bed, *TMW* 237n.

beild *v.past p.* festered (*fig.* filled with rancour), *TMW* 164; **beildit,** built, *TC* 97; as *n.* storehouse, *TMW* 345

beirit *v.past p.* bellowed, *CK* 211

bejaip *v.inf.* play tricks on, *TMW* 452

bek *n.* beckoning gesture, *TMW* 277

bellox *see* **ballox**

belyve *adv.* quickly, *TC* 331; **belyf,** *TMW* 49

bemys *v.pres.t.* 3 *pl.* resounds, *introd.* p. 35

ben our *prep.* from a distance, *TMW* 487

bendis *n.pl.* leaps, *CK* 43

bent *n.* grass, ground, *RM* 69

berdin *n.* burden, *TMW* 165

beriall *n.* as *adj.* beryl (greenish-blue precious stone), *GT* 23, 39; *introd.* p. 9

berne *n.* man, *CK* 123; infant, *CF* 133; consort, *TMW* 237; *pl.* fellows, *CK* 134; *TMW* 494

beseik *v.pres.t.* 1 *sing.* beseech; *OE* 164; *pres.p.* **beseikand**, *TDP* 54

besene *v.past p.* furnished, *TC* 416

beteiche *v.pres.t.* 1 *sing.* yield up, *TC* 577

beuche *n.* bough, *TMW* 6; **buche**, *CF* 174; **bewch**, *TMW* 205

bewrie *v.imp.* reveal *TMW* 41

beyt *v.inf.* relieve, assuage, *introd.* p. 36

bickert, bikkerit *v.past t.* 3 *sing.* and *pl.* assaulted, *CK* 186; *GT* 194

bikkir *n.* assault, commotion, *GT* 144

bill *see TC* 332n.

birkyn *n.* as *adj.* birch, *CF* 52

birs *n.pl.* bristles, hairs, *TMW* 95

bla *adj.* livid or bluish from cold or bloodlessness, *CF* 181; *TC* 159

blaiknit *v.past p.* made pale, wanting in colour, *TC* 410

blait *adj.* ashamed, *introd.* p. 15

blanchit *v.past p.* whitened, rendered colourless, *introd.* p. 36

blenking *vb.n.* fluttering of eyelashes, glances, *TC* 503

blenkis, *v.pres.t.* 3 *sing.* or *plur.* leer, glance, *TMW* 487; 2 *sing*, *OE* 382

blenkis *n.pl.* leers, glances, *OE* 355; *TC* 226; *TMW* 111, 486, 494, etc.

blomyt *adj.* blooming, *GT* 55

bo *v.inf.* make a face, *TMW* 276

boddum *n.* low-lying ground, *introd.* p. 36

bogill *n.* evil spirit, monster, *TMW* 111

bokkit *v.past t.* 3 *sing.* spurted, belched, *CK* 206

bone *n.* bane, woe, destruction, *RM* 54

boudin *v.past p.* swollen, *CK* 171; **bowdyn**, *TMW* 345

bougaris *n.pl.* rafters, *CK* 133

boun *adj.* ready, *TC* 600

bour *n.* boudoir, *TMW* 184

bourd *n.* joke, *TMW* 385, 476

boustuousle *adv.* roughly, *CK* 111

bout *n.* bolt (fired by crossbow), *CK* 124

bownys *v.pres.t.* 3 *sing.* and *pl.* makes ready, *introd.* pp. 10, 43

bra *n.* hillside, *introd.* p. 36

braid *n.* sudden alarm, *CF* 39

braid *v.past t.* 1 *sing.* reared, *TMW* 348

braid selit *adv.* sealed with a broad (seal), *TMW* 347

braith *adj.* broad, *introd.* p. 7

brand *n.* sword, *TC* 180

brankand *v.pres.p.* strutting, showing off, *TMW* 180

brayd *v.past t.* 3 *sing.* hurried off, *RM* 69

breid *n.* portion; **on breid**, openly, *TMW* 74; **breid of erd**, inch of ground, *TMW* 234

breif *n.* rage, *CK* 171

breif *v.inf.* tell, enlighten, *TMW* 385

breird *n.* first shoots; **on breird**, newly started to grow, *TC* 413

brent *adj.* high, smooth, *TC* 173

broddit *v.past t.* 1 *sing.* spurred, goaded, *TMW* 330

brok *n.* badger, *SPM* 70

broud *v.past p.* embroidered, *GT* 90

browderit *v.past p.* embroidered, *TC* 417

browdyn *adj.* embroidered, *introd.* p. 6

brows *n.pl.* eyebrows, *TC* 173

brukkilnes *n.* moral frailty, readiness to yield to temptation, 'brittleness', *TC* 86; *adj.* **brukle**, *LM* 7; *TC* 569

brute *n.* noise, *introd.* p. 35

brym *adj.* fierce, *TMW* 95

buche *see* beuche

buddis *n.pl.* bribes, *TMW* 142

bugill *n.* ox, *KQ* 36

bukky *n.* puffing out of the cheek

(like a 'buckie' or whelk shell), *TMW* 276

bullar *n*. bubble, *TC* 192

bumbart *n*. drone ('bummer'), *TMW* 91

bummill *n*. clumsy oaf, *CK* 154

burall *adj*. rustic, *Aen* Prol I, 48

burd *n*., **hard on burd** close at hand, hard on one's heels, *GT* 55

burelie *adj*. fine, handsome, stalwart, *TC* 173, 180

buschement *n*. ambush, *CK* 185

buskit *v.past p*. made ready, ornamented (especially of a woman), *TC* 255

bustfull *n*. boxful, *SPM* 54

bustouss *adj*. rough, massive, *CF* 5; *OE* 97; *TC* 153, 166, 195; *Aen* Prol. I, 48

but *prep*. without, *introd*. p. 9, etc.; **far but** *adv*. on the far side, *TMW* 494

bydand *v.pres.p*. awaiting, *TDP* 55

bylis *n.pl*. boils, *TC* 395

byre *n*. cowshed, *CK* 124

byrnand *v.pres.p*. as *adj*. burnished, *OE* 318, 330; as *v*., *introd*. p. 7

cabeld *v.past t*. 1 *sing*. haltered, *TMW* 354

cack *n*. excrement, *SPM* 59n.

caill *n*. broth, *SPM* 55

cairfull *adj*. gloomy, sad, *TC* 1, 541, 585; *OE* 317; **caerfull**, sober, *TMW* 418; *adv*. **cairfully**, sorrowfully, *TDP* 23

caiss *n*. circumstances, *CF* 89; plight, incident, *OE* 110

came *n*. comb, *CF* 58

campioun *n*. champion, *introd*. p. 22; *LM* 29

cape *v.imp*. take, *SPM* 25

cappill *n*. horse, *TMW* 355

cappis *n.pl*. bonnets, *CK* 133

carioun *n*. dead flesh, *TC* 577

carlingis *n.gen.sing*. old woman's, *introd*. p. 15

carmleits *n.pl*. carmelites, *introd*. p. 38

carpars *n.pl*. talkers, *introd*. p. 38n.

carybald *n*. monster (term of abuse of unspecified meaning), *TMW* 94

cassin *v.past p*. thrown, *TMW* 23

cative *adj*. wretched, *TC* 408

cautelouss *adj*. full of tricks and subterfuges, *CF* 6, 24

cavell *n*. rascal, base fellow, *CK* 65

cavillatioun *n*. piece of trickery, *CF* 65

ceder *n*. cider, *TC* 441

celicall *adj*. heavenly, *GT* 257

chaftis *n.pl*. jaws, *CK* 76; *TMW* 108, 290

chaip *v.inf*. escape, *TMW* 55; **chapit**, *past t*. 3 *sing*. escaped, *CK* 97

char (**on**) *adv*. ajar, bared, *introd*. p. 22

charbukkill *n*. carbuncle, *Aen* Prol. I, 7n.

charde *v.past p*. pierced, transfixed, *CK* 76; *past p*. of **cheir**

chaumerglew *n*. boudoir activities, bedroom sport, *CF* 122

cheise *v.inf*. choose, *TMW* 208

chenyeis *n.pl*. chains, *TMW* 53, 55, 366

cheverit *v.past t*. 3 *pl*. shivered, *TC* 156

chevist *v.past p*. obtained, acquired, *TMW* 292

chid *v.inf*. accuse, *TMW* 290; **chydand** *v.pres.p*. accusing, *OE* 413

chittirlilling *n*. morsel(?), *introd*. p. 15 (*chitterling*, N. Eng. scraps of pigs' guts)

chuf *n*. churl, *TMW* 290

chuk *v.inf*. caress, *TMW* 291

chydand *see* **chid**

chymys *n*. mansion, *TMW* 292

chyrmys *v.pres.t*. 3 *sing*. chirps, *introd*. p. 36

claggit *v.past p*. smeared, bedaubed, *introd*. p. 40

claik *n*. honk, *SPM* 38

claithis *n.pl.* garments, *TDP* 25

clampit *adj.* botched, *SPM* 14

clapper *n.* leper's instrument for attracting attention, *TC* 343, 387, 442

clawcht *v.past t.* 3 *sing.* seized, *OE* 126

cleikit *v.past t.* 3 *sing.* hooked on, *CK* 65

clevering *v.pres.p.* clinging, *KQ* 55

clewis *n.pl.* cliffs, *GT* 243

clippit *v.past p.* named, *SPM* 58; *OE* 38, 111

clokkis *n.pl.* beetles, *CK* 26

clowtit *adj.* patched, *SPM* 14

clynk *v.inf.* sing, *introd.* p. 36

collatioun *n.* late-night refreshment, *TC* 418

colleraige *n.* water-pepper plant, *SPM* 25

columbyn *n.* columbine, *introd.* p. 14

compile *v.inf.* give an account of, *GT* 72

complyng *n.* compline (last service of the day), *introd.* p. 10

conclud *v.inf.* bring to an end, *TDP* 23; say by way of conclusion, *TC* 586

conclusioun *n.* end, death, *TC* 614

conding *adj.* worthy, *TDP* 63; fitting, *Aen* Prol. I, 50

confountet *v. past p.* routed, *introd.* p. 22

connyng *adj.* learned, *GT* 273

consuetude *n.* custom, *TMW* 64

contenance *n.* demeanour, *KQ* 69

conyng *n.* coney, *KQ* 39

cop *n.* leper's begging bowl, *TC* 343, 387, 442, 579; *pl. TC* 492

cordeleirs *n.pl.* Franciscan friars, *introd.* p. 38

cornecraik *n.* landrail, corncake, *introd.* p. 43

cornys *n.(gen.sing.)* corn, *introd.* p. 9

corruscant *adj.* glittering, *TDP* 25

count *n.* female genitalia, *SPM* 35

countermaund *n.* prohibition, *CF* 86

courtyns *n.pl.* curtains, *GT* 11

cout *n.* colt, *TMW* 354

coverit *v.past t.* 3 *pl.* resuscitated, *CK* 118

cowit *v.past p.* as *adj.* cropped, *TMW* 275 and *n.*

cowpis *n.pl.* cups, drinking vessels, *TC* 419

cowschet *n.* wood-pigeon, *introd.* p. 36

cowth *v.past t.* 3 *sing.* could, knew how to, *OE* 53, etc.

crabit *adj.* ill natured, jaundiced, *TMW* 227; **crabitlie** *adv.*, *TC* 154

crampand *pres.p.* as *adj.* curling, *TDP* 22

crauch *exclam.* ejaculation admitting defeat, *introd.* p. 15

craudone *n.* coward, *TMW* 326

crelis *n.pl.* wicker-baskets, *TMW* 355

croce *n.* crucifix, *introd.* p. 22

crok *n.* old ewe, *introd.* p. 15

crowdis *v.pres.t.* 3 *pl.* coo (of birds), *introd.* p. 36

croyn *v.inf.* bellow, low (like a cow), *introd.* p. 34

crud *n.* excrement, droppings, curd, *SPM* 28

cruke *adj.* crescent (the moon) in its quarter, waning, *SPM* 43

crynd *adj.* shrivelled, *TMW* 278

cuitchours *n.pl.* lay-abouts, wasters, *introd.* p. 38

culit *v.past t.* 3 *pl.* cooled, *TMW* 509

cullour *n.* sense, *Aen* Prol. I, 121, 348 (passage ii, 10)

culome *n.* backside, *SPM* 28, 59*n.*

cumlie *adj.* handsome, *TMW* 34

cummerans *n.* encumbrance, *TMW* 118

cummerlik *adv.* like gossips, *TMW* 510

cundyt *n.* source, *Aen* Prol. I, 341 (passage ii, 3)

curage *n.* boldness, courage, *KQ* 91, *OE* 16, etc., *TMW* 67, 188, 215, 485, etc.; **curageouss** *adj.* spirited,

CF 20 (often with a sexual connotation)

curches *n.pl.* kerchiefs, *CF* 104; *TMW* 23, *sing.* 138

cure *n.* guardianship, *TC* 10

curyus *adj.* subtle, elegant, *introd.* p. 36; **curiouslie** *adv.*, *TMW* 21

cuvating *vb.n.* desire, *RM* 86

daill *n.* dale, valley, *RM* 75; *TMW* 10; **in daill** to deal with, *SPM* 49; *cf. RM* 39*n.*

daine *adj.* aloof, cold, *TMW* 132, 253

daiss *n.pl.* days, *CF* 15

dalis *n.pl.* heaps, *CK* 218

danger *v.inf.* be endangered, *TMW* 500

dangerus *adj.* disdainful, *TMW* 132

daynte *n.* esteem, *TMW* 376

deand *v.pres.p.* dying, *OE* 316

degoutit *v.past. p.* spotted, *KQ* 65

degre *n.* rank, *LM* 19

deificait *v.past p.* deified, *TC* 288

deir *n.* harm, *RM* 21; *v.inf.* to harm, *SPM* 3

deir *adj.* of high price, *SPM* 49

deming *n.* notion, chance to pass judgement, *TC* 118

denger *n.* power, outside influence, allurement (of opposite sex), *RM* 21

denteit *adj.* dainty, *SPM* 49

depaynt *v.past p.* painted, *GT* 66

depurit *v.past p.* as *adj.* purified, *GT* 5

deray *n.* disturbance, excitement, *CK* 2

derflie *adv.* boldly, *introd.* p. 40

dern(e) *n.* secret, under clandestine conditions, *RM* 22; *TMW* 9, 192, 242; *introd.* p. 18; **i derne**, in secret, *RM* 39

devaill *v.inf.* fade away, fall, *introd.* p. 9

dichis *n.pl.* ditches, *introd.* p. 36

dicht *v.past t.* 3 *pl.* got ready, *CK* 11

dill *v.pres.t.* 2 *sing.* sooth, assuage, *RM* 7

dink *adv.* neatly, *TMW* 377

dirige *n.* office, funeral oration, *CF* 53*n.*

dirkin *v.inf.* eavesdrop, *TMW* 9

disagysit *v.past p.* as *adj.* disguised, *TC* 95

discrive *v.inf.* describe, *GT* 64

diseis *n.* discomfort, *TC* 320

dises *n.* disease, ailment, *TMW* 281

dispern *v.inf.* dissipate, *introd.* p. 22

dispone *v.inf.* prepare, *LM* 98

disponyng *v.pres.p.* as *n.* administration, *OE* 343

dispyte *n.* scorn, animosity, ill-feeling, *TC* 304; **dispitous** *adj.*, malicious, *TMW* 253; **dispytit** *v.past t.* 1 *sing.* despised, *TMW* 271

dissimulait *adj.* deceitful, *TC* 225

disteyn *v.inf.* stain, besmirch, *Aen* Prol. I, 45; **disteynit** *v.past p.* as *adj. GT* 278

dogonis *n.pl.* worthless fellows, *TMW* 458

doif *adj.* spiritless, *TC* 32

dok *n.* arse, *introd.* p. 15

dollin *v.past p.* buried, *TMW* 410

donk *adj.* damp, *introd.* pp. 9, 36; **donkit** *v.past t.* 3 *sing.*, *TMW* 10, 512; *introd.* p. 18, **donkis** *n.pl.*, damp places, *introd.* p. 36

doolie *adj.* gloomy, dismal, mournful, *TC* 1, 344; **dolly**, *introd.* p. 36

dottit *adj.* foolish, *SPM* 11; **dotit**, *TMW* 377

douk *n.* dive, *SPM* 39

dow *n.* dove, pigeon, *SPM* 40; *pl.* **dowis**, *TMW* 263

draif *v.past t.* 3 *pl.* passed, *TMW* 511

dram *n.* liquid measure, *SPM* 39

dre *v.inf.* endure, *TMW* 443; *pres. t.*, *RM* 22

dregar *n.* dredger, *introd.* 25

dreggis *n.pl.* dregs or drugs (?), *SPM* 24

dress (him) *v.inf.* raise (himself), *KQ* 29; **dressit (tham)** *v.past t.* 3 *pl.* displayed (themselves), *KQ* 11

drest *v.past p.* as *adj.* afflicted, *RM* 53

drope *n.* village, *CF* 15

drug *v.inf.* drag, *introd.* p. 22; **druggit** *v.past t.* 3 *sing.*, *CK* 62

druggar *n.* as *adj.* slave, drudge (drudging), *KQ* 25

drumly *adj.* gloomy, *introd.* p. 36

drup(e) *adj.* wanting, feeble, *TMW* 192, 370.

dubbis *n.pl.* pools of mud, *introd.* p. 36

duke *n.* duck, *SPM* 39

dule, duill *n.* misery, *RM* 22, 53; *OE* 128; *TC* 472; *TMW* 242; *introd.* p. 22

dule *v.past t.* 1 *pl.* grieve, *TMW* 450

duleful *adj.* miserable, *TDP* 23; *OE* 134

dulis (halit the) entered the fray, *CK* 217

dully *adj.* slack, *OE* 134

dures *n.* injury, harm, *GT* 170

duschit *v.past t.* 3 *sing.* fell heavily, *CK* 112

dyall *n.* dial, clock, *Aen* Prol. I, 341 (passage ii, 3)

dynnit *v.past t.* 3 *pl.* made a noise, *TMW* 10

dyrkyn darken, *introd.* p. 9

dyte *n.* writing, poem, *CF* 11*n.*; *TC* 1

dyvour *n.* bankrupt, *TMW* 410

effereis *n.pl.* manners, *TMW* 49

egeis *n.pl.* eggs (? corrupt), *SPM* 23

eis *n.pl.* eyes, *introd.* p. 43

eke *adv.* also, *KQ* 83; *RM* 36; **eik** *v.inf.* increase, *RM* 94; past p., *introd.* p. 51

eldnyng *n.* jealousy, *TMW* 119, 126

elrich *adj.* fairy, *GT* 125

emerant *n.* as *adj.* emerald (green), *GT* 39

enbroudin *v.past p.* embroidered, *KQ* 3

engyne *n.* disposition, imagination, *TMW* 121; ingenuity, *Aen* Prol. I, 3

enlumynit *v.past t.* 3 *sing.* illuminated, *GT* 45

ene *n.pl.* eyes, *TPD* 4; *TMW* 111; **eyne**, *GT* 212

erd *n.* earth, *TDP* 40

etlit *v.past t.* 3 *sing.* aimed at, *CK* 123

evour *n.* as *adj.* ivory, *KQ* 28

examplair *n.* example, illustration, *TDP* 7

exeme *v.pres.t.* 2 *sing.* examine, *TMW* 156

fachioun *n.* curved sword, *TC* 187

failit *v.past t.* 3 *pl.* missed, *KQ* 82

fais *n.pl.* foes, *TMW* 405

fane *adj.* willing, enthusiastic, happy, *RM* 29; *OE* 384; *TMW* 341, 363

fang *n.* prize, booty, *introd.* p. 22

fang *v.inf.* take, *TMW* 363; **fangis** *pres.* 3 *pl.*; **fangis thame** take for themselves, *TMW* 62

fant *adj.* faint-hearted, *TMW* 86

farnys *n.pl.* ferns, *introd.* p. 36

fax *n.* hair, *OE* 365

faynt *v.pres.t.* 3 *sing.* becomes more impotent, *TMW* 210

fe *n.pl.* sheep, *RM* 2

fedderit *v.past p.* feathered, *TC* 168

feid *n.* enmity, *CF* 142; *TMW* 324, 405

feill *adj.* many, *RM* 117

feir *n.* mate, company, appearance, demeanour, *KQ* 22; *RM* 19; *introd.* p. 14

felloun *adj.* cruel, *introd.* p. 36; *SPM* 61

felterit *v.past p.* tangled, matted (of hair), *TC* 163

felye *v.inf.* fail to achieve, *introd.* p. 22

fepillis *v.pres.t.* 3 *sing.* makes a wry mouth, pouts, leers, *TMW* 114

ferly *n.* marvel, strange thing, *introd.* p. 14

fervent *adj.* biting, stinging, *TC* 4; passionate, *TC* 215

figurait *v.past p.* likened, *CF* 204; *cf. TC* 511*n.*, *TC* 511

flaft *v.past p.* puffed up, *SPM* 10

flaggis *n.pl.* flashes of lightning, *introd.* p. 36

flap *n.* blow, *introd.* p. 40; **flappis** *pl.*, *CK* 131

flatlingis *adv.* flat, *OE* 398

flauchter falis *n.pl.* large fragments of turf, *CK* 216

flaw *n.* blast of wind, *introd.* p. 36

flayn *n.* arrow, *CK* 73, 102; *GT* 188; **flanis** *pl.*, *TC* 167

fleggar *n.* 'scarer'; **foule fleggar** scare crow, *introd.* p. 15

fleittand, fleityng *v.pres.p.* floating, *introd.* p. 41

flet *n.* inner part of house, *introd.* p. 25

flodderit *v.past t.* 3 *sing.* overflowed, *introd.* p. 36

floschis *n.pl.* watery swamps, *introd.* p. 36

flyrit *v.pres.t.* 3 *sing.* fleers, looks lustfully, *TMW* 114

flyte *v.inf.* quarrel, argue, *TMW* 342

fontell *adj.* from a fountain or spring, *OE* 23

fordynnand *v.pres.p.* filling with noise, *introd.* p. 36

forfochin *adj.* exhausted by fighting, *CK* 215

forgeit *v.past t.* 3 *sing.* bent(?), *CK* 83

forlane *adj.* useless, *TMW* 137

forleyt *v.inf.* forsake, *CK* 55

forme *n.* physique, bodily strength, *TMW* 87

forthy *adj.* strong, full of force, pushing, *TMW* 85; **forsy**, *CK* 193; *TMW* 85

forvayit *v.past t.* 3 *sing.* reeled around, *GT* 204

fouth *n.* abundance, *Aen.* Prol. I, 58, 120

foynyee *n.* beech-marten, *KQ* 37

frak *v.pres.t.* 3 *pl.* rush, hasten, *GT* 237

fraward *adj.* bitter, *TC* 323, 352

fre *adj.* generous, liberal, *RM* 20

freikis *n.pl.* knights, warriors, *CK* 204

freke *n.* fellow, man, *TMW* 210

frely *adv.* marvellously, generously, *OE* 72

fremyt *adj.* strange, *GT* 225

fructuus *adj.* fruitful, *introd.* p. 10

fruster *adj.* vain, useless, *TMW* 190

fulyeit *adj.* failing, *TMW* 86

fumyll *v.inf.* handle, feel, *TMW* 134

fure *n.* person, *TMW* 85

fure *v.past t.* 3 *sing.* fared, *SPM* 17

furthwart *adv.* forward, at the fore, *TMW* 85

futher *n.* a lot (of people), *CK* 222

gair *n.* gore in garment or piece of cloth, *TC* 179

gaistly *adj.* terrifying, *TDP* 3*n.*

galys *v.pres.t.* 3 *sing.* sings (of the cuckoo), *introd.* p. 36

gammis *n.pl.* gums, *CK* 196

ganand *v.pres.p.* fitting, *SPM* 44; *Aen.* Prol. I, 355, 364 (passage ii, 17, 26)

ganecome *n.* return, *TC* 55

gant *n.* yawn, *SPM* 38

ganyeis *n.pl.* darts, *GT* 168

garth *n.* garden, *GT* 40, *TMW* 3

gavell *see* cavell

gayte *n.* goat, *KQ* 33; **gaitis** *pl.*, *CK* 18

geir *n.* possessions; **hard geir** virile member, *TMW* 232

geit *n.* jet, *TMW* 201

geldit *v.past p.* stripped (*lit.* 'emasculated'), *TMW* 392

gemilling *n.* variation (in music), *OE* 370*n.*

generabill *adj.* capable of being generated or created, *TC* 148, 171

gent *adj.* elegant, beautiful, *GT* 41; *TMW* 69, etc.; *see* **gentryce**

gentill *adj.* noble, *OE* 9, 27, 65, 112; *comp.* **gentillar,** *TDP* 44

gentilness *n.* noble qualities, *OE* 7

gentryce *adj.* ladylike, of aristocratic bearing, *TMW* 69*n.*

gerss *n.* grass, *SPM* 81

gesserant *n.* armour resembling fishes' scales, breastplate, *KQ* 14

gett *n.* offspring, *introd.* p. 15

geummill *v.inf.* interfere, meddle (*lit.* 'jumble'), *CK* 156

gib *n.* tom-cat, *TMW* 120

gif *adv.* how well, *CK* 52

gigotlike *adv.* wantonly, *TC* 83

gild *n.* clamour, shouting, *introd.* p. 35

gillot *n.* mare, *TMW* 114

gird *v.inf.* **leit gird** let fly, hit out, laid about them, *CK* 141

girnall *n.* granary, *introd.* p. 15

girnit *v.past t.* 3 *pl.* snarled, bared their teeth, *CK* 141

gladderit *v.past p.* besmeared, encrusted, *TMW* 98

glading *v.pres.p.* making glad, *GT* 6

glaid *adj.* glad, cheerful, *TMW* 7, 20

glaidsum *adj.* cheerful, *TMW* 359

glaikit *adj.* foolish, *SPM* 6, 59*n.*

glar *n.* mud, filth, *TMW* 99

glemys *v.pres.t.* 3 *sing.* glares, *TMW* 228

glete *v.inf.* glitter, *GT* 66

gobbis *n.pl.* mouths, *CK* 195

goif *v.inf.* gaze, *TMW* 287, 393*n.*

goldit *v.past p.* as *adj.* endowed with riches, *TMW* 361

goldspynk *n.* goldfinch, *introd.* p. 36

gole *n.* grief, *OE* 139

goreis *n.* filth, matter, *TMW* 98

goulis *n.* red in heraldry (gules), *GT* 41

gowk *see* guk

gowlis *n.* corn-marigolds, *introd.* 14

gowpene *n.* double measure (two handfuls), *SPM* 64

graif *n.* grave, *LM* 46

grane *n.* minute particular, *TC* 433

granis *n.pl.* groans, *CK* 141

granit *v.past t.* 3 *sing.* groaned, *CK* 174

grathit *v.past p.* dressed, *TMW* 18

gravin *v.past p.* buried, interred, *TC* 414

greissis *n.pl.* grasses, *TC* 425; *SPM* 81; *TMW* 20

grip *n.* vulture, *OE* 296

grome *n.* man, *TMW* 78

groundin *v.past p.* as *adj.* ground sharp, *TC* 181; **grundyn,** *GT* 199

gryce *n.* suckling-pig, *SPM* 65

guberne *v.imp.* govern, *introd.* p. 23

guk *n.* gowk, cuckoo, *SPM* 1, 64, 73; **cuk,** *SPM* 25*n.*

gukgo *n.* cuckoo, *introd.* p. 36

gummys *n.pl.* vapours, mist, *introd.* p. 9

gurl *adj.* stormy, *introd.* p. 36

guse *n.* rectum, *SPM* 65

gutaris *n.pl.* gutters, *TMW* 99

gymp *adj.* slender, *CK* 32; graceful, *TMW* 69; *n.* trivial point, *Aen* Prol. I, 125

gys *n.* manner, *introd.* p. 10; *see TC* 164*n.*, 260

gyte *n.* mantle, *TC* 164*n.*, 178, 260

habirgeoun *n.* sleeveless coat-of-mail, *TC* 186

haboundand *v.pres.p.* abounding, *OE* 75

hace *adj.* hoarse, *TC* 338, 445

hache *n.* ache, *TMW* 224

haill *adj.* whole, *RM* 35; *SPM* 53

hailsing *v.pres.p.* saluting, doing obeisance, *KQ* 102

hailsum *adj.* healthy, *introd.* p. 14

haire *adj.* grey (hoary), *GT* 114

hairt *n.* heart, *RM* 35, 78, etc.

haising *n.* hoarseness, *SPM* 62

hait *adj.* full-blooded, full of ardour, *TC* 29, 215, 237, 514

hakkit *v.past p.* cut up, *SPM* 30, 53

halit *v.past t.* 3 *pl.* scored (goals), *CK* 217; see **dulis**

hals *n.* neck, *TDP* 27

hanche *n.* hip, *TC* 187

hanyt *adj.* sexually inactive, restrained, denied, curbed, *TMW* 386

harbery *n.* refuge, *TC* 403; *introd.* p. 14

hard *adj.* stout, *TC* 186

harde *v.past p.* heard, *TMW* 6

hardy *adj.* valiant, *RM* 20

harnes *n.* armour, *TC* 186

harnis *n.pl.* brains, *SPM* 53

hate *n.* hat, *OE* 159

haunt *n.* hiding place, den, *KQ* 29

hautand *adj.* high-sounding, arrogant, *TMW* 12

haw *adj.* wan, leaden in colour, *TC* 257, 340

hawchis *n.pl.* level land by a river, *introd.* p. 9

hechar *adj.comp.* higher, *TMW* 160

hecht *v.past t.* 3 *sing.* was called, *TC* 213

hecht *v.past t.* 3 *sing.* promised, *CK* 103; 1 *sing.*, *TC* 23

hegeit *v.past p.* hedged in, *TMW* 4

heidit *v.past p.* as *adj.* tipped, headed, *TC* 168; **heildit** concealed, *TMW* 14

heill *n.* continued existence, health, *RM* 113; *LM* 1

hekill *n.* hackle, *CF* 58

heklit *v.past p.* as *adj.* fringed (hackle-shaped), *TC* 244

hensour *n.* young spark, *CK* 91

herknere *n.* as *adj.* hearkening, ever-alert, *KQ* 34

herle *n.* heron, *TMW* 382

hert *n.* hart, *KQ* 39

heryit *v.past p.* harried, *TMW* 378

hewit *v.past p.* as *adj.* coloured, *TMW* 11

hewmound *n.* helmet, *TC* 186

heynd *adj.* skilful, *CK* 92; pleasant, gentle, *TMW* 14

heynd *n.* man, young blade, *TMW* 32

hicht *n.* height, *TMW* 4

hird *n.* herd, shepherd, *OE* 97

hissill-rys *n.* hazel branch, *CK* 151

hogeart *n.* (?) (*lit.* swineherd) (abusive), *TMW* 272

hoir *adj.* hoary, *TC* 163; hoarse, *TC* 338, 445

holkit *v.past p.* as *adj.* hollowed, *TDP* 4, 21, 32

holyn *n.* holly, *TMW* 11

host *n.* cough, *SPM* 71

hostit *v.past t.* 3 *sing.* coughed, *CK* 47; *TMW* 272

how *adj.* hollow, *TDP* 21; *TC* 157

howis *n.pl.* thighs, *CK* 188; haunches, *introd.* p. 40

howp *n.* hope, *RM* 113

huche *n.* cliff, *RM* 127

hude *n.* hood (of medical degree), *SPM* 2; (of cloak), *introd.* p. 30

hufing *v.pres.p.* waiting, *KQ* 53

humyll *adj.* gentle, *introd.* p. 6

hur *n.* whore, *TMW* 168

hurcheon *n.* hedgehog, *SPM* 30; *TMW* 107

hutit *adj.* derided, scorned, hooted at, *TMW* 465n.

iceschoklis *n.pl.* icicles, *TC* 160

inclusyt *v.past p.* enclosed (of a sound), reverberating or echoing, *introd.* p. 35

incubus *n.* spirit, *GT* 125

indoce *v.inf.* endorse, *introd.* p. 22

infern *adj.* from the nether-regions, *introd.* p. 22

innatyve *adj.* innate, natural, *Aen* Prol. I, 97

inthrang *v.past t.* 1 *sing.* pushed in, *TMW* 13

ipotdorica *adj.* hypodorian (a term in medieval music), *OE* 369 and *n.*

ische schouchlis *see* iceschoklis

jatouris *n.pl.* trouble-makers, rowdies, *CK* 156

josit *v.past t.* 1 *sing.* possessed, enjoyed, *TMW* 201

keik *v.inf.* peep, *TMW* 81, 125

kell *n.* women's headdress, *GT* 60

kemmit *v.past p.* combed, *TC* 222; *TMW* 21

kendillis *v.pres.t.* 3 *sing.* kindles, *TC* 30

kennatis *n.pl.* hounds, *CF* 149

kenrik *n.* kingdom, *TMW* 216

kerffis *v.pres.t.* 3 *pl.* carve, cut and serve (meat), *TMW* 484

kirsp *n.* delicate fabric, *TMW* 23

kirtyll *n.* gown, dress, *introd.* p. 40

kittokis *n.pl.* paramours, *CF* 137*n.*

knaip *n.* lad, *TMW* 125

knoppis *n.pl.* buds, *introd.* p. 9; **knopis** *GT* 22

kythe *v.inf.* show, reveal, *introd.* p. 21; **kythis** *v.pres.t.* 3 *sing.* and *pl.*, *TMW* 433; **kythit** *past t.*, *introd.* p. 36

laggerit *v.past p.* as *adj.* bemired, smeared with cow-dung, *introd.* p. 36

laichly *adv.* lowly, *TDP* 20

laif *n.* rest, remainder, *LM* 45; *TMW* 240, 395, 506

lair *see* lare

laist *v.past t.* 3 *sing.* held, fastened, *CK* 176

laitis *n.pl.* behaviour, conduct, manners, *TMW* 37, 147

lakar *adj.comp.* more debased or deficient, *Aen* Prol. I, 346 (passage ii, 8)

lance *v.inf.* spring, *CK* 52

langour *n.* longing, *OE* 363

lap *v.past t.* 3 *sing.* leapt, *introd.* p. 40

larbar *n.* impotent fellow, *TMW* 133; **larbaris** *pl.*, *TMW* 67; as *adj.* *TMW* 175

lare *n.* learning, *RM* 17; *TDP* 45

lathlyit *v.past t.* 1 *sing.* loathed, *TMW* 381

latis *see* laitis

lattit *v.past p.* prevented, *TC* 27; *RM* 116*n.*

lauch *v.inf.* laugh, *TC* 231; **lauchand** *pres.p.*, *TMW* 240*n.*

lawdis *n.pl.* lauds, hymns of praise, *introd.* p. 36

lawitnes *n.* ignorance, *SPM* 16

lawrean *n.* laurel, *SPM* 29

lawrer *n.* laurel, *Aen* Prol. I, 6

lazarous *n.* leper, *TC* 343; *introd.* *n.* 30

ledderyn *adj.* leathern, *introd.* p. 10

lege *n.* liege-lord, superior, *introd.* p. 36

leid *v.inf.* lead, *CF* 106

leid *n.* lead (metal), *TC* 155

leid *n.* man, person, *TC* 449; *TMW* 44; people, *TC* 451, 480; **led,** *TMW* 441

leid *n.* language, speech, *Aen* Prol. I, 372, 384 (passage ii, 34, 46)

leir *v.inf.* learn, *TC* 269, 479, 480*n.*; *TMW* 257; **leird** *v.imp.*, *SPM* 75

leme *v.inf.* gleam, shine, *GT* 30; **lemand** *pres.p.*, *introd.* p. 9

lemmane *n.* lover, paramour, *CF* 106

lemys *n.pl.* rays, *GT* 29

lenage *n.* lineage, *OE* 18

lendis *n.pl.* limbs, *CK* 45

lesty *adj.* enduring, long-lived, *KQ* 41

lever *n.* liver, *OE* 298

levyn *n.* lightning, *introd.* p. 36

lewar *n.* louvre, hole in roof, *CF* 189

lewche *v.past t.* 3 *sing.* laughed, *RM* 123; *pl.*, *TMW* 506

lewit *adj* crude, *Aen* Prol. I, 21

leyis *n.pl.* pastures, *introd.* p. 36

leyne *adj.* emaciated, *introd.* p. 37

licht *v.past p.* light (real), *CK* 15

lichtlyit *v.past t.* 1 *sing.* treated lightly, *TMW* 328

liggis *v.pres.t.* 3 *sing.* lies, *CK* 138; **liggit** *v.past p.*, *RM* 44

lik schilling *n.* 'licker of husks of corn', i.e. a beggar, *introd.* p. 15

lincum *n.* lincoln green, *CK* 15

linget *n.* flax, *SPM* 29

lipper-ludge *n.* lodging-house for lepers, *TC* 438; *introd.* n. 31

list *v.pres.t.* 3 *sing.* wishes, *OE* 2; 2 *sing.*, *RM* 55; *inf.*, *TMW* 187; 2 *pl.*, *TMW* 258

lob *adj.* clumsy (oaf), *TMW* 387, 114n.

loife *v.inf.* flatter, *CF* 207

loik *adj.* luke (warm), *TMW* 498

loppin *v.past p.* covered (sexually), *TMW* 387

losingeris *n.pl.* deceivers, *TMW* 258

lougis *n.pl.* ears, *SPM* 10

loun *n.* lad, *CK* 116; **lowne** lout, *TMW* 328

louring *v.pres.p.* scowling, *KQ* 67

loutit *v.past t.* 3 *sing.* bowed down, *TMW* 322

low *n.* flame, *GT* 45

loweouss *adj.* loose, immoral, *CF* 136

luffage *n.* lovage (herb used as diuretic), *SPM* 29

lugeing *n.* lodging, *TMW* 478

luifferis *n.pl.* lovers, *TC* 140, 308, 561; *TMW* 375

luikit *v.past t.* 3 *sing.* looked, gazed, *TC* 372

lumbart *n.* banker (Lombard), *TMW* 362

lume *n.* tool (penis), *TMW* 96, 175

lurdan *n.* lazy fellow, *introd.* n. 43

lusty *adj.* pleasant, *KQ* 1

lyart *adj.* grey, *TC* 162

lychtlyit *v.past t.* 3 *sing.* despised, *TMW* 328

lyddir *adj.* slow, sluggish, *Aen* Prol. I, 383 (passage ii, 45)

lyking *vb.n.* sweetheart, *CK* 138

lykly *v.inf.* make attractive or accurate, *Aen* Prol. I, 124

lymmis *n.pl.* limbs, *CK* 28

lyne *v.past p.* lain, *introd.* p. 22

lyntall *n.* portal, lintel, *introd.* p. 20

lyntquhite *n.* linnet, *introd.* p. 36

lyre *n.* skin, *CK* 34; face, *TC* 339

lyst *n.* hem, *introd.* p. 10; **listis** *pl.*, *TC* 179

lyte *adj.* little, *GT* 71; *TC* 271

lyth *v.imp.* listen, *TMW* 257

maculait *v.past p.* as *adj.* spotted, stained, *TC* 81; **maculate**, *introd.* p. 40

magnifie *v.inf.* make greater, *OE* 2

mait *adj.* worn-out, *CK* 213

makdome *n.* figure, *TMW* 73

malis *n.pl.* packloads, *CK* 214

mangit *v.past p.* dazed, *CK* 214

manifest *adj.* clearly revealed, *TC* 305; *v.inf.*, reveal, show off, *TMW* 73

marrit *v.past p.* upset, *RM* 13

martrik *n.* marten, *KQ* 37

matutyne *adj.* morning, *GT* 4

mauch *adj.* maggotty, *introd.* p. 15

maw *n.* gullet, *OE* 298

mawgre *adv.* nevertheless, in spite of, *RM* 45

mawis *n.* mavis, *TC* 430

maynsworn *v.past p.* perjured, *Aen* Prol. I, 422, 428 (passage ii, 84, 90)

meit *n.* food, *CF* 46, 96

meldrop *n.* hanging drop of mucus, *TC* 158

mell *v.inf.* join, mate, *TMW* 56

mellie *n.* conflict, *LM* 23

mellit *v.past p.* mingled, blended, *KQ* 7

menskit *v.past t.* 2 *sing.* honoured, *TMW* 152

merle *n.* thrush, blackbird, *TC* 430

merrens *n.* affliction, nuisance, *TMW* 57

merse *n.* ornamented top of mast, *GT* 20

meys *v.inf.* soothe, *introd.* p. 9

middingis *n.pl.* midden, dung-heaps, *CF* 46

mis *n.* misdeed, sin, *TDP* 35

miskennyt *v.past t.* 1 *sing.* deceived, *TMW* 380

modern *adj.* of the present, *introd.* p. 22

moir *adj.* more, *TC* 102, 616

mokkis *n.pl.* mockeries, *CK* 22; **mokis**, *TMW* 279

molet *n.* bridle-bit, *TMW* 349

mone *n.* moon, *SPM* 43

monische *v.pres.t.* 1 *sing.* warn, *TC* 612

morgeound *v.past t.* 3 *sing.* grimaced at, *CK* 22

mowis *n.* light matter, joke, *CK* 182

mowlit *adj.* mouldy, *TC* 441

moy *adj.* mild, docile, *TMW* 349

mude *n.* mood, state of mind, *RM* 13

mudlit *v.past t.* 3 *sing.* mowed down, *CK* 153

muris *n.pl.* moors, *CF* 46

muttoun *n.* mutton, *introd.* p. 15

mycher *n.* thief, *introd. n.* 43

myddret *n.* midriff, *OE* 298

mydlis *n.pl.* middles, waists, *GT* 63

myngit *v.past p.* mixed up, *SPM* 68; *imp. SPM* 43; *TC* 613

mysdirt *n.* mouse-droppings, *SPM* 68

mystirs *n.pl.* needs, business, *TMW* 128

na *conj.* no, nor, than, *TC* 263, etc.

naple *n.* apple, *OE* 282

nar *adj.comp.* nearer, *TC* 263

narratioun *n.* tale, *TC* 65

neddir *adj.* lower, *introd.* p. 9

neddirmair *adv.* lower still, *OE* 345

neiff *n.* fist, grasp, *TMW* 486

nevell *n.* wallop, *CK* 67

nicht *v.past t.* 3 *pl.* approached, drew near (poss. with an obscene connotation), *CK* 17

nobbit *v.past t.* 3 *sing.* knocked, *CK* 184

noddill *n.* head, *TMW* 275

nois *n.* nose, *TC* 158

none *n.* noon-hour, *TC* 114

nowis *n.pl.* heads, *CK* 184

noy *n.* annoyance, *TMW* 116

nurice *n.* nurse, dogfish, *SPM* 67

nyce *adj.* wanton, *KQ* 26; *CK* 17; extravagantly fine, elegant, *TC* 220; **nys** with fine distinctions, *introd.* p. 36

oftsyis *adv.* frequently, many times, *TC* 525

onone *adv.* immediately, *TMW* 239

onwemmyt *adj.* unsullied, *Aen* Prol. I, 51

oppin *adv.* plain, *TC* 305

oritionis *n.pl.* prayers, supplications, *TDP* 53

orlege *n.* measure of excellence, *Aen* Prol. I, 340 (passage ii, 2) (*lit.* 'a clock')

oster *n.* oyster, *SPM* 66; *n.* **ostir dregar**, oyster-dredger, *introd.* p. 15

ouirfret *v.past p.* covered over, *TC* 163

ouirquhelmit *v.past t.* 3 *pl.* covered over, *TC* 401

oulkis *n.pl.* weeks, *TMW* 177

ourhailing *v.pres.p.* pondering, *KQ* 46

ourhelit *v.past p.* obscured, *CF* 191; *GT* 93; **ourheld**, *introd.* p. 10

ourstraught *past p.* stretched across, *KQ* 86

oursyld *adj.* overcast, *OE* 170

outwaill *n.* outcast, *TC* 129

oyss *v.inf.* use, *Aen* Prol. I, 117

paikis *n.pl.* blows, *CK* 227

paisit *v.past t.* 3 *pl.* lifted, *CK* 115

pako *n.* peacock, *TMW* 379

palmester *n.* palmist, fortune-teller, *TDP* 42

palpis, pappis *n.pl.* breasts, bosoms, *TDP* 27

papingay (papyngo) *n.* parrot, *TMW* 382, *introd.* p. 39

participant *v.pres.p.* partaking, *TC* 289

pary *v.pres.t.* 1 *sing.* wager, *SPM* 78

paupis, *n.pl.* breasts, *OE* 69

peilit *adj.* hairless, fleshless, *TDP* 4; *introd.* p. 15; **pelit**, *introd.* p. 10

peir *adj.* worthy of, the equal of, *TMW* 314

peirsyng *vb.n.* piercing, blinding (of vision), *TC* 207

pene *n.* penny, *TMW* 135

pennownys *n.pl.* pennons, *introd.* 10

pens *v.imp.* think, meditate, *TDP* 34

percace *adv.* by chance, *Aen* Prol. I, 383 (passage ii, 45)

percyng *v.past p.* as *adj.* keen-sighted, *KQ* 27

peronall *n.* wanton woman, young girl, *TMW* 231

persewis *v.pres.t.* 3 *pl.* frequents, *TMW* 478

pertlyar *adj.comp.* livelier, *TMW* 244

pete *n.* pity, compassion (in courtly love relationship), *TMW* 314

pew *n.* plaintive bird call, *introd.* p. 41

phary (fary) *n.* fairy, fairyland, *OE* 119

phisnamour *n.* physiognomer, *TDP* 42

pietie *n.* pity, regret, *TC* 84

pik *n.* pitch, resin, *SPM* 33

piking *v.pres.p.* stealing, *CF* 27

pikis *n.pl.* thorns, *OE* 292

pilis *n.pl.* pointed blades of grass, *introd.* p. 9

piscence *n.* influence, power, *LM* 33

pitht *n.* virility, *TMW* 80

plaigis *n.pl.* plagues, *OE* 332

plane *n.* flat land, *KQ* 1; *RM* 31; *adj.*
flat, *introd.* p. 36; **in plane** at court, *TMW* 244

pleid *n.* argument, *CK* 167

plesance *n.* pleasure, *TC* 83

plet *adj.* plaited, *TMW* 15

ply, plyse *n.* plight, *OE* 363; *TC* 501

poleist *adj.* decorated, *TDP* 26

pollecy *n.* sagacity, *Aen* Prol. I, 97

pollis *n.pl.* heads, skulls, *TDP* 4

porpapyne *n.* porcupine, *KQ* 26

port *n.* mien, bearing, *TC* 446

pottingary *n.* apothecary's art, *SPM* 15, 76

poweir *n.* might, *RM* 23

prattily *adv.* elegantly, *KQ* 11

precelling *v.pres.p.* excelling, *TC* 446

preckit *v.past p.* inflamed, stung, spurred, *OE* 101

preiss (the) *v.imp.* press on, strive, *RM* 23; **preissis** *pres.t.* 3 *sing.*, *RM* 95; **preissit** *past t.* 3 *sing.*, *CK* 113

prene *n.* pin, brooch, *TC* 423

prettik *n.* practice, *SPM* 15; skill, art, *TC* 269

prevelie, privelie *adv.* stealthily, without attracting attention, *TC* 94, 387, 529, *TMW* 525

previe *adj.* discreet, *RM* 24

properte *n.* style, propriety, *Aen* Prol. I, 121

propir *adj.* private, *introd.* p. 21

proyss *n.* prose, *Aen* Prol. I, 139

pulder *n.* powder, *GT* 203

pungitive *adj.* stinging, *TC* 229

purly *adv.* poorly, *TMW* 135

purpur *adj.* shade of red, *GT* 7n.

purspyk *n.* pickpocket, *introd.* 25

put *n.* thrust, jab, nudge, *TMW* 231

pykis *n.pl.* thorns, prickles, *TMW* 15

pyne *n.* toil, *KQ* 25; torment, *Aen* Prol. I, 144

pyrkis *v.pres.t.* 3 *sing.* perches, *introd.* p. 36

quair *n.* book, *TC* 40, 61n.; *introd.* n. 15

quha *pron.* who, *TC* 60, 64, 131, etc.

quhaill *n.* whale, *SPM* 51

quhairon *rel. pron.* on which, *TMW* 5

quhais *poss.adj.rel.* whose, of which, *TC* 146

quham *pron.* whom, *LM* 87

quhat *pron.* and *adj.* what, *TC* 70, 351, 367, etc.

quhele, quheill *n.* wheel, *KQ* 55; *OE* 270, 272

quhetting *v.pres.p.* whetting, sharpening, *TC* 193

quhidder *adv.* whether, *CK* 95

quhilk *pron. rel.* which, *TC* 33, 52; *adj.* which, 47; **the quhilk** *pron.* 89, etc.; **quhyle . . . quhyle** sometimes . . . at other times, *TC* 49

quhilum *adv.* occasionally, *KQ* 66; *introd.* p. 33

quhirling *vb.n.* whirling, spinning, *OE* 270

quhisling *v.pres.p.* whistling, *TC* 20

quhitlie *adj.* whitish, *TC* 214

quhome *pron.* whom, *TC* 31, etc.

quhou *adv.* how, *Aen* I, 414 (passage ii, 76)

quintacensours *n.pl.* seekers after the fifth essence (quintessence) by which base metals might be transmuted into gold (i.e. money-grabbers), *introd.* p. 38

quotidiane *adv.* daily, *TDP* 15

quyk *adj.* vital, alive, *LM* 75

quynchyng *v.inf.* go out (of a light), *introd.* p. 9

quytteris *v.pres.t.* 3 *sing.* chatters (sound of a quail), *introd.* p. 36

radem *v.inf.* redeem, bring back to glory, *introd.* p. 7

raffell *n.* doeskin, *CK* 13

rage *n.* turmoil, *TC* 31; *TMW* 386

ragment *n.* discourse, tale, *TMW* 162

raid *n.* sexual encounter, 'ride', *TMW* 141, 391

raiffis *v.pres.t.* 3 *pl.* rave, *TMW* 481

rak *n.* crack, *GT* 240

rak *v.inf.* stretch, *TMW* 350

rakit *v.past t.* 3 *pl.* went, *TMW* 524

rakles *adj.* recklessly adopted, *TMW* 43

rak sauch *n.* gallows bird, *introd.* p. 15

ralyeis *v.pres.t.* 3 *pl.* jest, *TMW* 480; **ralyeit** *v.past t.* 3 *pl.* jested, *TMW* 149; **ralis** *pres.t.* 3 *sing.*, *TMW* 193

range *n.* path, *KQ* 45

rankild *adj.* rankled, continuously painful, *TMW* 163

ransonis *n.pl.* ransoms, *introd.* p. 22

rappit *v.past t.* 3 *sing.* showered, *GT* 195

raucht *v.past t.* 3 *pl.* passed, handed, *TMW* 148

ravischit *v.past p.* entranced, *TC* 142

rawe *n.* row, *KQ* 17; *RM* 12n.; **rawis** *pl.*, *TMW* 35

rawk *adj.* hoarse, *TC* 445

rax *v.inf.* prevail, control situations, *CF* 143

reboytit *v.past p.* repulsed, *GT* 180

rebute *n.* repulse, *GT* 181

recure *n.* remedy, *TC* 335

rede *n.* voice, song, *introd.* p. 6

rede *adv.* quite, *TMW* 141

refet *v.inf.* recover, *OE* 365n.

reffys *n.pl.* stolen objects, *introd. n.* 43

regester *n.* fixed criterion, *Aen* Prol. I, 6

reguler *n.* regulator, *Aen* Prol. I, 340 (passage ii, 2)

regyne *n.* queen, *introd.* p. 22

rehator *n.* scroundrel, *introd.* p. 15

reherss *v.inf.* speak, relate, *OE* 7; **reheirs**, *TC* 57

reid *v.pres.t.* 1 *sing.* advise, counsel, *RM* 34

reivis *v.pres.t.* 2 *sing.* rob, *RM* 49

rejoisit (him) *v.past t.* 3 *sing.* made (him) happy, *TC* 48

reke *n.* smoke, *GT* 239

rele *v.inf.* spin, revolve, *KQ* 98

releschand *v.pres.p.* carolling, *introd.* p. 36

remeid *n.* cure, *TC* 33; *LM* 97

remeid *v.inf.* cure, *TC* 473

remufe *v.inf.* move, *TC* 21; **remuffit** *v.past t.* 3 *sing.* dispersed, *TMW* 514

renk *n.* man, *CK* 42; **rinkis** *pl.*, knights-at-arms, retainers, *TC* 432; **rynk**, *OE* 12

renyeis *n.pl.* reins, *TMW* 350

repair *n.* subject for contemplation, recourse in thought, *TDP* 47

rerde *n.* din, *CK* 135; *introd.* p. 35

rerdit *v.past t.* 3 *pl.* roared, *introd.* p. 36

responsaill *n.* assurance, *TC* 127

ressavit *v.past p.* received, *TC* 44

rest *n.* respite, *TMW* 141

rethoris *n.pl.* poets, masters of rhetoric, *LM* 38

reuth *n.* pity, sorrow, *LM* 91; *OE* 371

reveill *v.imp.* confess, *TMW* 43

revest *v.past p.* attired, *GT* 7

revin *adj.* torn, *introd.* p. 37

rew *v.imp.* be sorry for, *RM* 4; **rewit** *v.past t.* 2 *pl.* regretted, *TMW* 43

rif *v.inf.* tear, *TMW* 350

riggis *n.pl.* backs, *CK* 136

rilling *n.* rawhide-shoes, *introd.* p. 15

ring *v.inf.* rule, *TDP* 61

rinkis *see* renk

rispis *n.pl.* sedges, *GT* 56

rivere *n.* robber, *CF* 180; *introd.* p. 15

rochis *n.pl.* rocks, *introd.* p. 36

roif *n.* rest; **roif and rest** peace of mind, *RM* 49

roising *adj.* rosy, *TC* 464

rokkis *n.pl.* distaffs, *CK* 28

rosere *n.* rose garden, *GT* 3

rosyne *n.* rose, *introd.* p. 22

rotting *vb.n.* putrid matter, *TC* 464

roun *v.inf.* whisper, *TC* 529; **rownis** *v.pres.* 3 *pl.*, *TMW* 480

roust *n.* rust (a source of corruption), *TMW* 163

roustie *adj.* rusty, blood coloured, *TC* 187, 188; **rousty** unvigorous, stiff, *TMW* 141

routis *n.pl.* shouts, *CK* 117

ruch *adj.* rough, *introd.* p. 15

rude *n.* face, complexion, *OE* 354

ruffill *n.* upsetting, *TMW* 332

ruffill *v.inf.* upset, *SPM* 4

ruggis *n.pl.* tugs, pulls, *SPM* 37

ruggit *v.past t.* 3 *sing.* wrenched, pulled violently, *OE* 299; *past p.*, *CK* 68

ruke *n.* rook, *SPM* 37; *TC* 445

rummyss *v.inf.* rumble, *introd.* p. 34

rungis *n.pl.* clubs, *CK* 136

ruse *v.inf.* praise, *TC* 573

rute *n.* root, bottom, *TMW* 162; **rute and ryne** root and branch, 'from the roots up', *introd.* p. 23

ruth *see* reuth

ryall *adj.* royal, *OE* 12

rym *n.* frost, *introd.* p. 9

ryne *n.* branch, *introd.* p. 23

rypelie *adv.* fully with consideration, *TC* 303

rys *n.* twig, branch, *introd.* p. 36

ryvand *v.pres.p.* tearing, *CF* 93

ryver, *see* rivere

sable *n.* species of marten, *KQ* 37

sadwyse *adj.* sober, *OE* 19

saipheron *n.* as *adj.* made with saffron (an orange-coloured confectionery), *TC* 421

sakles *adj.* innocent, *TMW* 97

salt *n.* assault, *GT* 198

salust *v.past t.* 3 *pl.* salute, *GT* 95; **saluse** *pres.t.* 3 *pl.*, *GT* 101

samin *adv.* same, *TC* 58, 484; *GT* 100

sanative *adj.* health-giving, *TMW* 8

sanctis *n.pl.* saints, *introd.* p. 15

sane *v.pres.t.* 1 *sing.* cross, *TMW* 444

sanyne *n.* blessing, *TMW* 102

sarar *adj.comp.* more violent, fiercer, *GT* 198; *CK* 164

sary *adj.* sorry, miserable, *TMW* 96

sat *v.past t.* 3 *sing.* oppressed, *CK* 164

satlingis *n.pl.* dregs of wine, *SPM* 27

sauch *n.* willow (as halter), *introd.* p. 15; *see* **rak**

sawis *n.pl.* salves, *SPM* 20

sawrand *adj.* pleasant, savoury, *SPM* 82

say *v.past p.* related, *RM* 89; *n.* **saw** chatter, *TMW* 115; **sege** *inf.*, *TMW* 196

schaiffyne *v.past p.* as *adj.* shaven, *TMW* 105

scaill *v.inf.* fall around, disperse itself, *introd.* p. 9

scaith *n.* loss, *CK* 72; *TMW* 358

scantlie *adv.* hardly, scarcely, *TC* 7

scapit *v.past t.* 3 *sing.* escaped, eluded, *TMW* 358

scart *v.inf.* scratch, *TMW* 93

schaikand *v.pres.p.* shaking, brandishing, *TC* 190

schalk *n.* lout, *TMW* 105

schankis *n.pl.* legs, *OE* 100

schaw *n.* thicket, *CF* 23, 85; wood, *OE* 96; *TMW* 516

sched *v.past p.* parted, *TC* 222

schent *v.past p.* destroyed, *RM* 71; *inf.*, *GT* 146

schevill *adj.* wry, twisted, *TMW* 106

schill *adj.* as *adv.* clear and loud, shrilly, *CK* 53

schilling *see* **lik**

scho *pron.* she, *SPM* 54*n.*, etc.

schore *vb.n.* threatening, *TMW* 110

schowis *v.pres.t.* 3 *sing.* shoves, *TMW* 106

schrift *n.* confession, *TMW* 251

schyre *adv.* clear, *TMW* 22

science *n.* knowledge, wisdom, *TDP* 45

scippis *v.pres.t.* 3 *sing.* skips, *TMW* 357

sclander *n.* slander, libel, *TC* 284

scrippit *v.past t.* 3 *sing.* scoffed, *CK* 21

scunner *n.* disgust, *TMW* 93

scutarde *n.* dirty fellow (*lit.* 'squirter'), *TMW* 92

sedull *n.* writing, *SPM* 21

sege *n.* man, *TMW* 469; **seggis** *pl.*, *SPM* 22

sege *n.* sage, *SPM* 27

seid *v.pres.t.* 1 *sing.* see (it), *SPM* 18

seir *adj.* separate, *introd.* p. 36

selch *n.* seal, *SPM* 31

selit *v.past p.* sealed, *TMW* 344, 347

selwyn *pron.* self, *Aen* Prol. I, 119

semelyer *subs.* seemlier (one), *TMW* 217*n.*

sentence *n.* style, *LM* 75; sense, substance, *Aen* Prol. I, 39, etc.

settis *v.pres.t.* 3 *sing.* suits, becomes, *TMW* 196

sey *n.* sea, *TC* 217

seysit *v.past p.* occupied, *introd.* p. 10

siching *v.pres.p.* sighing, *TC* 100

sickir *adv.* securely, *LM* 13

sike *n.* water-course, stream, *introd.* p. 36

skabbit *adj.* scabby, *TMW* 92

skarth *n.* monster (*lit.* 'cormorant'), *TMW* 92

skeich as *adj.* skittish, *TMW* 357

sker *adj.* scared, *TMW* 357

sklys *n.* slice, *CK* 157

skuggis *n.pl.* shadows, *introd.* pp. 9, 34, 56

slak *n.* soft seaweed, *SPM* 42

slake *v.inf.* relax, *KQ* 67

sle *adj.* cunning, *LM* 7; *Aen* Prol. I, 108*n*

sleiffull, sleeveful, *SPM* 42

sloknyt *v.past p.* extinguished, *TMW* 522

sloppar *adj.* slippery, *KQ* 79

sluss *n.* slush, *SPM* 42

smaikis *n.pl.* rascals, *CK* 223

smak *n.* taste, *SPM* 56

smake *adj.* rascally, miserably mean and contemptible, *TMW* 113

smaragdyne *n.* emerald, *KQ* 23

smolet *n.* grimace (?), *TMW* 113

smy *adj.* as *n.* weakling, wretch, *TMW* 113

snypand *v.pres.p.* cutting, biting, *introd.* p. 36

sobbis *n.pl.* yelps, sobs, *SPM* 51

son *adv.* soon, *SPM* 60

soppis *n.pl.* clouds, patches of mist, *introd.* p. 36

sottin *v.past p.* as *adj.* mixed in, sodden(?), soiled(?), *SPM* 34

sound *adj.* healthy, *SPM* 20; *LM* 10

soutar *n.* shoemaker, *CK* 171

sowch *n.* sighing, *TMW* 519

sowkand *v.pres.p.* sucking, *LM* 26

sowrokis *n.pl.* sorrel, *SPM* 27

soyr *adj.* sorrel, rusty brown, *TC* 211

span *n.* measurement of nine inches, *TMW* 160

spedelie *adv.* quickly, *TMW* 40

speedful *adj.* necessary, *introd.* p. 6

speir *v.inf.* ask, *OE* 117; *pres.t.* 2 *pl.*, *TMW* 52

sperkis *n.pl.* sparks, *GT* 24

sport *n.* diversion, entertainment, pastime, *TC* 40

spray *n.* shoots, *TMW* 29; *introd.* p. 36

spulyeit *v.past p.* despoiled, *TMW* 397

spynist *adj.* newly-opened, *TMW* 29

stad *v.past p.* beset, *TC* 542

staiffis *v.pres.t.* 3 *sing.* rams, *TMW* 486

stanneris *n.pl.* gravel, little stones, *GT* 36

starklie *adv.* strongly, severely, *TC* 280

starnis *n.pl.* stars, *TC* 170

staw *n.* stall, *introd.* p. 22

steir *v.inf.* move into action, *CK* 71; *CF* 168n.; *TC* 352; **steiris** *v.pres.t.* 3 *sing.*, *TC* 469

stendis *n.pl.* strides, *CK* 41

stert *v.past t.* 3 *sing.* sprang, *TC* 538

stevin *n.* voice, cry, *TC* 491; **stevynnys**, *introd.* p. 36

stew *n.* rush, burst of vapour or dust, *TMW* 339

stingis *n.pl.* poles, *CK* 143

stobbis *n.pl.* branches, *introd.* p. 42

stoppell *n.* stopper, *TMW* 339

stoppit *v.past p.* blocked, *TMW* 99

stound *n.* thrill of pain or delight, *TC* 538; *TMW* 340; **stoundis** *pl.*, *TC* 542

stour *n.* battle, *LM* 29; *GT* 202

straik *n.* stroke, blow, *TMW* 234

straik *v.past t.* 3 *pl.* struck with, struck, *CK* 143n.

straitis *n.* Moroccan leather, *CK* 14

stramp *v.pres.t.* 1 *sing.* stamp, *TMW* 493; **strampit** *past t.* 3 *sing.*, *OE* 105, 124

strandis *n.pl.* streams, *GT* 61

strange *adj.* aloof, *introd.* p. 20

strong *adj.* strange, *KQ* 80

sturt *n.* strife, discord, fighting, *CK* 71

styll *n.* plight, *RM* 57

styrlyng *n.* starling, *introd.* p. 36

substantious *adj.* weighty, *TMW* 248

sudron *n.* southern (i.e. English), *Aen* Prol. I, 111, 113; *introd.* p. 34

suelt *v.past t.* 3 *sing.* passed away, swooned, *CF* 49, 52; *TC* 591

sueving *n.* dream, *GT* 244

sugeorne *n.* delay, *TMW* 176

supple *v.inf.* help, *LM* 43

supplie *n.* aid, *TC* 138

surcote *n.* upper-garment, *KQ* 57

surrigianis *n.pl.* surgeons, *LM* 42

swage *v.inf.* assuage, reduce, *SPM* 31

swak *v.past p.* threw, *TC* 522

swalme *n.* swelling, *TMW* 167

swanquhit *adj.* swan-white, *TMW* 243

swatterit *v.past t.* 3 *pl.* splashed, *introd.* p. 41

sweir *adj.* lazy, *introd.* p. 38

swerf *n.* faint, *TMW* 225

swonne *n.* in a state of limpness, *TMW* 175

swyngeours *n.pl.* scoundrels, *introd.* p. 38

swyre *n.* shallow valley, *introd.* p. 10; *TMW* 519

syde *adv.* at such length, extravagantly, *TMW* 196

syld *v.past p.* hidden, *introd.* p. 10; **sylit**, *TC* 10

sympill *adj.* simple, nothing much (to look at), *TMW* 468

syne *adv.* then, afterwards, *OE* 84

syphareitt *n.* sybarite, *introd.* p. 15

syphyr *n.* cypher, person of no value, *TMW* 184

syre *n.* man, husband, *TMW* 145

taidis *n.* toads (creatures said to devour corpses), *TC* 578

taiknyng, takning *n.* token, symbol, *TC* 232

taillis *n.pl.* skirts; **syde-taillis** long trains, *introd.* p. 40

takill *n.* weapon, *CK* 93

tauch *n.* tallow, *introd.* p. 15

techrys *n.pl.* dewdrops, *introd.* p. 9

temperance *n.* restraint, moderation, *TC* 194

tendouris *n.pl.* tutors, advisers, *OE* 20

tene *n.* anger, *TC* 194; **teyn**, *introd.* p. 35

tent *n.* heed, attention, *RM* 33

tern *n.* gloom, *introd.* p. 22

terne *adj.* fierce, *TMW* 261

testament *n.* will, dying declaration, *TC* 576

teynd *v.past t.* 3 *sing.* enraged, annoyed, *CK* 94

thewis *n.pl.* habits, *TMW* 119

thoillit *v.past t.* 3 *sing.* endured, *TC* 70

tit *v.past t.* 3 *sing.* took, *CK* 93

to bald *adj.* impertinent, over-bold, *Aen* Prol. I, 411 (passage ii, 73)

tod *n.* fox, *CF* 147

tolter *adv.* carelessly, unsteadily, heedless of security, *KQ* 88

to-wrye *v.inf.* spin about, *KQ* 88

traisting *v.pres.p.* trusting, *TC* 51

trammis *n.pl.* shafts, *CK* 194

translait *v.past p.* changed, turned, *TDP* 40

trawe *n.* trick, *TMW* 124

trip *n.* tripe, *OE* 298

trist assignation, *TMW* 124

trymmillis *v.pres.t.* 3 *pl.* trembles, *introd.* p. 22

tun *n.* cask, barrel, *Aen* Prol. I, 59

turtoris *n.pl.* turtle-doves, *TMW* 262

twychyng *v.pres.p.* as *prep.* touching, referring to, *Aen* Prol. I, 380 (passage ii, 42)

twystis *n.pl.* branches, *introd.* p. 36

tyde *n.* occasion, *KQ* 57

tyring *v.pres.p.* as *n.* wearying, *TC* 210

tyrit *v.past t.* 3 *sing.* tired out, *TMW* 176

unabaisitly *adv.* unabashedly, *GT* 194

unbald *adj.* stripped of courage, *TDP* 8

unbrisde *adj.* unbruised, *CK* 147

ungird *v.past p.* unprotected, *CK* 195

unricht *adv.* in the wrong way, *TC* 205

unyoldin *v.past p.* as *adj.* resolute, unwilling to surrender, *CK* 177

upe *adv.* open, *introd.* p. 20

upricht *adj.* undoubted, true, *CF* 74

upspred *v.past p.* spread out, carpeted, *TMW* 29

upwith *n.* upward (movement), way up, *TMW* 401

vacandis *n.pl.* free creatures on holiday, *TMW* 206

vainegloir *n.* pride, *CF* 78, 216

valyeand *adj.* valiant, *TMW* 183

vardour *n.* verdure, *TMW* 30

vent *n.* discharge, outrush (of words or feeling), *TMW* 166

vertu *n.* outstanding merit, good qualities, *TMW* 189, 397

wa *adj.* sad, *TC* 350

waif *v.inf.* wave, *introd.* p. 36

waillit *v.past p.* as *adj.* chosen, choice, *TC* 440; **wale** *inf.*, *GT* 186; **waill**, *TMW* 76, 530

wailyeit(d) *v.past t.* 3 *sing.* availed, *OE* 148, 187

waistit *adj.* emaciated, *TMW* 90

wait *adj.* wet, soggy, *introd.* p. 36

wait *v.pres.t.* 3 *sing.* knows, can say, *TC* 64, etc.

walcryif *adj.* as *n.* sleepless, *CF* 103

wallidrag *n.* lazy fellow, sloven, weakling, *TMW* 89

wallit *adj.* encircled by a wall, *KQ* 51

wallowit *v.past p.* withered, wasted away, *TDP* 21; *OE* 350

walteris *v.pres.t.* 1 *sing.* turn, toss, *TMW* 213

wambe *n.* belly, stomach, *CK* 105; *TMW* 131; **wame**, *CF* 45

wan *v.past p.* 3 *sing.* hid, *CF* 145

wane *adj.* grown wan, pale, *OE* 350

wanhope *n.* despair, *TC* 47

wanis *n.sing.* and *pl.* dwelling(s), *CK* 145

wanrufe *adj.n.* restlessness, *RM* 28

wap *n.* wallop, *CK* 105

war *adj.comp.* worse, *TC* 460; *TMW* 200; **wer**, *TMW* 176, 469

warblis *n.pl.* warblings, *introd.* p. 36

ware *v.inf.* pass, spend, *OE* 156; **waris** *v.pres.t.* 3 *pl.* pour out, *TMW* 39; **warit** *past t.* conceived, *TMW* 229; **warit** *past p.* expended, *TMW* 394

waresoun *n.* reward, *OE* 374

warly *adv.* cautiously, *Aen* Prol. I, 107

warpit *v.past t.* 3 *sing.* uttered, addressed, *TMW* 150; *pl.* tossed about violently, *introd.* p. 36

warsche *adj.* pallid, *OE* 350

wauchtit *v.past t.* 3 *pl.* quaffed, *TMW* 39

wed *v.inf.* wager, *CK* 104

wedder *n.* wether, castrated ram, *CK* 104

wedder *n.* weather, *TC* 4

weid *n.* dress, clothing, *TC* 165

weid *n.* weed, *TDP* 21; **wed**, *introd.* p. 36; **weedis**, *introd.* pp. 6, 40

weildis *v.pres.t.* 3 *sing.* possesses, *TMW* 372

weir *v.inf.* ward off, *TC* 182; **woir** *past t.* 3 *sing.*, *TC* 165

weir *n.* war, *TC* 196

weird *n.* fate, destiny, *TC* 385, 412, 436

wellis *n.pl.* streams, *TC* 588n.

weltering *v.pres.p.* rolling, *KQ* 78; **welterand**, *introd.* p. 41

welterit *v.past p.* overturned, *TC* 436

wend *v.past t.* 2 *sing.* thought, imagined, *RM* 108

went *n.* course, *Aen* Prol. I, 378 (passage, ii, 40)

werd *n.* fate, destiny, *OE* 156

werely *adj.* aggressive, warlike (bristling with armour), *KQ* 26

weyn *v.pres.t.* 1 *pl.* think, *Aen* Prol. I, 131

wicht *adj.* strong, heady, *TMW* 39

wichtis *n.pl.* creatures, *TC* 435

wickir *n.* willow, *LM* 14

widdercock *n.* weathercock, *TC* 567

widderit *v.past p.* as *adj.* worn, *TC* 165

wilsum *adj.* wild, twisting, *OE* 155, 290

wirreit *v.past p.* worried, attacked, *CF* 147

witting *v.pres.p.* knowing, *TC* 497

wlonkes *n.pl.* beautiful women, *TMW* 36

wod(e) *adj.* furious, mad, *CF* 92; *TMW* 141, 294; *introd.* 25

woir *see* **weir**

wolroun *n.* wild boar, *TMW* 90

wolx *v.past t.* 3 *pl.* grew, *introd.* p. 36; **woxe** 1 *sing.*, *TMW* 329

womenting *v.pres.p.* as *n.* lamenting, *OE* 147

worschip *n.* dominance, sovereignty, *TMW* 372

wortis *n.pl.* plants, roots, *KQ* 35

wowaris *n.pl.* suitors, *CK* 5

woxe *see* wolx

wraggers *n.pl.* wranglers, *introd. n.* 43

wraik *n.* revenge, *TC* 370

wraikfull *adj.* vengeful, *TC* 329

wrait *v.past t.* 3 *sing.* wrote down, narrated, *TC* 64

wraith *n.* anger, *TC* 182

wrangwyss *adj.* wrongful, *Aen* Prol. I, 444 (passage ii, 106)

wrears *n.pl.* traitors, betrayers, *introd. n.* 43

wrewche *adj.* angry, wrathful(?), *RM* 125

wrinkand *v.pres.p.* wringing, *OE* 131

wrything *v.pres.p.* distorting, *TC* 189

wyppit *v.past p.* tied, *GT* 62

wysnyt *v.past p.* as *adj.* wizened, shrivelled, *introd.* p. 36

wyte *n.* fault, reproach, *TC* 134; *Aen* Prol. I, 448 (passage ii, 22, 110)

yadswyvar *n.* 'copulator with old mares', *introd.* p. 15

yaip *adj.* keen, *CK* 121; *TMW* 170

yeid *v.past t.* 3 *sing.* went, *TC* 481

yeld *v.pres.t.* 3 *pl.* yelled, shouted, *introd.* p. 35

yerd *n.* sexual organ, *TMW* 130, 220*n.*

yerne *v.imp.* desire, wish for, ask for (us to be redeemed), *introd.* p. 23

yet *n.* gate, *TC* 388

ying *adj.* young, *OE* 96; *TMW* 41, 79, 306

yokkit *v.past p.* 3 *pl. adj.* set to, *CK* 202; as *adj.* yoked, harnessed, *TC* 209

yoldin *v.past p.* as *adj.* relaxed, *TMW* 220*n.*; as *v.* yielded, given up, *GT* 209

yolk *v.inf.* clasp, *TMW* 220

youngkeiris *n.pl.* stalwarts (young fellows), *CK* 202

youtheid *n.* state of youthfulness, *TC* 30

yowis *n.pl.* cattle, *introd.* p. 40

yporlerica *adj.* hypolocrian, a term of medieval music, *OE* 370

ythrungin *v.past p.* thrust, *KQ* 94

yuillis yald *n.* odd man out (*lit.* 'one who does not get a Christmas present'), *introd.* p. 22 (**yald**, worn-out mare)

yuke *v.inf.* itch, *TMW* 130

yulestok *n.* winter cabbage, *SPM* 72